UNDERSTANDING THE SUNDAY SCRIPTURES

A Companion to
The Revised Common Lectionary
Year C

by H. King Oehmig, D. Min.

Contributing Editors:
Isabel Anders, M.A.
Paula Franck, M.T.S.

READMARK PRESS

Chattanooga, Tennessee

Printed in the United States of America by:

R E A D M A R K P R E S S
www.readmarkpress.com
P.O. Box 11428
Chattanooga, TN 37401

Telephone: 800.722.4124
Fax: 423.242.4266
info@readmarkpress.com

$21.95
ISBN Number 978-0-9795581-2-2

INTRODUCTION

here is a story that takes place in the 8th chapter of the Acts of the Apostles that makes for a fitting way to end this final volume, *Year C*, of *Understanding the Sunday Scriptures: A Companion to the Revised Common Lectionary.*

To set the stage, an angel comes to the disciple, Philip, and gives him the following message: "Get up and go toward the south to the road that goes down from Jerusalem to Gaza" (v. 26). Philip obeys the guidance of the angel, and heads south in faith. On the road, Philip encounters a court official of the Queen of the Ethiopians. The eunuch, who was in charge of the royal treasury, had been in Jerusalem to worship, and was on his way home. He was sitting in his chariot engaged in Bible study, reading from the scroll of Isaiah.

The Holy Spirit directed Philip to go over and join the eunuch in his chariot, and, in breathless obedience, he ran over and jumped into the first-century Lexus. Next Philip poses one of the key questions in all religious faith, especially in the study of sacred texts that contain the core revelation. He asks the eunuch, "Do you understand what you are reading?" To which the Ethiopian replies—in unison with people in search of truth for all the ages—"How can I, unless someone guides me?" (vv. 30-31). It is at this moment that Philip interprets the passage from Isaiah that the eunuch had been reading, and introduces him to the Lord Jesus through the text. And, without months of baptismal instruction under his belt, the eunuch spots a mud puddle and has Philip immediately baptize him into the "blessed company of all faithful people."

The point here is obvious. Scripture does not interpret itself—like anything else that is read through the lens of humanity. We read it with our eyes, and it passes through our heads, and occasionally into our hearts. It is read through our predispositions, our belief systems, and our genetic makeup—and through the faith community. But it is not a magical Word. It is brought alive by sound teaching and informed instruction inspired by the guidance of the Holy Spirit.

Let me give you an example. During the summer of our junior year at seminary, a friend who had been assigned to do his Clinical Pastoral Education work in a mental hospital in Mississippi came back saying he had a patient under his care—a serious, ardent, Bible-believing Christian—who was missing a right eye and a right hand from self-mutilation. He had savaged himself in front of his own family to fulfill the Scripture he knew to be unyielding and inerrant. The man had taken literally the words of Jesus in the Sermon on the Mount: "If your right eye causes you to sin, tear it out ... and if your right hand causes you to sin, cut it off and throw it away; it is better for you to lose one of your members than for your whole body to go into hell" (Mt. 5:29-30). Never mind that Jesus went about healing all kinds of blind people—who, no doubt, had been sinners before the Lord too. But this man had literalized the Bible to the point of sickness.

That is why it not only takes a village to raise a child, but it also takes the community to interpret Scripture. No wonder seminary curricula require at least a year's worth of Scripture study, let alone the study of Greek and Hebrew, so that the stewardship of the Book will be responsible and edifying, not terrifying. The Hippocratic oath should apply as well to teaching the Word: "First, do no harm."

Me-and-my-Bible, just like Me-and-my-God, can and does lead to inspiration and new birth, but it can also lead to pathology. When not understood in its appropriate context—that is, read through the eyes of the *summum bonum*: God's *agape* enfleshed in Jesus Christ and mediated through the Holy Spirit—the Bible can be perverted, justifying everything from slavery, to mass slaughter, to handling rattlers, to self-mutilation. Need we note that the devil quoted Scripture to tempt Jesus (Mt. 4:5-7).

It has been a great gift, and an equally great responsibility, for your writers and Editors at Synthesis to collaborate on *USS*, Years A, B, and C. And a significant note of thanks goes out to the Rev. Dr. J. W. H. Rhys, noted biblical scholar from the School of Theology at the University of the South. His insights into Scripture have been invaluable to me as a student and as the Editor-in-Chief of *Synthesis: A Weekly Resource for Preaching and Worship in the Episcopal Church*.

Isabel Anders, our Managing Editor and noted author in her own right, has been a Godsend for Synthesis and *USS*. Her unflagging commitment to excellence in writing, editing, proofing—ensconced in her deep, rich faith—have been a huge blessing to me, and to the Church-at-large. Exceptionally well done, good and faithful servant.

Paula Franck, our Christian educator and exegete, has been able to go beyond the "church speak" that often accompanies religious teaching, and has made the truths of Scripture come alive for the rank and file. Her sense of balance with inspiration, of truth in love, has made *USS* a truly cross-denominational work, as well as a source of edification for the Episcopal Church.

I also must convey profound appreciation to our older son, Henry Oehmig, although he has now moved on to graduate business school at Vanderbilt University. Henry came from being the Acquisitions Editor at Jefferson Press and stepped in to help his old dad make Read Mark Press the kind of first-class publishing operation it ought to be. His advice, counsel, and wisdom are far beyond his years. I already miss him and my granddog, Tank, more than I can say. Being in the office just ain't the same, guys.

Finally, I appeal to you, sisters and brothers, who have found previous volumes of *USS* to be of value (and this one as well)—that you will tell your friends and neighbors about the resource. After being at this ministry for 21 years, I still have not found the secret to marketing to folks in the Episcopal Church. Space advertising is expensive—and of questionable value. Direct sales pieces rarely work and can be downright annoying. Third-class mail is a joke. And small, independent bookstores seem to be on the endangered species list.

The best way to help us is the old-fashioned one, the one that Jesus himself used to spread the good news of the Kingdom: *by word of mouth*. Go and tell. Give as a gift to a friend, relative, or colleague, and ask them to do likewise. Give it to vestry folks, or Sunday school teachers, or a child at school. And we'll take it from there. Otherwise, left undone, the great coming together that Philip and the eunuch from Ethiopia had on that fateful day—when one told the other about the good news of the Gospel and changed his life—will remain on the pages of the Book, not embodied in the present in a way that can make a difference to someone today.

H. King Oehmig
Season of Pentecost, 2009
Chattanooga, Tennessee

CONTENTS

Pentecost

Season After Pentecost

LOOKING FOR DELIVERANCE

Jeremiah 33:14-16; Psalm 25:1-9; 1 Thessalonians 3:9-13; Luke 21:25-36

As we begin a new Church Year, preparations to celebrate the *first* Advent of Christ in history are balanced with anticipation of his *second* Advent in the unknown future. Likewise, the Lectionary for this first Sunday of Advent presents us with contrasting images: predictions of cosmic destruction balanced with corresponding words of hope.

The Prophet Jeremiah lived during one of the most turbulent times in Jewish history—the period of defeat and exile in Babylon. Jeremiah had correctly predicted the fall of Judah to Babylon; but he also held up God's promise to restore the people. During the period of exile in the sixth century, B. C., Jeremiah preached a message of hope in which Jerusalem would be rebuilt and the people returned to their homeland under a new covenant with God.

In today's passage Jeremiah foretells the reign of a mighty king, a descendant of David (33:15a), who would bring righteousness, justice, and safety to the land. In the aftermath of the destruction of Judah and Israel, God's promise of restoration would be total, and would include their land. Here the branch of David is identified with the Holy City of Jerusalem, which will be called "The Lord is our righteousness" (in the sense that *God is present*, v. 16b).

Psalm 25 tells us what we are to do as we wait for God's deliverance. We are to put our trust in God and ask the Lord to show us the Divine ways. As we seek forgiveness for our sins, we remember that God is gracious in teaching sinners and in guiding the humble to do right.

Luke's Gospel predicts even greater upheavals than those in Zechariah. Luke's discourse on the end of history comprises almost all of chapter 21, with the verses assigned for today focusing on the cataclysmic events surrounding the return of the Son of Man. In contrast to Mark's account, in which the prophecies are largely against the temple and Jerusalem, Luke shifts attention to the end times. He introduces *Jesus, the victorious Son of Man*, as the messianic Lord who has control over the chaotic forces of wars, cosmic signs, and unruly seas.

If the people to whom Jesus spoke were to understand his message, he had to use images that were familiar to them. Thus we read of the signs in the sun, moon, and stars that are matched by "distress among nations confused by the roaring of the sea and the waves" (v. 25).

For the Hebrews, the sea was bound up with the chaotic abyss of the earliest, formless creation covered by darkness (Gen. 1:2). The sea always had the capacity to burst the bounds that God had set for it and sweep away all that human endeavor had constructed.

In the midst of this terrifying cosmic and terrestrial upheaval, the Son of Man will come with power and glory in a cloud (v. 27). Like the cloud present at the Transfiguration (Lk. 9:34) and the Ascension (Acts 1:9), this cloud was both opaque and luminous, revealing the visible presence of God without unveiling the Divine mystery (cf Ex. 34:5). Here in Luke, too, the cloud will manifest the Divine presence.

PRAYER FOR THE DAY

Almighty God, we pray for the grace to forsake darkness, and to put on the armor of light, now in this life, in which your Son Jesus Christ came to us in great humility; and in the last day, when he comes again in glory to bring us life immortal. *Amen.*

Luke describes two basic human reactions to these cataclysmic events. Most people will "faint from fear and foreboding" (v. 26). But Jesus commands his faithful followers to "Stand up and raise your heads, because your redemption is drawing near" (v. 28). They are to respond with *hope*. For the believing community, the coming of the Son of Man in glory is a joyful, ecstatic experience. The cosmic order will convulse at the return of the Lord; but these signs are side-effects to the final act of deliverance by Jesus the Redeemer.

A new order, a new creation under the complete rule of God will emerge, in which the Divine purpose will prevail under the kingship of Christ. For the disciples of Jesus, therefore, the end is not a catastrophe of terrible doom, but the world's final deliverance from evil and the restoration of the entire cosmos.

In the brief parable of the fig tree and its interpretation (vv. 29-31), we see that just as the budding of the tree foretells the approach of summer, so these events foretell the coming of God's Kingdom. In this we can find assurance that "the kingdom of God is near" (v. 31).

The final verses add a sense of urgency. We cannot know for sure when these things will come to pass; but what we *can* know is the everlasting truth of these words of Jesus. "Heaven and earth will pass away, but my words will not pass away" (v. 33). Thus Jesus exhorts his followers to live rightly, to pray, and always

ON REFLECTION

Early Advent is about the future. The future of the world. The future of society as we know it. The future of you and me.

What's going to take place? How can we be prepared? What are the clandestine signs of today that carry the seeds of what will be tomorrow? How can we discern them—what is under our control, and what remains outside of human purview?

Beneath the burgeoning holiday spirit, and the echo of jingle bells in the malls across America, the future remains a mystery, more ominous and daunting than many of us want to admit. Signs and portents causing worry dot our lives like billboards lining an interstate highway.

What are we to do? To whom can we turn?

Harry Emerson Fosdick, noted minister of Riverside Church in New York City, moved in retirement to Bronxville, New York. Nevertheless, he would travel daily by train into the city where he kept an office. Fosdick soon noticed that every morning a fellow commuter, who always caught the same train, would pull down the window shade as the train passed 128th Street. Having observed the ritual for a while, and knowing the man at least casually by now, Fosdick asked him why he pulled down his shade every morning at that particular place. The other man explained: "I was born in that slum, and I find it painful to be reminded of those early days of my life. Besides, there is nothing I can do about the pain."

After a sympathetic silence, Fosdick responded: "I don't mean to poke around in your private life, but if you want to deal with your pain, you might want to begin by leaving the shade up."

Rather than leaving the shade down on our lives—on haunting memories from the past, or the potentially grim prospects for the future—Advent says to raise your shade up. It is exactly in the midst of this darkness that the new light of God's love shines and will shine most brightly. Lift up the shade, and let the light of the Gospel of Jesus stream in and inform your present—as you gather strength to face the days ahead.

—H. King Oehmig

to be alert, ready to "stand before the Son of Man" (v. 36).

The community to which Paul wrote in 1 Thessalonians was eagerly awaiting this final reign of Christ, and believed that it would occur in their lifetime. This earliest book in the New Testament begins with a note of thanksgiving, as Paul writes with affection and appreciation to the community at Thessalonica. Paul and the other leaders pray night and day for their growth in faith, for the gift of whatever is lacking, and that they may soon see each other face to face (3:10).

Here present-day concerns are reflected, and not future predictions, as in the Old Testament and Gospel passages. The Christian experience is seen as *present joy* for which Paul would have

all believers offer thanksgiving. It is this joy that serves to warm their hearts to one another and keep them on the Way.

Paul was needed in so many places that these hopes of a face-to-face meeting were somewhat wistfully expressed. But this Epistle shows how truly he loves these converts, as he prays for an opportunity to do more for them. He believed God would, however, use his prayers even in his physical absence.

His closing words here are in the form of a blessing on the people and their situation. But this last phrase is also an expression of promise as we anticipate "the coming of our Lord Jesus with all his saints" (v. 13b). This is our hope and our joy as we enter the Advent season.

POINTS TO PONDER

1. Try to visualize the events that Jesus describes in the Gospel passage. How do you think those who heard Jesus might have responded to these prophecies? What is your reaction as you read them today?

2. Why do you think this passage in Luke is read as we begin the season of Advent?

3. Jesus tells his followers that they are to "stand up ... because your redemption is drawing near" (Lk. 21:28). What do these words mean for you? How would you define redemption? What events in your own life, and in the world around you, are examples of redemption?

4. Refer to the Old Testament reading for today found in Jeremiah 33:14-16 and contrast the prophet's prediction of a "Branch" of righteousness with the words of Jesus in the Gospel passage.

5. In the Epistle for today in 1 Thessalonians 3:9-13, Paul asks for an increase in faith, holiness, and love for one another as we await the coming of the Lord. What are some of your hopes for the world as we await the coming of Christ?

_____

_____

_____

_____

_____

_____

_____

"PREPARE HIS WAY"

Baruch 5:1-9; Canticle 4 or 16 (Lk. 1:68-79); Philippians 1:3-11; Luke 3:1-6

"You, my child, shall be called the prophet of the Most High, for you will go before the Lord to prepare his way" (Canticle 16, Lk. 1:76). With these words, the mission of John the Baptist is foretold. For the next two Sundays the Gospel Lectionary focuses on the prophetic voice of this Forerunner of Christ.

Luke's Gospel begins with the infancy narratives of John and Jesus as a prologue for their respective ministries. John, whose name means "God is gracious" in Hebrew, was the long-awaited only son of Zechariah, a rural priest. His wife, Elizabeth, was a kinswoman of Mary, the mother of Jesus. Like Isaac and Samuel before him, John was God's gift to his aged parents.

Zechariah was stricken mute when he did not believe the angel Gabriel's announcement to him that Elizabeth would bear a son (Lk. 1:18). Zechariah did not regain his speech until it was time for the child to be named and circumcised; whereupon Zechariah uttered a prophecy in response to the question of "What then will this child become?" (Lk. 1:66a).

Zechariah's prophecy, the Song of Zechariah, or the *Benedictus*, is read today in place of the Psalm. In this hymn of praise, Zechariah recalls the fulfillment of God's promises to Israel and declares that this child will be the one to prepare the way for the Lord, bringing a message of forgiveness and salvation. The hymn ends with a beautiful expression of hope for a world in which there will be light and peace.

As the account of Jesus' ministry begins, Luke is careful to locate the life of Jesus firmly in world history. This is no timeless redeemer myth, like those of existing mystery religions of the time. Jesus was a figure who lived in a specific time and place.

Thus, the first act in this historical drama, the preparatory witness of John the Baptist, can be dated in the fifteenth year of the imperial reign of Tiberius Caesar (A. D. 14-37). At that time, Rome controlled the world from the Euphrates River to what was called the "Pillars of Hercules," or the Strait of Gibraltar.

Luke is likewise very precise about where Jesus lived. These events took place in Judea, where Pontius Pilate was governor (A. D. 26-36), and in Galilee, where Herod Antipas reigned as its puppet ruler. Luke goes on to mention adjoining areas and their rulers (3:1-2).

In earlier days the Word of the Lord had come to such prophets as Amos and Isaiah; now that Word has come to John the Baptist. Previously Luke told us that John was the long-awaited only son of Zechariah, a rural priest, and his wife Elizabeth, and also that he was a kinsman of Jesus (Lk. 1:5-80). All four of the Gospels contain accounts of John's life and ministry.

John made his home in the wilderness. But when "the word of God came to John" (v. 2b), he went to the people of Judea to warn them of impending judgment. It was a hard message, preached by an austere man in the stark setting

PRAYER FOR THE DAY

Thank you, Lord, for your messengers the prophets, who preach repentance and make plain the way of salvation. Give us grace to listen and to forsake our sins, as we await the coming of Jesus Christ our Redeemer. *Amen.*

of the lower Jordan Valley. He called for a baptism of repentance for the forgiveness of sins (cf Is. 40:3-5; 52:10).

John came to "prepare the way of the Lord" so that all the world would see God's salvation. Even nature would be affected by this preparation: valleys would be filled, mountains leveled, and a smooth and even way made ready. Yet there was nothing permissive or sentimental in John's message.

The sinner who was received was not to remain a sinner. Judgment was near, and all people—even those who thought of themselves as righteous—were to heed the call to forsake past transgressions.

Thus, with John the Baptist, the fulfillment of God's promise of a new exodus from sin and death into *newness of life in God's Son* is proclaimed. Representing the last of the prophets in the Old Testament tradition, John has come forth to awaken the world to a new reality.

Like the Isaiah text John undertook to fulfill, the apocryphal Book of Baruch—composed

ON REFLECTION

The sun-drenched, God-drunk preacher, John the Baptist, has arrived on the scene, announcing what he has heard from on high. From the Divine impulse—not from speculation or philosophizing—John speaks for the One behind him as he points to the One before him. And the talk of fire and brimstone, at first glance, seems more akin to the ranting of a pagan storm-god than a message from the Holy One of steadfast love. But the fire of God that John announces (Lk. 3:9) is not the fire of thunderbolts or of volcanoes. It is another kind of fire.

The "fire of God" is not the fire that maims or disfigures or kills. That is the "fire of sin." The fire of God, as disclosed to Moses at the burning bush, is a fire that never consumes or destroys. It is a refining fire. A cleansing fire. A fire that loves us too much to let us get away with twistedness and destructiveness. As George Macdonald, C. S. Lewis' mentor said, the further we move away from God's love, the more it burns; the closer we come, the more it soothes and sustains us.

Grant M. Gallup has written: "What we are doing today in our nations, states, cities, villages and hamlets—whether we like it or not—is 'preparation' for what's coming. … You get what you prepare for. We are preparing for the dustbin of history. But John the Baptist says 'Prepare ye the way of the Lord.' Fill up the valleys of poverty, pull down the mountains of privilege, selfishness, and greed.

"Are you preparing the way of the Lord? Are you preparing for a way to continue racism, class privilege, continued expenditure of your tax money and your own future on militarism and continued bullying of the Two Thirds World? If so, you are preparing the way of death and hell."

The particular circumstances of the world in John's day might have been different from ours. But the message is the same: Prepare! *As part of seeking a restoration of closeness to God, we must not forget that healing and renewal always begin with repentance. Redemption begins with change. With truth that exposes untruth, that displaces denial with personal amendment of life. This is the "preparation" John calls us to—even if it means losing what we hold most dear and trusting ourselves completely to God's care.*

John the Baptist says: Prepare the Way of the Lord.

—H. King Oehmig

as a celebration of return from the Exile in Babylon—proclaims deliverance. While both Isaiah and Baruch speak of mountains being made low, Baruch also includes the manner in which the heirs of the Exile would return. Baruch personifies Jerusalem as standing on the heights, looking to the east to welcome her returning children. Exiles had gone out on foot, prodded by enemies. In contrast, those who returned would travel in luxury. Nature would join in giving them ease; woods and fragrant trees would shade them as God would lead Israel home with joy.

Whereas John the Baptist and Baruch described God leading the people on a journey to salvation, the Apostle Paul expressed the imminent manifestation of salvation as "the day of Jesus Christ" (Phil. 1:6b). Paul looked for his converts in Philippi to share in Christ's glory, and already saw in them the good work of redemption.

Paul begins his letter to the community in Philippi with the usual greetings from himself, and from his companion Timothy, and gives thanks for their prayers and shared work in spreading the Gospel. The letter was written from prison, but Paul does not say exactly where.

He reminds them that it is Christ's work to produce in them the virtues and perseverance with which they can praise God. Paul loves these converts, and he expects love to increase among them all. This love will help give them good judgment when it is most needed in their lives (1:9-10). In faithfulness they will be able to present themselves as pure and blameless, because they will have learned the compassion of Christ.

We too live in the time between the two Advents of Christ. And we also look to the first as a source of hope, and anticipate the second as the fruition of the work Christ has begun among us.

POINTS TO PONDER

1. Why do you think Luke makes such a point of noting the historic time and place of Jesus' ministry? What difference does this make with regard to our understanding of the story itself?

2. John the Baptist is the last of the prophets in the Old Testament tradition. John proclaimed a "baptism of repentance for the forgiveness of sins" (Lk. 3:3). What do you think he means by this?

3. As you read verses 4-6, what kind of world is described here? How can this world become a reality?

4. Refer to the Old Testament reading in Baruch 5:1-9. How does this text relate to the words of John the Baptist? What Advent themes do you find here?

5. John calls us to prepare the way so that Christ can come. What can we do in this season of Advent to prepare the way for Christ to enter into our individual lives?

_____

_____

_____

_____

_____

_____

_____

_____

THE ONE WHO IS COMING

Zephaniah 3:14-20; Canticle 9 (Isaiah 12:2-6); Philippians 4:4-7; Luke 3:7-18

Our Old Testament passage for today carries forward the Advent theme of joyful hope: "Rejoice and exult with all your heart" (Zeph. 3:14).

The Prophet Zephaniah wrote in the 7th century B. C., chastising Israel for idolatry and corruption, and warning of the coming day of the Lord. However, in this last chapter of the book, Zephaniah holds out the hope of salvation.

God has turned the enemies of Israel away; thus Israel is protected from harm and freed from fear. Although Zephaniah recognizes that disloyalty to God's way must call for punishment, he declares that God will establish a new day.

The Lord is already gathering those who had been dispersed by the burden of their sins. Truly a new time of glory is coming, and as it approaches, Zion must rejoice and sing "as on a day of festival" (v. 18a).

With God's presence established among them, the people have nothing to fear—now or in the future. Their oppressors will be banished and their fortunes restored. God will preserve the lame and the outcast, turn their shame into praise, and bring them renown among all the peoples of the earth.

Today's response to the Old Testament text is a song of praise from Isaiah 12:2-6 that offers thanksgiving for the power and goodness of God. As a conclusion to the messianic promises of the preceding chapter, these verses express confidence in God's protection, and call for praise at God's saving deeds toward all nations.

The Lord's restorative power is like water drawn "from the wells of salvation" (v. 3). Thus Israel is to sing and shout for joy, for the "Holy One of Israel" (v. 6) is among them!

This sense of profound joy in the Lord's presence is also echoed in Paul's letter to the Philippians. The Third Sunday of Advent is often referred to as *Gaudete* Sunday, from the Latin word for "rejoice." This theme is repeated in the opening verse of the passage for today: "Rejoice in the Lord always; again I will say, Rejoice" (4:4).

Paul urges his converts to rejoice now and to renounce all anxiety. They are not to worry about anything, but to submit their requests to God in prayer. As they do so, they are also to offer sincere thanksgiving and be grateful that the Lord supplies all their needs (v. 6). The Lord, who is coming soon, will keep safe the hearts and minds of the faithful.

The Gospel reading continues the account of John the Baptist from last week, focusing on the prophet's call to repentance. John makes it very clear that it is a mistake for anyone to portray the call of God as indulgent generosity. The sternness or even harshness of John's message—addressing his hearers as "offspring of vipers" and threatening them with the "wrath to come" (v. 7)—made his proclamation memorable. And the people listened, turning to him as one who could show them a new way.

John's message stressed the power of God

PRAYER FOR THE DAY

We ask for your power and your mighty presence, O Lord, that your merciful grace may embrace us and deliver us from our sins, through Jesus Christ our Lord. *Amen.*

and the truth that God cannot be moved by mechanical acts of worship, or swayed by inherited privilege. No one could rely on protection due to having had a patriarch as an ancestor. God could turn the very stones into true children of Abraham. Whatever a person's heritage, the ax was about to fall; and nothing short of the fruits of genuine repentance could deflect its severing action.

In a passage unique to Luke, this repentance is described in answer to the crowd's question of what they should do (v. 10). For ordinary people, the message is to remember compassion for the helpless and unfortunate as prescribed in the laws of Leviticus and Deuteronomy, and as proclaimed by the prophets. Those who have more than they need are to provide for those who are in want of food and clothing.

Representatives of various groups also come to ask what the fruit of their repentance should be. No group of people was thought to have more need for repentance than the tax collectors, who could demand any amount they pleased in profit. John's warning to them was

ON REFLECTION

What John the Baptist proclaimed hardly sounds like good news! The ax is about to fall to the root of the unproductive tree! This announcement leaves us knee-deep in Advent, left to draw upon the last part of the Gospel reading, retrieving from it the hope we so desperately need.

Clearly, we—as individuals and as a nation—do not forsake our petty narcissism and become moral and loving in the way John commands simply because we should. Have you ever tried to love someone? To what extent have you been able to be "just" and "loving"—before the self-preservationist part of you shut down those energies in a heartbeat, as soon as your personal interest became threatened?

"I baptize you with water, but the One who is mightier than I is coming, the thong of whose sandals I am not worthy to untie. He will baptize you with the Holy Spirit and with fire."

He is coming to baptize us with empowerment to live the life God intends us to practice toward our neighbors, our world, our selves.

He will baptize us with the fire to burn away narcissism at its roots and replace it—not so much with white-knuckling moral rearmament as with a new heart and a new mind and a new vision from Above. This is the fruit of the Holy Spirit released within us.

Advent is the ideal time, as we wait, longing in faith for the joy of Incarnation, to remind ourselves that Christians are never natural born. They are virgin born—born, if at all, through the Spirit and fire.

Lane Denson writes: "Reverence. An Advent sound of gentle stillness, a silent and holy moment can prepare us once again for such due respect and kindness toward all of life—and toward ourselves, for we are God's beloved. The church can, the church must have a hand in this. We must turn from our crippling narcissism to the practice of reverence."

Only then can we begin to bear fruits worthy of repentance.

—H. King Oehmig

very clear: they were to collect no more than was due them (v. 13).

Next came John's warning to the soldiers. As Jews were not required to serve in the Roman legions, these were probably foreign soldiers under Herod Antipas. Here we see Luke's themes of reversal and God's love for the outcast. John declares that they must be content with their wages and not turn to threats and blackmail. The prophetic preaching of John is to be worked out in terms of acts of justice and loving-kindness in day-to-day living.

The power of the message, and the assurance of the messenger *that he was proclaiming the Word of the Lord* and not his own, led the crowds to see that God's gift of prophecy had been reborn in John.

Such a rebirth was understood to signify that the age of the Messiah was dawning, and it prompted speculation that John himself might be the anticipated leader. John firmly denied any such status by declaring: "I am not worthy to untie the thong of his [the Messiah's] sandals" (v. 16).

The Messiah's work, as John saw it, would be the bringing of judgment—a separation of those who would repent from those who were unmoved in their rebellion. The just would find the security of God's protection, while the wicked would be consigned to utter ruin.

In contrast to the other readings for today, which include a strong call to rejoice, John's message is one of repentance. But this too is part of the Good News that John proclaimed.

POINTS TO PONDER

1. What is the image of John the Baptist that emerges from the Gospel passage? Why do you think people came to hear his preaching? How do you think they might have reacted to his words?

2. How does John describe the actions of God and of the coming Messiah? Discuss the specific images he uses so vividly. How do we respond to his words as we read them today?

3. How does John understand his mission as contrasted with that of the coming Messiah? How would you describe the difference between John's baptism with water and the Messiah's baptism with the Holy Spirit and fire?

4. In Luke 3:10-14, John tells the people how they should conduct their lives in order to "bear fruits worthy of repentance" (v. 8). How does John characterize our responsibilities to others here? If John were to appear today, what do you think he might tell us to change in our lives?

5. In the letter to the Philippians, what does Paul say about how we are to conduct our lives as we await the Lord's coming?

_____

_____

_____

_____

_____

THE VISITATION

Micah 5:2-5a; Canticle 3 or 15 or Psalm 80:1-7; Hebrews 10:5-10; Luke 1:39-45 (46-55)

As we look forward to the birth of Christ, the Old Testament readings remind us of the promises made to the house of King David. With the Prophet Micah, the expectation was of one who would stand and rule in the strength of the Lord. Moreover, this deliverer would not only descend through David's lineage, but would also come from Bethlehem (5:2).

Micah also speaks of a woman who is in labor bringing forth the One who would draw the rest of Israel home (v. 3b). Then the Shepherd of Israel would stand and feed his flock. The strength of his presence would bring security, for all Israel had awaited this time of victory. Moreover, this Savior would be great not only in his own time and place, but for all people in all times.

This Advent hope is mirrored in Psalm 80, a prayer of lament for a better future. Calling upon God as their shepherd to save them (vv. 1-2), the people ask how long the Lord will be angry and make them the scorn of their neighbors. Tears have been their food and drink. The appeal repeated in verses 3 and 7 expresses their heartfelt prayer for deliverance as they wait for God's salvation. "Restore us, O Lord God of hosts; show the light of your countenance, and we shall be saved" (v. 7).

The letter to the Hebrews relates the fulfillment of the hoped-for restoration of Israel in terms of the person of Jesus Christ and his sacrifice. In his coming into the world, the Savior takes the lines from Psalm 40:6-8 as the charter of his ministry (Heb. 10:5b-7). The sacrifices of the Old Covenant are no longer effective. If one presents burnt offerings with the thought that they may take away sins, the truth is that they do not.

One thing alone can be truly pleasing to God, and that is obedience—the effort to perform God's will. This is what Jesus Christ comes into the world to do. His life replaces the outmoded sacrificial law. Jesus has come, bringing the reality of the self-emptying of the Cross. This act not only makes holy the Messiah who offers it in his capacity as High Priest for the human race; it equally sanctifies all those who put their trust in the Lord's offering.

Thus we turn to the specific events that set the stage for the One who will offer himself for the whole world. Luke, in the first two chapters of his Gospel, weaves together the annunciation and birth stories of John the Baptist and Jesus.

The story of the meeting of Mary and Elizabeth for today follows soon after Mary was visited by the angel Gabriel, who told her she would bear a son to be called the "Son of the Most High" (Lk. 1:31-32). When Mary questioned how this could happen, since she was a virgin, Gabriel quoted God's words to Sarah (Gen. 18:14): "For nothing will be impossible with God" (v. 37). As further evidence, the angel tells Mary that her kinswoman Elizabeth, said to be barren (v. 36), is in the sixth month of pregnancy with a son. Mary replies with the familiar words, "Here am I, the servant of the Lord" (v. 38).

PRAYER FOR THE DAY

O God, purify our hearts today, we pray, that your Son Jesus Christ, at his coming, may find prepared within us a fit abode for his presence. *Amen.*

Mary then sets off for Judea to visit Elizabeth. As Mary enters the house, Elizabeth joyfully greets her; whereupon Elizabeth's child, John, leaps in her womb (v. 44), witnessing to the lordship of Jesus. The infant's response is also the sign in which Elizabeth recognized the mother of the Messiah, the coming Lord of all. "Blessed are you among women, and blessed is the fruit of your womb" (v. 42).

The passage continues with Mary's response to Elizabeth, or the Magnificat (vv. 46-55). The content of this extraordinary canticle actually reflects Elizabeth's formerly childless state more than Mary's, and echoes the Song of Hannah (1 Sam. 2:1-10). However, the song belongs to Mary as a model of faith and obedience.

The first part (vv. 46-50) is an expression of Mary's personal thanksgiving to God, who was active in the conception of Jesus. Her experience of what God has done for her is then expanded to encompass God's deliverance for the whole world.

The proper relationship of an obedient servant of God is one of praise and joy. Even though Mary is of "low estate," through her obedience to God's call and her receptivity to the Spirit, she will be called *blessed* by future generations (v. 48). Verse 49 contrasts the lowliness of Mary with the might of God. In verse 50, the mercy of God displayed in Mary has become universal and extends through her to all who fear God.

ON REFLECTION

Mary is the exemplary believer of the Christian faith. She embodies the trust God expects from us in order to accomplish the Divine work in the world.

Mary is an archetype of faith—the mother of believers—in much the same way that Abraham is the father of a nation. Both launched out on a journey without maps, trusting God fully with no guarantees or contractual assurances. Faith and obedience paved their path.

Mary's glorious hymn rings through to our spirits today, speaking of ironic reversal, transforming her personal "Yes" into a universal cry for God to be God in the world.

When Mary uses the past tense to refer to the restructuring of the world (Lk. 1:51-55), she reflects her conviction that all of this is an accomplished fact. God's full and final deliverance of the world—the revolution of Jesus, the vindication of the poor—is already underway and stirring in her womb.

It is a stirring, like all stirrings, that will cause her joy, anxiety, anger, and heartbreak. It is also the Ultimate breakthrough of a new way of salvation that the peasant God-bearer believes on faith.

Who is Mary? Rowan Williams describes her as "she who literally makes a home for the Creator of all things, the strangest reality we can conceive, in her own body and in her own house, she whom we meet again in the Gospels struggling with the strangeness of her son, from the finding in the temple to the station at the cross."

Perhaps she can fathom the outcome of this revolution—the manifestation of this great salvation in its fullness—only NOW in her status as foremost of the saints, united with her Son in glory: Mary, favored one, full of grace.

—H. King Oehmig

God has lifted up the lowly, and filled the hungry. God has done these deeds in the history of Israel, and will continue to work in the future through Jesus. In the past, God has remembered Israel, whose hope for a Messiah is linked with the original Abrahamic Covenant. The never-ending compassion of God overflows to generations of those who open themselves to grace in Christ Jesus.

In Christ the last shall be first and the first shall be last. The proud are brought down and the lowly lifted up; the hungry are filled and the rich sent away empty. This theme is fully brought to light in the choice of Mary to give birth to the Messiah, for those of low degree will be exalted in God's Kingdom.

Mary herself is a model of faith, humility, and obedience; yet she also exemplifies an extraordinary courage and strength of purpose. Her "yes" to God becomes the means of grace for the whole world.

POINTS TO PONDER

1. After Mary has learned from the angel Gabriel that she is to bear the Son of God (Lk. 1:26-38), she goes to spend time with her kinswoman Elizabeth, who is also pregnant. What do you imagine they might have shared during their time together?

2. The meeting of Mary and Elizabeth is commemorated on the calendar of the Church as The Visitation, and is celebrated on May 31. What is the example that Mary and Elizabeth set for us as individuals and as the Church?

3. Read the Magnificat in Luke 1:46-55. What kind of world is described here?

4. What themes of the Gospel message are presented in Mary's song? How is the ministry of Jesus anticipated in these words? How are we called to change by this proclamation of Mary?

5. How would you describe Mary and her influence on the traditions of the Church? How is she a model for you personally?

JESUS' BIRTH

Isaiah 9:2-7; Psalm 96; Titus 2:11-14; Luke 2:1-14 (15-20)

The waiting is finally over. The words of the prophets over the centuries are about to be fulfilled, and our own Advent anticipation to be realized: "For a child has been born for us" (Is. 9:6).

Luke finally brings us to the birth of Jesus the Messiah—the climactic figure in God's plan for human redemption. The narrative leading up to the birth itself was presented in the context of fulfillment for Israel. But in today's reading, Luke sets the birth within the wider background of the Gentile world, as "a light for revelation to the Gentiles" (Lk. 2:32a), as well as "for glory to your people Israel" (v. 32b).

Thus Luke refers to both historical and geographical details in Roman life. However, theological concerns far outweigh the attempt at exact facts. The census decreed by the Emperor provides the means to place Mary and Joseph in Bethlehem—the messianic city of David. Joseph's lineage connects Jesus to the Davidic line as foretold in the prophetic tradition; thus, Jesus is a son of the house of David as well as the Son of God.

Luke tells us that Joseph traveled to Bethlehem to comply with the census decree, along with Mary, to whom he was engaged, and who was expecting a child. While Joseph and Mary were in Bethlehem, the time came for Mary to deliver her child (v. 6). We are told that there was no room for them at the inn, so that the child was born in a stable and placed in a manger.

This Child, who is God's only Son, entered human life in the humblest of circumstances. However, the absolute requirements of the birth had been met. And this Jesus, who was born with the barest essentials of hospitality, became, in his ministry, the host to the dispossessed and displaced of the world. At his Nativity, the world's rejection of the Messiah had already begun.

How then was the world to know of this miraculous event? The birth of a child of royalty is announced with trumpet fanfare and great ceremony. But in keeping with Luke's theology, the birth of the Messiah was told of first to the poor and lowly, not the powerful.

Verses 8-13 tell of the first proclamation of the birth to a group of shepherds from the fields surrounding Bethlehem. They received a privilege greater than a crown when "an angel of the Lord stood before them, and the glory of the Lord shone around them" (v. 9).

Their first response was terror; no one is prepared to face the reality of Divine majesty. The angel acted quickly to calm their fears: Here in the city of David, a Savior had been born for them who was "the Messiah, the Lord" (v. 11). They could find this Child lying in a manger. Although this Child was God's own Son, he shared the origins and living conditions of these ordinary people of the world.

Then an entire heavenly choir is pictured, praising God and promising peace to the world that God loved enough to save. *Glory to God in the highest heaven, and on earth peace among those whom God favors* (v. 14).

PRAYER FOR THE DAY

On this festival day, O God, we celebrate the birth of your only Son, Jesus Christ, our Liberator from sin and death, who now reigns with you and the Holy Spirit in glory everlasting. *Amen.*

Verses 15-20 record the initial responses to this news. First, the shepherds went immediately to Bethlehem to see for themselves what the angel had told them. After finding Mary, Joseph, and the Child, they told others, who in turn were amazed by this incredible news.

Mary herself "treasured all these words and pondered them in her heart" (v. 19). These sentiments are echoed again in 2:51, as Jesus continued to mature. Just as every mother marvels at the birth of her child, Mary continued to reflect on implications of all the events surrounding this son whom God had entrusted to her.

The other readings today tell us more about what the coming of this Child would mean. The Prophet Isaiah announces that the people will no longer walk in darkness (9:2). The world now rejoices as it is freed from bondage and oppression. The Child who has been born for us is a son with authority upon his shoulders, to whom special names are given.

The Holy Child we celebrate is born to rule, and we know him as a Wonderful Counselor. His coming is divinely planned, so we declare that he is the Mighty God, the expression of God's presence with us. We can call him Everlasting Father because we know that he and the Father are one. As the Prince of Peace he brings us reconciliation with God and true fellowship with one another.

His authority will continue to increase, and with his reign will come endless peace. He will establish and uphold his Kingdom with justice and righteousness from now until the end of time. This is God's plan—God's "zeal" to save the world.

Thus the letter of Titus can proclaim: "The grace of God has appeared, bringing salvation to all" (2:11). In response to this gift of God's

ON REFLECTION

Jesus will not always be found where we expect to find him. We tend to look for him in the easy, the nice, the clean, the predictable: in churches and in other Christians, in the Bible and in our Christmas hymns, in church-sanctioned activities and clearly defined tasks of ministry.

But if these are the only places we are looking for him, then we're not looking in the stable, in the dirt and straw and deprivation where the real story, the actual birth took place. Michael Quoist wrote in his book Prayers:

I am not made of plaster, nor of stone, nor of bronze. I am living flesh throbbing, suffering. I am among [you] and ... I am poorly paid, I am unemployed, I live in a slum. I am sick, I sleep under bridges, I am in prison. I am oppressed, I am patronized. I sweat men's blood on all battlefields. ... And yet I said to them: "Whatever you do to My brothers [or sisters], however humble, you do to Me."

Gathered at Bethlehem's manger, we are poised between love's completion or frustration, between love's triumph or tragedy. God's enfleshment in Jesus is love's risk. It is God's vulnerability. God's fullness made empty. God's richness made poor. God's "otherness" become flesh and blood—for us and for our salvation. The power of response is in our hands.

Let us pray, then, for the gift of recognition, which is indeed the message of Christmas. As we contemplate together what has unfolded at Bethlehem, let us acknowledge the meaning of Jesus as the holiest, riskiest sacrament of God's love that ever occurred.

—H. King Oehmig

salvation, we are to renounce all thought and action that is not consistent with the way Jesus lived on earth—as we "wait for the blessed hope" of Jesus Christ (v. 13).

As he gave himself for us, so we now give ourselves to him in a disciplined life of righteousness. He alone was able to purify our souls from all sin and iniquity. And through his marvelous work of salvation, he has united to himself "a people of his own who are zealous for good deeds" (v. 14). As we seek to perform these deeds to which Jesus inspires us, we find the fullness of Christian believing here and now.

On this festival day, the Psalmist gives us words with which to express our joy and thanksgiving, as we sing a new song to proclaim God's salvation and glory among all the nations. The world is called to "worship the Lord in holy splendor" (96:9a). So today we can truly celebrate with the Prophet Isaiah and say that *our joy is increased* (9:3).

POINTS TO PONDER

1. The words of the Prophet Isaiah have become familiar to us through the music of Handel's *Messiah*. As you read the images from today's Old Testament Lesson, what other words and phrases with special meaning for you would you use to describe Jesus as Messiah?

2. As we look back to the birth of Christ, and forward to his coming again, how does the Epistle of Titus suggest that we are to conduct our lives?

3. As you read the Gospel account of the birth of Jesus, imagine what it might have been like to be any one (or all) of the various characters in the story. How do you feel as the events unfold, and how is your life changed by what you have witnessed?

4. Reflect on the message that the angels brought (Lk. 2:14). How are these words relevant to us today?

5. We read that the shepherds returned to their flocks "glorifying and praising God." How do we as a faith community give God praise on this day? How has your own life been transformed by God's gift of Jesus?

– 15 –

ONE WITH THE FATHER

Isaiah 61:10—62:3; Psalm 147 or 147:13-21; Galatians 3:23-25; 4:4-7; John 1:1-18

The Gospel reading for the Sunday after Christmas is the eloquent Prologue from the Gospel of John. Here John affirms that *the Word became flesh* in Jesus of Nazareth, who is the second person of the Trinity. This is what Christmas really means: God the Father, whom none of us has seen, has been revealed to us in Christ. He manifests all the fullness of salvation as God's essential being, having *become flesh* in the way that we too are flesh.

The Prologue tells us that Jesus existed in the beginning with God the Father and was active in creation. He became incarnate and dwelt among us in human flesh. As the source of light and life in the world, he is the one who makes God the Father known to us.

In the beginning there was the Word—the *Logos*—who gave form or voice to the purpose or intention of Abba the Father. And the *Logos* was with God, never separated from the Father, whose purpose the *Logos* expressed.

This *Logos was* God, the second person of the Trinity—the glory equal, the majesty co-eternal. All things came into being through him. The *Logos* was the agent who gave reality to the Father's design of creation. In him was *life*, such as was the life breathed into the still figure of Adam; and he is the *newness of life* for all who are in Christ.

There was a man sent from God whose name was John. The *Logos* or Word of God came to him, and enabled him to testify to *the light.* However, the Gospel makes clear that John the Baptist was not the light (1:6-8).

The *Logos,* who was life, came to his own that he had brought into being. Yet those who were his own failed to recognize him (v. 11). There were, however, some who did recognize him and put their trust in him. To them he gave the privilege of becoming children of God. This was not a matter of human ancestry, or of their own impulses and endeavors, or of the influence of their culture. This adoption was strictly given by God's grace.

"And the Word became flesh and lived among us ... full of grace and truth" (v. 14). This is the meaning of Christmas, of the human birth of the *Logos* in Bethlehem. He made his dwelling (literally, "pitched his tent") among us, and thus we were able to see his glory— the grace and truth that is the Divine nature. "From his fullness we have all received, grace upon grace" (v. 16).

Law, instruction, and guidance for a way of life were given long ago through the ministry of Moses (v. 17). Grace and truth have now come to us through the ministry of Jesus Christ. No one has ever been able to see God, for the intensity of light and holiness would be overwhelming. Nevertheless, we who are disciples have seen the only Son, the one who became what we are, and who yet remains forever one with God the Father. He has made God truly known to all of us (v. 18) through the Incarnation,

Thus Paul can write with confidence to the Galatians that the "fullness of time" (4:4) has come with the appearance of God's Son,

PRAYER FOR THE DAY

O God, cause us to manifest in the world the light of your incarnate Word: Jesus Christ our Lord, who lives and reigns with you and the Holy Spirit, one God, now and forever. *Amen.*

who was born of a woman and lived as one of us. For centuries the Jewish people had found identity in the Law, a pattern of instruction that Paul refers to as "our disciplinarian until Christ came" (3:24). The Law was something people had obeyed; but Paul knew from his own personal experience that there were those who counted on their own performance of the Law rather than on the graciousness of the God who had given the Law.

Paul makes a distinction here between a renewed faith that has been fulfilled through the coming of Jesus Christ, and the former faith under the discipline of the Law. Now the earlier instruction has been turned, by Jesus, into the freedom of grace. Through his obedience to the will of the Father, Jesus Christ brought reconciliation and new life to believers.

Now, as heirs with Christ, we are no longer slaves to the discipline of the Law, but are adopted as God's children. We can call God "Abba," as Jesus did, and live with confidence in God's love for us.

While Paul and the Gospel of John could describe the reality of the Incarnation, the prophets of old and the Psalmists could only anticipate the coming of the Messiah. In the reading from Isaiah, the prophet rejoices in the expectation of a new era. "My whole being shall exult in my God" (61:10). The prophet sees the people clothed with garments of salvation and righteousness. Writing after the Exile, Isaiah would have experienced Israel's struggles for renewal. But the prophet describes a *new era* in

ON REFLECTION

The prologue to John's Gospel, always read on this day, offers us the Christmas message in its eternal significance.

Today we see Jesus, not as the Babe in the manger, but as the Word of, from, and about God … the Holy One who has "tabernacled" among us.

Michael Ramsey wrote that: "Christmas says: Christ has taken humanity to himself, and so every man and woman and child in the world is lovable and infinitely precious. And, in response, men and women can treat one another—whatever their race or color—in the light of Bethlehem; or they can, in rejecting the human dignity of their fellows, reject their own dignity too."

Christ is the one who has become flesh in order to dwell among us. Only Jesus has come from the Father, "full of grace and truth." Only Jesus will return to reign as the Eternal Word.

As Leo the Great (d. 461) put it: "Invisible in his own nature, he became visible in ours. Beyond our grasp, he chose to come within our grasp. Existing before time began, he began to exist at a moment in time. Incapable of suffering as God, he did not refuse to be a man, capable of suffering. Immortal, he chose to be subject to the laws of death."

As Life he was Light for humanity through his coming into the world. Yet that world which was made by him refused to acknowledge him.

But there were those who did acknowledge the Logos who had come into the world and had been made flesh as they were. To them, as they perceived his true though hidden splendor, he gave the capacity to become children of God.

How will we, his heirs, make his name known and honor him in this Holy Season?

—H. King Oehmig

which Israel will be vindicated. Zion's glory will become a shining lamp for all the nations, and a transformed community will be called by a new name.

Thus we can proclaim along with the Psalmist: "Hallelujah! How good it is to sing praises to our God!" (147:1). As the defender of the people, God restores Jerusalem and gathers the exiles. The Lord has established peace on the frontiers, and has declared statutes and judgments to the people. There is no limit to the Divine wisdom and power.

As Creator, the Lord counts the stars and calls them by name. God has command over the forces of nature. The Lord shows compassion by healing the brokenhearted and lifting up the lowly.

Today as we celebrate the priceless gift of the Incarnation, may we too become witnesses to the true light, which is *Jesus Christ*.

POINTS TO PONDER

1. What is your understanding of "the Word" as used in the Prologue to the Gospel of John? How is the Word manifested in our world today?

2. This is a familiar and powerful passage. What do we learn here about the life and ministry of Jesus? Which images or phrases are especially meaningful for you and why?

3. In what ways would you characterize the relationship between God the Father and God the Son as expressed in this passage?

4. How would you explain the difference in John 1:17 between the Law of Moses and the grace and truth of Christ? How have you experienced this grace and truth in your own life?

5. Both the Epistle for today (Gal. 3:23-25; 4:4-7) and the Gospel refer to us as being *children of God*. What does it mean for you to be adopted as a child of God?

THE NAME OF JESUS

Numbers 6:22-27; Psalm 8; Galatians 4:4-7 or Philippians 2:5-11; Luke 2:15-21

Even after religious custom forbade voicing the personal name of God, the first syllable, *Jah* or *Jo*, continued to be used in combination with other syllables in individual names. Jonathan, Saul's son's name, meant "given by YHWH." Elijah meant "YHWH is God."

Of course, Christians think most readily of Joshua (YHWH saves), which sometimes is written Yeshua, and which, through Greek and Latin, got into English as *Jesus*.

The Gospels, Matthew 1:21 and Luke 1:31 and 2:21, tell that the name of Jesus has been given by angelic command. Matthew gives as the reason that *Jesus shall save his people from their sins.*

Our Gospel reading for today tells how the Bethlehem shepherds respond to their vision of angels and find the stable where Mary and Joseph are caring for the Holy Child, cradled in the manger. So the shepherds tell of what has been made known to them, while Mary seeks to understand more fully the significance of the task to which God has called her.

In Luke's account, the name is conferred on the eighth day from birth at the time when the child is circumcised. Of course, the name had already been determined by God's inspiration.

The only unique verse in today's reading is verse 21, and it is the only one that specifically pertains to today's subject. In fact, it is the only verse in all of the Gospels that describes the naming of Jesus. From this verse is derived the Feast of the Holy Name itself.

The verse introduces a passage of Scripture that Luke intends primarily to show that Joseph and Mary are thoroughly devoted to their faith and observe all the requirements of the Mosaic Law, which prescribes three ceremonies to follow the birth of a male child: circumcision (Lev. 12:3); dedication of firstborns (Ex. 13:12-13): and purification of the mother (Lev. 12:4-5).

Through circumcision (as later through baptism), Jesus the Messiah gains solidarity with humanity and becomes subject to the Law along with his people.

In Matthew's birth narratives, where the angel addresses Joseph rather than Mary, and where Joseph does the naming, there is at least a nod toward the significance of the name when the angel tells Joseph, "She will bear a son, and you are to name him Jesus, for he will save his people from their sins" (Mt. 1:21).

Matthew affirms that Jesus kept and endorsed the provisions of the Law of Israel, and he assumes that this meant being circumcised and presented; but he never mentions these events.

For us, the message is that the Holy Family obeyed both God's Word, in heeding the command of the angel and the dictates of the Law, in presenting Jesus for circumcision and dedication.

On this Feast of the Holy Name, we consider especially how this Holy Child is related to God the Father, to Israel, and to the community—as

PRAYER FOR THE DAY

Heavenly Father, you gave your incarnate Son the holy name of Jesus as the sign of our salvation. Now bestow on each of us, we pray, increased understanding and love of him who is the Savior of the world. *Amen.*

well as to the entire human race as *the Name that saves.*

Our Old Testament passage today is the Aaronic benediction, the ancient wording used in the Jerusalem temple to conclude worship: "The Lord bless and keep you; the Lord make his face to shine upon you, and be gracious to you; the Lord lift up his countenance upon you, and give you peace" (Num. 6:24-26). This is God's promised blessing on those who seek his Name.

The Galatians passage (4:4-7) compares our own relationship with God, as true children, to the wonderful example of Jesus himself coming from God, through his mother Mary, to be our Savior. "And because you are children, God has sent the Spirit of his Son into our hearts, crying, 'Abba! Father!' So you are no longer a slave but a child, and if a child then also an heir, through God" (vv. 6-7).

In Philippians 2:5-11 we read that we are to have that same mind in us that was in Christ—

ON REFLECTION

What's in a name?

Grant Gallup writes in "Homily Grits" (Jan. 1, 2003):

"Names used to mean something, and still ought to. For our Biblical religion makes the Naming of People of highest importance. The first official words spoken over us in church used to be 'Name this child.' The old Prayer Book assumed that Naming took place then, at Baptism; alas, nowadays that is lost when months or years later the Sponsors mumble out, 'I present N. to receive the Sacrament of Baptism.' To Name someone is to bestow an identity for them to live up to, and into. Indeed, to know the name of someone is to have power over them, some influence. Name, rank, and serial number are the first things a surrendered soldier must give to captors. In the Prayer Book, 'N.' stands for Name, and is asked for in many places...

"Jesus is given a Jewish name—a good Jewish name, but it's a name that some Spanish speaking people use quite a lot for their own kids. ... Jesus is the English version of a Greek rendering of an Aramaic slant on a Hebrew name. The Hebrew name was Jehosha, or Joshua for short. Yeshua in Aramaic. It means 'Yahweh saves.'"

In Matthew 1:21, Joseph was told in a dream that he was to name the coming child Jesus, "for he will save his people from their sins." He is named to be our savior and deliverer. When the angel Gabriel appeared to Mary, Gabriel too declared that the baby was to be called Jesus (Lk. 1:31).

Thus, in naming the child Jesus, Mary and Joseph are obedient to God and follow the requirements of their ancestral faith, which include the purification of Mary and a dedication sacrifice for a first-born child (Lk. 2:22-24).

Names in Scripture have great meaning as an indicator of who an individual is and what that person is called to do. Mary and Joseph did not name this child; the naming was part of God's unfolding plan of salvation.

As we invoke his Name—especially today—we proclaim that he embodies all that God intends for us: blessing now and life eternal.

—H. King Oehmig

in humility and obedience, to the glory of the Father. Jesus "emptied himself" for us; and God also highly exalted him, so that at the name of Jesus every knee should bend (v. 10).

Psalm 8 reminds us of the exalted nature of God's name, the marvelous works of God's hands, and the true confidence we can have in the One who has made us "a little lower than the angels."

In Christ we find the fulfillment of God's purpose, to bring us to eternal life through his Name.

POINTS TO PONDER

1. Today's readings revolve around the theme of the importance of naming and blessing. As you read these passages, what is revealed about the nature of God and God's relation to humanity?

2. What response are we to have to the holy names for God and the name of Jesus?

3. What is revealed here about the mission of Jesus and our part in this ministry?

4. As you read the Gospel passage, imagine that you are the parents of the infant Jesus. How do you think you would respond to the events described here? What do you think Mary treasured and pondered in her heart?

5. Reflect on your own name. What does it mean for you? If you were to change your name, what name would you choose, and why?

JESUS IN THE TEMPLE

Jeremiah 31:7-14; Psalm 84; Ephesians 1:3-6, 15-19a; Luke 2:41-52

On the Second Sunday After Christmas, there is a choice of several Gospel passages. Today we read in Luke of Jesus in the temple as a young boy.

As we celebrate our Savior's birth, we realize that our salvation is the act of God, Father, Son, and Holy Spirit. The design for our Lord's redeeming ministry begins in the mind of the Father, and every act of that ministry manifests the work of the Holy Spirit. This is shown by the bodily descent of the Spirit as Jesus rose from the water of his Baptism.

So the letter to the Ephesians will bless and thank *the Father of our Lord Jesus Christ* for blessings provided for us in the heavenly places to which Christ leads us. As we give that thanks to our heavenly Father, we remember that the Lord sought us before we ever thought of seeking God.

There are many ways of saying that we love God because God first loved us. Ephesians expresses it that *God chose us in Christ* before the foundation of the world, and that through Jesus Christ we were destined for adoption as God's children.

For those whose adopting manifests God's glorious grace, the writer of Ephesians gives thanks. Moreover, there is the further prayer that the Father will grant a *spirit of wisdom and revelation* to enlighten our hearts. Then we will know the greatness of God's power in fulfilling the hope that God sets before us (vv. 17-19).

While joyous thanksgiving for God's goodness becomes most complete for those who have known adoption in Jesus Christ, trust in what the Lord would do or was doing was well developed among many of the Old Testament prophets.

Jeremiah saw the overthrow of Judah, but he was convinced that it was not the end. As people were marched off into exile, Jeremiah was ready to promise that they would preserve their identity even in an alien land. Therefore God would reclaim them.

The Lord would gather them from the ends of the earth (31:8). This would include not only those capable of finding their own way: the blind and the lame would be able to travel with them; and provision for pregnant women would be made as well. With compassion God would guide them, and supply them with water—while leveling the road before them.

Even after imposing judgment, God is forever a Father to Israel. God will guard the people as a shepherd guards a flock. On the heights of Zion a restored people shall rejoice over grain and wine and oil, over sheep and cattle. The mourning over exile will be turned to joy as God's people experience the complete Divine bounty.

Probably Psalm 84 represents the feelings of worshipers at the pilgrim feasts while Solomon's temple was the primary place to meet with God. Yet it could equally well represent the joy in entering God's presence in a temple that was erected to replace that of Solomon after the return from exile.

God's house was a place of refuge for the people, and that sense of security could be represented by the sparrow or swallow finding a nest near the Lord's altars.

PRAYER FOR THE DAY

O God our Creator, we ask that we may graciously share in the abundant life of your Son, Jesus Christ our Lord, who came to us and humbled himself in order to share our humanity. *Amen.*

Those privileged to dwell in the house of the Lord can be constant in their praise. Those who must come as pilgrims, often traveling through harsh country, will find springs to sustain them on their way.

Resting places along the journey will be found in hilltop villages; and on the height of Zion the Lord will reveal the Divine presence to them.

To the people, the Lord God is both light and protection, and the house of God is the place most to be desired in all the world (v. 10).

Pilgrimage was a part of Jesus' experience as he grew up. From Nazareth to Jerusalem would be a three-day march for infantry. A pilgrim party that would include at least older children would take more than a week each way.

Jews avoided dealing with Samaritans; instead of following the direct route, they would go over to the east side of Jordan to avoid confrontation. And when they crossed the Jordan again near Jericho, it would still take two days to reach Jerusalem.

The whole of Nazareth, perhaps joined by some nearby villages, was an extended family. Any member would gladly care for neighbor children.

So the Holy Family reached Jerusalem. They came to the temple, purchased lambs along with their neighbors, and saw them roasted so that they could eat the Passover.

Even as a boy, Jesus felt that this was where he belonged. When the pilgrim party started home, he stayed. Might he be one to dwell in

ON REFLECTION

Today we read that Jesus traveled on foot with friends and family from Nazareth to Jerusalem when he was twelve years old—and then walked back again. But it is what happens at the temple in Jerusalem that reveals the most to us of what his life was to be about.

He was there to observe Passover, in the company of neighbors and kindred from Nazareth who were no doubt excited and realizing the fulfillment of true worship through this journey.

On the way home, a head count would be needed. At meal time, the individual households would gather; but at the end of the day's journey, Jesus did not appear. When aunts and cousins had not seen him either, Mary and Joseph had no choice but to retrace their weary steps.

Where on earth would a twelve-year-old boy be found? After three days of fruitless search it must have seemed a wild gamble to go looking for Jesus in the temple! Yet there he was, sitting and listening to religious professionals discuss the proper way to live life, and even dealing with questions that no one would ever expect a twelve-year-old to ask.

This turn of events was as astonishing for Mary and Joseph as for anyone else present. Their anger must have been stilled by the amazing sight of Jesus sitting and talking with teachers many times his age, listening and asking questions—exuding presence, even in his obvious youth.

They had a right to demand to know: Why weren't you with us as you were supposed to be?

But Jesus asked them: "Where else would you expect me to be?" He knew his priorities and was fulfilling their mandate, stretching his capacity to receive wisdom in that holy place.

Luke's Greek literally translates: "Didn't you know I had to be among what belongs to my Father?" The King James Version makes this read "about my Father's business"—and newer translations just say "in my Father's house." What could be clearer?

—H. King Oehmig

the Lord's house and praise God continually? He contrived to get in touch with the learned scholars of his people.

He got to ask them questions, and they were the most perceptive questions that the teachers had ever been asked. Indeed, his questions were so good that the leaders would rather answer his concerns than send him away.

Mary and Joseph came back to look for Jesus. Even in Jerusalem, bad things could happen to a boy. It didn't occur to them to start looking in the temple.

When they finally did locate him, Jesus told them that they ought to have known that *he had always thought of God as Father*, and there was nowhere else that he wanted to be.

Yet he accepted that it was not the time to stay. The family started back to Nazareth, although it may well have been too late to catch up with the pilgrim party. Jesus went on learning obedience from Joseph and Mary.

Because he was fully human, there was need for Jesus' mind to grow along with his body. His mother treasured all of these things in her heart, as Jesus increased in wisdom and years, and in Divine and human favor.

POINTS TO PONDER

1. As you read today's Gospel, describe what you imagine the thoughts and feelings of Mary and Joseph might have been when they realized that Jesus was missing and began searching for him. How did they react when they finally found him in the temple? What didn't they understand (Lk. 2:50)?

2. What do we learn in this story about Jesus as he grew into adulthood? How would you describe the relationship between Jesus and his family as depicted here? In verse, 51, what specifically do you think Mary might have treasured in her heart?

3. The first words Jesus speaks in the Gospel of Luke are found in verse 49. What do these words reveal about his understanding of his relation to God at this point in his life?

4. In this story we see that Jesus was brought up in a family with strong religious traditions. How do you think this fact might have influenced his life and ministry? What elements in your own upbringing have most strongly influenced your spiritual formation?

5. This story of the boy Jesus in the temple is found only in the Gospel of Luke. Why do you think Luke included this incident?

_____

_____

_____

_____

_____

_____

THE LIGHT OF CHRIST

Isaiah 60:1-6; Psalm 72:1-7, 10-14; Ephesians 3:1-12; Matthew 2:1-12

Epiphany marks the end of the twelve days of Christmas. The readings for the Day of Epiphany reveal how the Gentiles come to acknowledge the glory of the Lord, the Light of Christ.

In contrast to the Gospel of Luke (2:1-20), Matthew's nativity story has no journey from Nazareth, and no angels proclaiming the birth of the Messiah to shepherds in the fields. Instead, we read that "Jesus was born in Bethlehem of Judea" (Mt. 2:1), and are given no further details. Bethlehem was the ancestral home of David, and in the opening genealogy, Matthew has already established that Jesus is the Messiah, the Son of David (1:1).

Matthew today presents to us the story of the Epiphany. Herod the Usurper, very able man that he is, occupies the throne of David in Jerusalem. A few miles away in what was thought of as David's city, the Holy Family can be found. As Matthew tells it, they have now been able to leave the stable.

When the Wise Men find them, they enter a house to present their worship and their treasures. Their pilgrimage has been lengthy and arduous, and now they have reached the goal of all their journeyings.

Generally we think of these Wise Men as skilled in astrology, but that may not have been the case. Changes in the sky would have been quickly noticed by all, and few would miss the appearance of an especially bright star formed by the conjunction of our largest planets, Jupiter and Saturn. The sight was visible in Palestine and in much of western Asia in 7 B. C.

So the Wise Men surmised that the star proclaimed the birth of one who would be a great king. Its western location indicated the land of the Jews. Thus they loaded their pack animals for the journey, and brought along precious gifts: gold, frankincense, and myrrh.

They came to Jerusalem and went to see King Herod. If a star meant a King of the Jews, Herod's court should have known about it. They were not aware that Herod was sure to see any such king as a threat to destroy, as he had slain his own three sons, whom he suspected of being rivals.

So he sent the Wise Men to Bethlehem as scouts for his own murderous purpose. The star led the men to the humble surroundings where Mary and the Child dwelt. They worshiped him and offered their gifts. But there the story ends abruptly, as they are warned in a dream not to return to Herod's court, but rather to go back to their homes by a different route.

Even in those days, God was protecting the Anointed One, Jesus, for his future work. A way of escape to Egypt would be provided so that he could avoid Herod's destruction of the innocents.

We understand from this familiar story how much the Light of Christ was needed in those early days. And it is no less needed today, now that "the mystery of Christ" has come forth and is for all nations—the Gentiles as well as his people Israel.

PRAYER FOR THE DAY

O God, by a star you revealed your only Son to all the people of the earth. Lead us now, we pray, to shine forth in his presence, that we may continue to reveal him in the world. *Amen.*

Jesus was God's anointed one. In the Isaiah scroll reading for today, we see his foreshadowing in a celebration for the return of God's people from the Exile. "Arise, shine; for your light has come" (60:1). He is the climax of the Divine self-revelation to Israel. And he is also *our* Light, our salvation.

Paul wrote of this mystery in Ephesians 3: *Now we can know, and the spiritual powers in the heavenly places can know.* The Light of Christ has been unveiled for us, showing us God's eternal purposes for mankind.

There is no need for Gentiles to become Jews, since the Gentiles share in the same promises of salvation that were made to Israel. This salvation is manifested through the community of the Church so that "the wisdom of God in its rich variety might now be made

ON REFLECTION

Martin Luther's sermon on the coming of the Magi may have captured the true feeling that surrounded this event—what has become the favorite, biblical parish-pageant ever.

The great reformer described how perplexed the "wise men" were upon arriving in Jerusalem. Not only were they "saddle sore" after having come all the way from Persia, not only were they tired and weathered after weeks of relentless travel, but they were ready for a celebration. They were all set for torches and feasting, merrymaking and dancing in the streets—yet when they arrived, Jerusalem was as quiet as a library.

Expecting something like Mardi Gras or Junk-a-noo, the wise men found only quiet. No one stirred. Luther in his sermon went on to say, "the birth of a puppy would have caused more excitement" than the birth of Jesus in Jerusalem.

The disappointment for these near-Eastern astrologers (we conclude that there were only three of them because they had three gifts to give Jesus) must have been large. They must have been haunted by the uncertainty: Had their stargazing been wrong? Had this light from the heavens actually pointed to another reality—something wholly different from the birth of the "king of the Jews"? Had they journeyed all this way in vain?

The only "king" of the Jews they encounter in Jerusalem is Herod. And he is no surprise whatsoever. Like other "kings," he wields great power, with dragoons under his command. And this potentate extraordinaire has also accomplished the extravagant renovation and enlargement of the temple. Yet he appears concerned about someone out there in diapers who is purported to be more powerful than he!

A band of weary "outsiders" looking for a "king of the Jews" makes him more nervous by what they tell him—and the teachers of the law and the ruling class of religious leaders are also worried (Mt. 2:4).

The actions of God should always make the well established a little nervous. Just when we think we are in control, just when we think we have managed everything the way we want it to go, just when we believe we have worked out our security and certainty—the disruptive Light comes. Grace happens—in ways beyond our wildest dreams.

—H. King Oehmig

known to the rulers and authorities in the heavenly places" (v. 10). All are now members of the Body of Christ and share in the promises made by God through Christ.

Psalm 72 calls on God to inspire an ideal king with virtue to rule on behalf of the poor, and to crush oppressors. The reign of such a king, or at least of his dynasty, should be eternal. The righteous would flourish and peace would be established for everyone. Rulers of other nations would pay him tribute. Thus glory will be given to the Lord, the God of Israel, who "does wondrous things."

He would redeem the poor and needy from oppression and violence. Even nature would provide abundant harvests of grain and fruit. All nations would call him blessed. All of this must be the Lord's doing. In light of this, *the whole earth will be filled with God's glory.*

Epiphany, then, means that all of the nations, including our own, may become fellow-heirs of all God's promises through the ages. This day begins a season of "revealing" of the purposes of God as they touch us now. For God's Anointed is alive and among us in power and glory.

POINTS TO PONDER

1. Describe the changes that will take place, according to the Prophet Isaiah, when the light comes into the world.

2. Today's Psalm 72 describes the qualities of the ideal king. How is the mission of the Messiah also reflected here?

3. In the letter to the Ephesians, Paul describes the mission to the Gentiles as the "mystery of Christ" (3:4). What significance does this passage have for us as Gentiles as we read it today?

4. As the Wise Men set out on their quest, what do you think their expectations might have been about the child "born king of the Jews" (Mt. 2:2)? What kind of men were they, and what can we learn from them as we read about their journey today?

5. In the Epiphany season, the emphasis is on how Christ is made known to the world. What is our own role in making the light of Christ shine out to the lives of those around us?

BAPTISM OF THE BELOVED

Isaiah 43:1-7; Psalm 29; Acts 8:14-17; Luke 3:15-17, 21-22

In this season of Epiphany, the Church commemorates three specific occasions of the *revealing of Christ*, beginning with the visit of the Magi, who brought their gifts and worshiped the Holy Child (Mt. 2:1-12). Their homage represented the adoration of all nations: that Jesus was to be the source of salvation and blessing for the whole world. The other two occasions are the Baptism of Jesus, which we celebrate today; and the wedding at Cana on the Second Sunday of Epiphany.

The Gospel reading begins with speculation about whether John the Baptist might be God's Messiah. John was an impressive figure whose ascetic lifestyle and prophetic voice brought to mind the Prophet Elijah. However, John knew his place in God's planned action. He was not the long-awaited Messiah, and he would not have people thinking that he was. So he proclaimed a greater figure soon to come, one whose sandals he was unfit to tie.

In common with other peoples, the Hebrews were accustomed to using water for religious purification. A specialized form of this washing was the practice of proselyte baptism, one of the ceremonies by which new converts were admitted to Judaism. For John, the ethical significance of the rite became prominent, as he inveighed against the Pharisees and Sadducees to "bear fruits worthy of repentance" (Lk. 3:8). Thus John's baptism was one of *repentance*, as well as a proclamation of the coming reign of God.

However, the one to come would bring a greater baptism—a baptism of empowerment by the "Holy Spirit and fire" (v. 16b). Here we see one of the major themes of the Gospel of Luke: the emphasis on the role of the Holy Spirit in the work of Jesus and the Church. Jesus'

baptism of Spirit and fire anticipates the wind and fire of Pentecost (Acts 2:1-4), when the gathered community was filled with the power of the Holy Spirit. The one who is to come will also be the judge who will separate the wheat from the chaff.

Luke's concise account of the Baptism of Jesus differs in several details from the other synoptic accounts. First of all, John is not specifically mentioned here. Luke tells us that he had been imprisoned by Herod (3:19-20); thus in this story there is a separation of the ministry of John and Jesus. The focus of attention is now fully on Jesus, who was among a crowd of people when he was baptized.

Luke tells us that, immediately after his Baptism, Jesus prayed; none of the other accounts includes this information. While Jesus is at prayer, the heaven is "opened" to declare God's glory; and the Holy Spirit descends upon him in the form of a dove (vv. 21b-22). Jesus is thus empowered by the Spirit for his ministry. Then a voice from heaven speaks directly to Jesus, declaring, "You are my Son, the Beloved; with you I am well pleased" (v. 22b). Similar words are spoken to Jesus at another critical moment in his ministry at the Transfiguration (9:35-36).

PRAYER FOR THE DAY

Our Father in heaven, who at Jesus' Baptism in the Jordan River called him your Beloved Son and anointed him in the Spirit, give to all of us who are baptized in his name a ministry in the world, as we boldly profess his message and power. *Amen.*

Thus anointed and affirmed, Jesus was prepared to live out the ministry for which God had chosen him. He made God real in ways never known before and manifested the true potential of humanity. He made clear that God's love is both unconditional and impartial, and in him, God's love reaches out to every nation.

The Servant Songs of Second Isaiah express what we have come to identify as the essence of Jesus' ministry. Time and time again he told his followers that the only way to attain greatness in God's Kingdom was through service. The servant figure of Second Isaiah is not a single person but the personification of the nation. The sufferings of the servant are those of Israel's Exile. The prophet hoped that the nation would be so purified through their suffering that they would become a true light for all nations.

In Isaiah 42 the nature of the servant is described as one who brings justice and compassion. In the opening verses of chapter 43, Israel is revealed as God's unique possession: "I have called you by name, you are mine" (v. 1b). God walks with the people of Israel through all their trials; thus they shall not be overcome. God will gather together and ransom the people as their Savior. God gives grace to "everyone who is called by my name, whom I created for my glory, whom I formed and made" (v. 7).

There is more in other songs: God's servant takes our suffering upon himself and is wounded by our iniquities (Is. 53:5). But it is by his suffering that we are healed. God grants the servant the patience and humility by which he

ON REFLECTION

In the apocryphal work, The Gospel of the Nazareans, *Mary, the mother of Jesus, invites her son to go and be baptized by his cousin John. Jesus responds: "Where have I sinned to go and be baptized by John?" Mary's reply is left unstated.*

Matthew, in his version of the Baptism, seems to lessen the potential denigration inflicted on Jesus—that of undergoing a cleansing rite administered by a "lesser" spiritual light—by saying that John would have prevented him from doing so. Nevertheless, Jesus insists that he should be baptized as a way of fulfilling "all righteousness" (3:15). Jesus is never on record as making a mistake.

In Luke's version of the event that we read today, the people are questioning in their hearts about whether John is himself the Christ. John answers, "I baptize you with water; but one who is more powerful than I is coming ... he will baptize you with the Holy Spirit and fire" (3:16). And so, while all the people are being baptized, Jesus also takes on the fulfillment of this rite quite naturally. But as Jesus himself is baptized, there is dramatic endorsement by the Holy Spirit in the form of a dove, and a heavenly voice proclaiming him as the Beloved (v. 22).

This event illustrates Jesus' obedience to the Father, and says, "Here I stand." It could have been otherwise—an announcement delivered by Jesus from one of the temple porticos, or a long speech given at the peak of a sacred mountain. But Jesus chose what God wanted him to do. And so he went. Even if it didn't feel exactly fitting to his position, as the One who brought with him a more powerful Baptism—he agreed to it.

And so, in this scene, we see a visual tableau of the Trinity before us, Father (voice), Son (body), and Holy Spirit (Dove), all in concert as participants in Jesus' act of obedience.

—H. King Oehmig

will preserve even a "bruised reed" as he establishes his way on earth (42:3). This is the story of Jesus. This is what it meant for him to be empowered by the Spirit as the Messiah.

In Acts 8 we read that the mission of Jesus had begun to spread outside Jerusalem. So Peter and John went to Samaria to pray for the believers there to receive the Holy Spirit. For although they had been baptized, the Spirit had not yet come to them. Thus the Apostles laid hands on them, and "they received the Holy Spirit" (v. 17).

In Acts, the Spirit is seen as a gift that is not automatically conferred at baptism. Rather, it is bestowed with prayer, accompanied by the laying on of hands, thus affirming the connection between prayer and the Spirit. *The gift of the Spirit cannot be bought.*

When a former magician named Simon witnessed the power of the Spirit, he sought to grasp this power for himself. When he offered Peter money, Peter harshly rebuked him (v. 20). The coming of the Spirit is always a gift granted by God, and a grace associated with the baptism of true believers.

For the gift of the Holy Spirit we offer God praise and glory. The Psalmist in Psalm 29 reminds us that believers are always to "ascribe to the Lord glory and strength" (v. 1), and to worship God in holy splendor. The power of the Lord is expressed here with images of nature's majesty and strength: the voice of the Lord is more powerful than all that the wind and sea can unleash.

On this day, as we commemorate the Lord's Baptism, may we also give thanks for our own baptism and gift of the Holy Spirit, which empowers us for our vocation as followers of our Lord Jesus Christ.

POINTS TO PONDER

1. Describe the events of the Baptism of Jesus as told in the Gospel passage. If you had been an eyewitness to this event, what exactly would you tell someone else about what you observed?

2. Why do you think people thought John might be the Messiah? What do we learn in Luke 3:15-16 about the ministry of John and of Jesus?

3. What is the difference between John's baptism with water and the baptism of the Messiah "with the Holy Spirit and fire" (v. 16)? What does this passage tell us about the Holy Spirit?

4. Immediately after he is baptized, Jesus prays (v. 21). What does this tell us about the role of prayer in the ministry of Jesus? What do you think he might have prayed about?

5. What do you think was the significance of Jesus' Baptism?

MIRACLE AT CANA

Isaiah 62:1-5; Psalm 36:5-10; 1 Corinthians 12:1-11; John 2:1-11

The theme of this Epiphany season, the *manifestation of Jesus' glory* as the *culmination of God's revelation,* receives striking evidence in John's Gospel. Today we witness the beginning of miracles or "signs"—in the story of the wedding at Cana. This opportunity becomes an occasion for revelation of the *glory of Jesus.*

Jesus understood his vocation. He had heard the Father's voice that proclaimed his status: "You are my Son, the Beloved; with you I am well pleased" (Lk. 3:22b). He was aware of how he was empowered to demonstrate the true nature of God as love, not only in great crises, but also in the ordinary situations of human life.

Jesus' mother was attending a wedding at Cana in Galilee, to which Jesus and his disciples had also been invited. Jesus had gathered his first disciples in the two days preceding this event as he traveled through Galilee (1:35-51).

A wedding feast was a major social event that often lasted a week, with new guests arriving every day. The wine flowed freely on such occasions; but when the wine ran out during the celebration, Mary informed her son of the shortage.

Jesus replied that this was no concern of his, for his hour had not come. His words here appear harsher than they really are. Referring to his mother as "Woman" is not a rebuke or an indication of a lack of affection or respect, but rather the way that Jesus often addressed women (Mt. 15:28; Lk. 13:12; Jn. 4:21). Jesus is reluctant to act here because his actions are controlled by the Father alone, and not by human intervention (Jn. 5:19). However, Mary does not seem to doubt that her son will do something, and instructs the servants to "Do whatever he tells you" (2:5).

Thus Jesus tells the servants to fill with water *six stone jars* meant for ritual washing. He then orders them to "draw some out, and take it to the chief steward" (v. 8). The miracle itself is expressed very simply and without any explanation: "When the steward tasted the water that had become wine ... " (v. 9a). The steward does not know the source of the wine, and praises the bridegroom for keeping the good wine for last. John concludes the incident by telling us that this was the first of the signs Jesus did that "revealed his glory; and his disciples believed in him" (v. 11).

There are many levels on which this incident, unique to the Gospel of John, has been interpreted. However, the story accomplishes two main objectives. First, *Jesus reveals his glory to the disciples so that they believe.* This event is actually the conclusion of their call to follow Jesus. Second, as with all the "sign" stories, *Jesus is revealed as the one who has been sent by the Father* to bring salvation to the world. The abundance of wine, 120-150 gallons, draws attention to the extravagance of the messianic age, as we see again in the feeding of the five thousand (Jn. 6: 1-14).

Here we also see the power of the Word: With the words, "Fill the jars with water" (v. 7), an ordinary event, a wedding, takes on

PRAYER FOR THE DAY

Almighty God, your Son our Savior Jesus Christ is the Light of the world; so help your people, enlightened by your Word and Sacraments, to shine forth and make Christ known to the ends of the earth. *Amen.*

cosmic proportions. A potential social disaster is averted, and we see the first evidence that the world is forever changed.

We expect songs of joy to accompany festive occasions, and the final chapters of the Isaiah scroll provide such songs to celebrate the return of exiles from Mesopotamia. For God's people to once more take possession of Mount Zion was a victory. However, this was not a military victory, as there was no vanquished foe. Rather, the opportunity to rebuild Judea came as a gift of God through Cyrus of Persia, who allowed the exiles to return home.

They have come to rebuild the walls of Zion and to restore the temple site as a place of worship for God. This is the Lord's doing, and God's victory must be made more resplendent. As the glory of Jerusalem rises, Israel will be vindicated against the nations that had mocked the Holy City's ruin. The Lord, who has provided the power to renew the place where the Divine name dwelled, will bestow a new name on the people. They will be seen as a glorious crown, a royal diadem in God's hand (62:3).

The worshipers can forget that their nation was once thought forsaken by their God. The land they love will no longer be thought of as desolate. The Lord God will delight to see Judea ploughed and irrigated to bring forth bounteous produce.

ON REFLECTION

How do we "read" the Epiphany story of Jesus' turning water into wine? There seem to be two pitfalls in incorporating its message into our lives. The first lies in overemphasizing the literal; the other in putting too much weight on the symbolic.

Looking too literally at the marriage feast in Cana makes Jesus appear solely as the wonder-working vintner, the party-saver, the reluctant rescuer of a bridegroom's oversight.

It represents Jesus as "God-when-you're-in-a pinch" or Jesus as the super-capable caterer. Or maybe Jesus, in this reading, becomes the new expression of the "foxhole God"—a Hebrew equivalent of Bacchus.

Or maybe we see Jesus as having defied the laws of nature with the central intent of dazzling the crowd. If turning water into wine is the whole story, an end in itself, it comes too close for comfort to the image of TV evangelists commanding people to stand up out of their wheelchairs and dance off stage.

On the other hand, to view the wedding feast as hovering in a symbolic mist abstracts the wonderfully human dimensions of the story. This view says the water doesn't really become wine—that is, intoxicating—but is some divine, nonalcoholic nectar that actually stands for the sweet new life Jesus brings.

But taking an overly symbolic view substitutes a sort of ethereal Jesus who glides into Cana a foot off the ground, aura burning brightly, with disciples following dutifully at a distance looking like their Master—very spiritual. This picture leaves little room for a Jesus who arrives tired and thirsty, ready to relax and enjoy himself—one who delights in the high occasion of this wedding.

What if Jesus hadn't turned water into wine, saving the party? It is said that every problem in life has hidden within it an opportunity so powerful that it literally dwarfs the problem. What if the literal and symbolic wine hadn't flowed on that occasion? It would be the greatest tragedy of life to miss the experience of Jesus' offering of the New Being.

—H. King Oehmig

Using the imagery of a wedding of the Almighty to the people, the prophet proclaims that "as the bridegroom rejoices over the bride, so shall your God rejoice over you" (v. 5b).

A different form of rejoicing and a different set of powers come into being in Paul's letter to the people of Corinth, who had received gifts beyond what they could understand. Here Paul seeks to help his converts make sense of the fullness of life they now experience through Jesus Christ. He does this by contrasting their *new life in Christ* with their former pagan life.

Now they find their own capacities enhanced and even *taken over* by powers that did not originate within themselves. How are they to understand the work of God and the gifts by which the work of God's Holy Spirit was made manifest in their lives?

Paul offers an initial test by which believers may know whether they are being guided by the Holy Spirit or are listening to some other voice. Does what we feel impelled to *do* or *say* or *think* glorify Jesus as Lord and Savior? Nobody will acknowledge Jesus as Lord except through the inspiration of the Holy Spirit. Likewise, no one speaking by God's Spirit ever curses Jesus.

Paul then goes on to identify the spiritual gifts that God needs and uses. Although there are a variety of gifts, they all have their source in the one Holy Spirit. Some gifts may be more necessary in one particular time and place than another, but all are apportioned to each one of us as God wills.

However, as the Psalmist tells us, the greatest of God's gifts is God's steadfast love. This love extends to the heavens; and God is the Holy One whose righteousness is like mighty mountains. God is the judge who saves animals and humans alike, and in whom God's people can take refuge. The Lord brings *light and life*. In a celebratory atmosphere, like that of the wedding at Cana, "They feast on the abundance of your house, and you give them drink from the river of your delights" (36:8).

POINTS TO PONDER

1. Imagine that you are one of the guests at this wedding in Cana. Describe the atmosphere of the occasion. What is the reaction when the wine runs out and is replenished with even finer wine? Why do you think Jesus was reluctant at first to do anything about the depleted wine supply? Why do you think he changed his mind? How would you characterize Mary's role in this incident?

2. What does this passage tell us about the world in which Jesus lived and about Jesus himself?

3. What do you think the effect of this event might have been on the disciples, on the servants who drew the water, and on the other guests?

4. In John 2:11, we read that the glory of Christ was revealed through this miracle. What is meant by the "glory" of Christ? Read the Epistle for today in 1 Corinthians 12:1-11, and reflect on the spiritual gifts you have been given in order to show forth God's glory.

5. John tells us that the "disciples believed in him" (Jn. 2:11) after this event. As you read this story, what is its meaning for you?

_____

_____

_____

_____

GOD'S WORK OF DELIVERANCE

Nehemiah 8:1-3, 5-6, 8-10; Psalm 19; 1 Corinthians 12:12-31a; Luke 4:14-21

The Old Testament and Gospel readings for today both illustrate the power of God's Word in Scripture. Nehemiah and Ezra read and interpret the "book of the law of Moses" (Neh. 8:1b) to the gathered people who have returned from Exile. The ministry of Jesus is revealed as he reads from the Prophet Isaiah in the synagogue in Nazareth.

When the exiles from Mesopotamia returned to their ancestral homeland, they faced two vital tasks. One was the physical rebuilding. Jerusalem lay in ruins. Solomon's temple and the royal palaces had been looted and burned. The city's defense walls had been demolished, and a vast amount of material construction was needed before proper life could resume. To rebuild such a land and city demanded more perseverance than had been needed in regaining possession of the land.

But even more important was the renewal of the spiritual foundation of the nation's common life. Lacking a uniform understanding of life as set forth by Moses and the Commandments, the people were headed toward the same behavior that had reaped national disintegration in the past.

To guard against such failure, Nehemiah and Ezra resolved to set before *all the people* the revealed way of life that was God's intention for their welfare. Thus, in the seventh month, the people were gathered together before the Water Gate, and the "priest Ezra brought the law before the assembly" (8:2). As he opened the book, the people stood up in reverence, bowed their heads in worship, and then Ezra began to read.

As a representative of both the hereditary priesthood and the tradition of scholarship, Ezra read from the scroll, while the governor,

Nehemiah, along with Ezra and the Levites, interpreted the meaning. After three generations away from Judea, many of the people no longer understood the language, so the appointed scribes explained and translated the words.

When the people heard the words of the Law, they wept as they began to comprehend how far short their own lives were of God's will. Yet Nehemiah and Ezra assured them that this was not an occasion to mourn: " ... for this day is holy to our Lord; and do not be grieved, for the joy of the Lord is your strength" (v. 10b).

Such a message is an occasion for praise to God as expressed in Psalm 19, which reminds us that all creation is telling the story of God's work. In this hymn to God as the Creator of nature and giver of the Law, we see how emphasis on the Law (vv. 7-13) counterbalances the personification and poetry of verses 1-6.

The heavens are pictured here as a celestial choir, which praises God without ceasing; the skies are like a track on which the sun, like an athlete, runs its daily course. But it is through the Law that God's servants find *how to live in obedience and righteousness*.

Luke's Gospel shows Jesus reading the Word of God and offering his interpretation in

PRAYER FOR THE DAY

We pray for grace, O Lord, to respond to the call of our Savior Jesus Christ. May we proclaim the Good News of his salvation to the whole world, that all may know the glory of his redeeming work. *Amen.*

the synagogue of Nazareth. In Luke's chronology, this event follows directly after Jesus' experience in the wilderness following his Baptism, where he overcame temptations and defined his understanding of his vocation.

Thus, empowered by the Holy Spirit, Jesus began his ministry in Galilee. His message was well received, and he "was praised by everyone" (4:15). He traveled to Nazareth where he had grown up, and went to the synagogue on the Sabbath as he usually did. The synagogues were the central focus of Jewish community life and worship, and the presence of Jesus in the synagogue puts the actions of Jesus firmly within the context of contemporary Judaism. The worship service itself would have included prayers, the reading of Scripture, and comments on the readings.

Jesus stood up, took the scroll that was handed to him, and began to read from the Prophet Isaiah. The text he was given is what we know as Isaiah 61:1-2, which begins, "The Spirit of the Lord is upon me" (v. 18). This fact had been made clear to Jesus as the Dove descended at his Baptism. Therefore, he was empowered—anointed—to be a herald of joy to the poor, to release the captives and oppressed, to bring sight to the blind, and "to proclaim the year of the Lord's favor" (v. 19).

Jesus then returned the scroll to the attendant and sat down. He had the complete attention of the people in the synagogue, who were watching him closely. Then he began to teach them saying, "*Today* this scripture has been fulfilled in your hearing" (v. 21)—not in the vague, distant future. The Kingdom of God was

ON REFLECTION

Today's Gospel poignantly reminds us that it is as important to know to whom *we are speaking as to be certain* what *we are saying.*

William H. Willimon has written in an article entitled "Shaped by the Bible" (in Christianity Today, *Nov. 11, 1991, and just as relevant today): "Because we have been so willing to accommodate the message of the Bible to the limitations of contemporary culture, the modern world does not regard the church as a threat; I suspect that it regards us as merely boring. We are giving the modern world less and less in which to disbelieve because it senses no difference between what the church is saying and what is being said by a variety of secular voices. Thus, the modern world is not called upon actively to decide for or against the church, because it sees in the church so little against which to take a stand. The world which once imprisoned our ancestors now responds to an utterly enculturated church with mere indifference."*

Who is listening anymore? Is it possible to "wake up" an audience that is already more than saturated with Entertainment Tonight and Reality TV? What does it mean in our times to speak the language of Good News—of relief to the poor, release to the captives, recovery of sight to the blind, and freedom to the oppressed?

What strikes us most in this scene is Jesus' undeviating courage *to speak the truth God has given him to deliver. He doesn't soft-peddle his unsettling proclamation to ease all his listeners, with a minimum of discomfort, into the reality he proclaims. He doesn't give them applesauce; he tells the truth—in the power of the Spirit. And he trusts God to use the proclamation according to the Divine providence.*

—H. King Oehmig

truly present in the person of Jesus of Nazareth. But there was more to be done.

Thus, after Jesus concluded his teaching, as we find in verses 22-30 (not included in today's text), the mood of the people changed. Their response turned to anger, as Jesus told them that his message of liberation was not just for the people of Israel. The crowd then drove him out of the synagogue and tried to stone him. This experience foreshadows the later rejection and hate that would culminate in his being crucified.

How are we to carry out the mission that Jesus has spelled out for us? In a continuation of the Corinthians passage from last week, Paul uses the analogy of the body to emphasize the importance of the unity of the community. Paul states that the body has many parts or members; each Christian is an individual member of the whole. Everyone who is in Christ belongs to that one Body. In baptism it is the one Spirit of God who comes to us.

Into this unity we bring all that we have been before, including our ethnic heritage and social status—whether as "Jews or Greeks, slaves or free" (1 Cor. 12:13). The physical body has many functions: to move, to hear, to see, to smell. And no one part can claim to be more necessary than another. So it is with the Body of Christ, in which all members are essential to the well-being of the whole. If one member suffers, all the members suffer together.

God appoints the gifts to various individuals, and no one person can claim them all. However, there is one gift—the greatest gift—that all can claim. That gift is the unfailing loving-kindness of God.

POINTS TO PONDER

1. If you had been present in the synagogue on this particular day, how do you think you would have reacted to Jesus' proclamation in Luke 4:21?

2. In verse 16 we read that Jesus went to the synagogue "as was his custom." Why do you think this particular fact is mentioned? What else do we learn about Jesus and the world he lived in from this passage?

3. As you reflect on verse 18, from the Isaiah Scroll, how have you personally been freed from captivity, blindness, or oppression through the power of Jesus Christ?

4. As individuals, we are also called to carry on the ministry that Jesus describes. As you read the verses from the Epistle passage for today in 1 Corinthians 12, how are you personally called to ministry as a member of the Body of Christ?

5. The opening line of the Gospel reading states that Jesus was "filled with the power of the Spirit." What do you think this meant for Jesus at this particular time in his ministry? How do you feel the Spirit of the Lord working in your own life?

_____

_____

_____

_____

_____

JESUS' PRESENTATION

Malachi 3:1-4; Psalm 84; Hebrews 2:14-18; Luke 2:22-40

"How lovely is your dwelling place, O Lord of hosts!" Thus begins our Psalm for today, Psalm 84. With these beautiful lines, we appreciate the joy of dwelling in God's House—where even the sparrow finds a home, and the swallow a nest.

Today we read of Jesus' Presentation in the temple on February 2, which is also called "Candlemas." This refers to the custom of blessing and distributing candles and carrying them in procession to the altar, a custom that probably originated in the seventh century.

The candles are distributed among the congregation and the Nunc Dimittis is sung; after which the people make a procession to celebrate the coming of Christ, the "True Light," into the world.

On this day we commemorate the fortieth day of the infant Jesus' life, when he was presented and dedicated to God in the temple. This action was performed in obedience to revealed law. Every firstborn male was to be so dedicated (Lk. 2:22-23).

Also implied in the phrase, "When the time came for their purification" (2:22), is the purification of Mary, based on Levitical law (Lev. 12:6). After the birth of a son, the mother was ceremonially unclean for seven days until the circumcision. Then she had to remain homebound for another thirty-three days until the fortieth day, when she offered a sacrifice to the priest to make atonement on her behalf (Lev. 12:1-8). Thus, for Luke, the cleansing of the mother and the offering on behalf of the child occur in a single trip to the temple.

As the Holy Child was carried in, the holiness of God's people reached out to him in the person of Simeon. There are those whose unfailing trust in God's care leads them to await the nation's redemption with patient expectancy. They are people open to God's Holy Spirit—and Simeon is preeminent among them.

Simeon is convinced that he will live to see the Redeemer come to console his people. And Simeon is here in the temple at the right time, as Mary and Joseph enter with Jesus. Simeon reaches for the Child, and his thankfulness pours out in the poetic words that we call the Nunc Dimittis:

> Lord, now you let your servant depart
> in peace according to your word.
> For my eyes have seen your salvation,
> which you have prepared before the face
> of all people,
> a light to lighten the Gentiles and the
> glory of your people Israel.

Yet he sees more than Mary or Joseph can yet know. Some will desire redemption on their own terms and will stumble on its reality. Yet others will embrace it as Simeon does. The coming upheaval will bring grief to Mary—a sword to pierce her very soul. But all of this

PRAYER FOR THE DAY

O God, on this day when your only-begotten Son was presented in the temple, may we present our selves to you with humble and contrite hearts, through Jesus Christ our Lord. *Amen.*

will serve to manifest how her Son truly is the embodiment of our salvation.

Simeon is not the only inspired witness. There is the aged prophet Anna, who has persevered through bereavement and years of obedience, and now, freed of earthly ties, can live strictly for God. She had devoted her life to fasting and prayer to prepare the way for the redemption of God's people (v. 37).

She, too, was filled with the Holy Spirit. Anna also recognizes in the Holy Child the climax of God's redeeming love and proclaims the fact.

So now that the requirements of God's revealed religion have been performed, the Holy Family can return to their own town of Nazareth. There the Child would grow in strength and blessedness, "filled with wisdom" under God's own approval.

The Prophet Malachi had spoken of God sending One to prepare the way, a messenger in whom God delights. The prophet envisioned one who would represent God's Covenant, and would test and purify the descendants of Levi, refining them like gold and silver. Only in this way could Judah and Jerusalem once more

ON REFLECTION

Just as the angel Gabriel had not appeared to anyone else in Nazareth to make the fantastic "annunciation"—but only to Mary—so now at the temple no heavenly host sounds a trumpet signaling God's messianic "new thing" being done in this baby. No paparazzi are on hand for this Presentation. No CNN cameras are whirling. No motorcade or microphones are on hand. The magnitude and magnificence is clothed in the mundane. The sacrament of God's healing love is ensconced in the everyday world of dutiful young parents. In other words, God's saving revelation comes from the ground up, not from the sky down.

"God chose what is foolish in the world to shame the wise; God chose what is weak in the world to shame the strong" wrote the Apostle Paul (1 Cor.1:27), and nowhere might this truth be truer than with Simeon and Anna.

From among all the hundreds and thousands of parents who had been in the temple to dedicate their "firstlings," and of the innumerable squealing, shrieking neonates that had passed them by on the way to their own dedications, they recognize the One. Such is the sensitivity of "anointed faith."

"Flesh and blood" has not revealed this to Anna and Simeon, just as "flesh and blood" would not reveal to Simon Peter at Caesarea Philippi that Jesus was "the Messiah" (Mk. 8:27-29).

Likewise, "flesh and blood" alone were incapable of moving the centurion at the cross to exclaim, "Truly this man was God's Son!" (Mk. 15:39).

Nor did "flesh and blood" reveal to Thomas, the doubter, what came to be a summary faith expression in the New Testament: "My Lord and my God!" (Jn. 20:28).

In all of these instances, the Spirit of God "opened the eyes of faith" to recognize this "new thing" God was doing.

—H. King Oehmig

present offerings genuinely pleasing to God at the temple.

To this the letter to the Hebrews stresses the reality of the Incarnation by describing the effects of the messianic ministry. In 2:14 it highlights the coming of Jesus, who lived among us as human in order to liberate humanity. In this way, Jesus brings to us the reality of the priesthood that had been imperfectly represented under the Old Covenant.

As our High Priest, he replaces the imperfect sacrifices—that Malachi had only *hoped* might be made pleasing to God—with the absolute sacrifice that is *the offering of himself.* "He had to become like his brothers and sisters in every respect" (v. 17). It is a voluntary offering, a deliberate submission. And because he himself was tempted in his human life, he is able to help all of us today when we experience trials and testings.

POINTS TO PONDER

1. Why do you think the Prophet Malachi compares the coming messenger to a "refiner's fire" and "fullers' soap" (3:2)? What do these images tell us about the mission of the Messiah?

2. The Psalmist expresses delight in entering the dwelling place of the Lord. Compare your own feelings of being in God's presence with those of the Psalmist.

3. According to the letter to the Hebrews, what was accomplished by God's Son sharing our humanity?

4. In the Gospel passage, how do you think Anna and Simeon felt when the infant Jesus was brought to the temple? Why were Mary and Joseph amazed by Simeon's words concerning the future of their Child?

5. As you reflect on what today's passages tell us about the meaning of Jesus the Messiah for all the world, how are you also changed by the presence of Christ in your life?

REJECTED BY HIS OWN PEOPLE

Jeremiah 1:4-10; Psalm 71:1-6; 1 Corinthians 13:1-13; Luke 4:21-30

The Old Testament and Gospel passages for today illustrate the difficulty of speaking God's Word. As prophets, Jeremiah and Jesus experienced rejection and persecution as they spoke God's truth to a world that did not want to hear the message they came to bring.

The Prophet Jeremiah lived during one of the most tumultuous periods in Israel's history, as he witnessed the destruction of Jerusalem and the beginning of the exile in Babylon. Although he suffered along with the people and protested over the judgment he was forced to proclaim against the nation—he also declared the eventual redemption of Israel. Nonetheless, Jeremiah was persecuted and imprisoned and finally sent into exile in Egypt.

The Lord had appointed Jeremiah to be "a prophet to the nations" (1:5) even before his birth. Yet Jeremiah did not believe he was worthy, because of his youth and lack of rhetorical skills. And so God told Jeremiah not to be afraid; the Lord would be with him and give him the words to speak. "Now I have put my words in your mouth" (v. 9).

Jeremiah's message was not just for Israel, but for all peoples and nations. His words were intended to uproot and destroy false human structures so that the way would be clear to build and plant what the Lord intended: "to pluck up and to pull down, to destroy and to overthrow, to build and to plant" (v. 10).

Today's Gospel reading continues from Luke 4:14-21, and recounts the reaction of the congregation in Nazareth when Jesus proclaimed, "Today this scripture has been fulfilled in your hearing" (4:21).

Just as Jeremiah was consecrated and anointed as a prophet before his birth, Jesus had been anointed by the Holy Spirit as God's Beloved (Lk. 3:22). Now he understood that the words of the Isaiah scroll (4:18-19) defined his own vocation. The Holy Spirit had come upon him to bring good news to the poor, sight for the blind, and freedom for the oppressed. These were the manifestations of Jubilee—the year of the Lord's favor.

The initial response of the congregation was amazement "at the gracious words that came from his mouth" (v. 22). But this astonishment soon turned to skepticism and anger. They knew Jesus as the son of their neighbor Joseph. How could anyone they knew so well presume to make such a claim?

Jesus was aware of their reaction and responded by quoting the proverbial saying, "Doctor, cure yourself!" (v. 23), to demands that he perform his usual quality of miracles in Nazareth. He went on to proclaim that "no prophet is accepted in the prophet's hometown" (v. 24).

Jesus knew that his message of a universal invitation—not one restricted to Israel—would be unacceptable to the people of Nazareth. They were satisfied with their own heritage and understanding, and were offended by the notion that they did not possess an exclusive status with God.

PRAYER FOR THE DAY

Almighty God, all things both in heaven and on earth are in your hands. We your people ask today for your peace and blessing, through Jesus Christ our Lord, who lives and reigns with you and the Holy Spirit. *Amen.*

Thus, like his great prophetic predecessors, Jesus will turn to the Gentiles as he reminds the congregation of the examples of the prophets Elijah and Elisha. Elijah was Israel's prophet; but during the great famine, he was sent to a foreign widow of Zarephath to bring God's help and relief (1 Ki. 17:8-24).

Elisha, next in the line of Israel's prophets, cleansed a Syrian military commander and enemy of Israel, Naaman, of leprosy (2 Ki. 5:1-19). The people of Nazareth did not like to be reminded of these facts any more than they wanted to entertain the notion that Gentiles could be admitted to God's Kingdom.

Now the words of Jesus no longer seemed so gracious and admirable. The idea that God is present to all the poor and oppressed, regardless of their ancestral ties to Abraham, so enraged the people of Nazareth that they now sought to kill Jesus by driving him out of town and throwing him off a cliff.

They had their own preconceived ideas of how God was to act, and any challenge to these closely held beliefs shook them to the core. As Simeon had predicted at the birth of Jesus (Lk. 2:34), Jesus would encounter rejection and opposition.

Jesus miraculously escaped by passing "through the midst of them" as he continued on his way (v. 30). From there he traveled to Capernaum, where he was accepted as one who taught with authority.

Luke here establishes the pattern that was to characterize the ministry of Jesus—a cycle

ON REFLECTION

What would true willingness toward God look like? Gerald May, M.D., in his work Will and Spirit: A Contemplative Psychology *(HarperSanFrancisco, 1987), points out: "Willingness implies a surrendering of one's self-separation, an entering into, an immersion in the deepest processes of life itself. … It is mastery yielding to mystery. … More simply, willingness is saying 'yes' to the mystery of being alive in each moment. Willfulness is saying 'no,' or perhaps more commonly, 'Yes, but …'"*

The rage exhibited by the people of the synagogue toward Jesus, and his implying that pagans were more obedient to God than the elect, demonstrates to what a degree willfulness had replaced willingness in their religion. Their wills had placed defined limits on what God could and would do, and Jesus-as-Messiah was not in their cards.

What about our religion? How has it become suffused with willfulness to the detriment of willingness—and how, in the process, has the power of the Lord been curtailed among us?

Frederick Buechner wrote in The Clown in the Belfry *(HarperCollins, 1992): "Israel did not want to be a holy nation. Israel wanted to be a nation like all the other nations, a nation like Egypt, like Syria. She wanted clout. She wanted security. She wanted a place in the sun. It was her own way she wanted, not God's way; and when the prophets got after her for it, she got rid of the prophets; and when God's demands seemed too exorbitant, God's promises too remote, she took up with all the other gods who still get our votes and our money and our 9 a.m. to 5 p.m. energies, because they are gods who could not care less whether we are holy or not, and promise absolutely everything we really want and absolutely nothing we really need."*

Whom will we choose to follow?

—H. King Oehmig

of proclamation, rejection, and persecution, as he found rejection by his own people and was then accepted by outsiders. This would also be the pattern for his disciples.

The Apostle Paul puts special emphasis on teachings about spiritual gifts, as he reminds the Corinthians that *all the gifts of the Spirit are of equal importance* and are given for the common good of the community.

In the conclusion to the reading from last week (1 Cor. 12:12-31a), Paul tells the Corinthians that they are to strive for the greater gifts. Thus, in the eloquent hymn of chapter 13, Paul teaches that *the greatest spiritual gift is love.* Without love, the gifts of tongues, prophecy, knowledge, faith, and self-giving are as nothing (vv. 1-3).

Paul goes on in verses 4-6 to list the qualities of this love by contrasting what love is and is not. Love is patient and kind, but not jealous, boastful, arrogant, rude, irritable, or resentful. Love does not insist on its own way or rejoice in wrongdoing. Instead, love rejoices in the truth. Love acts through bearing, believing, hoping, and enduring (v. 7). While the other gifts are transient and incomplete, "love never ends" (v. 8).

Thus Paul urges believers to strive for spiritual maturity. In childhood we spoke, thought, and reasoned as children; but with maturity comes new insight. Yet even so, our present and incomplete way of knowing is like the dim and distorted image in a mirror made of polished bronze. But when we see Christ "face to face" (v. 12), we will be able to discern clearly and know the fullness of what we now know only in part.

Thus, while faith, hope, and love abide, the greatest of the spiritual gifts is love, for it is through love that we experience the glory of Christ. When love rules, we will at last see face to face, and we will know as fully as we are known.

POINTS TO PONDER

1. Imagine the scene at the synagogue in Nazareth as the people's response to the words of Jesus changed from amazement in Luke 4:22 to rage in verse 28. How would you explain what happened here?

2. What does the Gospel passage for today tell us about the ministry of Jesus and the response to his mission? How did this event in Nazareth foreshadow later responses?

3. The proverb about prophets in their own country in verse 24 is a familiar one. What are some other examples of prophets rejected by their own people? How do we continue to reject the message of Jesus in our own time?

4. Also refer to the Old Testament reading in Jeremiah 1:4-10. What do we learn from the experiences of both Jeremiah and Jesus about the role of a prophet?

5. What do you imagine would happen if Jesus were to appear in your own congregation? How would his message be received? What must we do to be prepared to receive him and his word today?

_____

_____

_____

_____

_____

THE MIRACULOUS CATCH OF FISH

Isaiah 6:1-8 (9-13); Psalm 138; 1 Corinthians 15:1-11; Luke 5:1-11

Through the witness of the Prophet Isaiah, Simon Peter, and Paul, we see how *God's glory is revealed in the world* by those who hear and respond to God's call.

The typical pattern of such a call is exemplified in the experience of the Prophet Isaiah, whose commission comes through an ecstatic vision set within the context of the salvation history of Israel: "In the year that King Uzziah died" (Is. 6:1a). This was probably sometime between 742 and 736 B. C.

Isaiah's vision unites heaven and earth as he sees the Lord enthroned in the temple. But God cannot be contained within the perimeters of the building, for the hem of the Lord's robe alone fills the temple. In this heavenly sanctuary, Isaiah also sees six-winged seraphim in flight around God's throne. These heavenly beings praise God in words that are echoed in the liturgy of the Eucharist: "Holy, holy, holy is the Lord of hosts; the whole earth is full of his glory" (v. 3).

Isaiah's response to this mystical revelation is a profound sense of his own unworthiness in the presence of the Divine. "Woe is me! I am lost, for I am a man of unclean lips" (v. 5a). He knew he was a sinner and that such a vision should destroy him. But he receives reassurance of God's grace and mercy as his "unclean" lips are cleansed by a live coal that a seraph brings to him from the heavenly altar. In this symbolic act, Isaiah is freed to hear and to speak God's word.

Now that his sin is purged, he is prepared to respond when the Lord calls for someone to send as a bearer of God's word. Isaiah responds by saying, "Here am I; send me!" (v. 8).

The optional portion of today's text contains the message that Isaiah is to deliver. It foreshadows the inevitable disobedience of the people and consequent desolation of the land. These will indeed be hard words to speak; but there is hope for the promise of the restoration of Israel in a "holy seed" (v. 13b) that will survive in the remaining stump of a tree.

In contrast to the heavenly vision of Isaiah, the call to the Apostles Simon Peter, James, and John came in the course of their everyday occupation as fishermen.

Although the message Jesus proclaimed was rejected by the people in his home village of Nazareth (Lk. 4:28-29), his reputation as a healer and teacher of power and authority spread throughout the region. As the Gospel passage for today begins, Jesus is standing on the shore of Lake Gennesaret (Sea of Galilee). There the crowd pressed around him, eager to hear the word of God.

When Jesus saw two boats near the shore of the lake, he entered the one belonging to Simon Peter. He asked him to anchor it where it was too deep for people to wade out, yet close enough for them to hear. Jesus then sat down, as rabbis did when teaching, and spoke to the crowd from the boat.

PRAYER FOR THE DAY

We pray that you may set us free, O God, from the burden of our sins, and grant to us the freedom of abundant life, through your Son, Jesus Christ our Savior. *Amen.*

When he had finished, Jesus told Simon to row out to deeper water and put down the fishing nets. Simon protested that they had worked all night but had caught nothing. Simon had spent his life fishing on this lake and knew that this was not the best time to expect much of a catch. Yet despite his misgivings, Simon acknowledged the authority of Jesus by addressing him as "Master," and once again cast out the nets.

The result of Simon's action in the midst of doubt was surely a miracle. Never had Simon and his partners seen such a catch of fish. When their nets began to break, they called for the second boat to help with the load. Both boats were so full that they began to sink. As with the miracle of the wine at Cana (Jn. 2:1-11) and the feeding of the multitude (Lk. 9:10-17), the Lord shows his power in an extravagant abundance.

When Simon Peter saw the unbelievable catch of fish, he fell to his knees saying, "Go away from me, Lord, for I am a sinful man!" (5:8). Simon's response is not so much a confession of moral unworthiness as an expression of awe in the presence of the Divine. While Simon's partners, James and John, were amazed by the catch of fish, Simon's focus was on the person of Jesus and on the grace he so freely offered.

Jesus immediately assured Simon, saying, "Do not be afraid; from now on you will be catching people" (v. 10).

Here Simon is depicted from the very beginning as spokesman for the disciples, as well as a man of faith. Jesus' command to let

ON REFLECTION

For Simon and his partners, the opening scenario in today's Gospel is a sadly familiar dilemma for working fisherfolk. They had done all in their human power to seek to fill empty nets through a night of fruitless fishing. All of their training as to when to catch the right tides—perhaps based on the most advantageous position of the moon, coordinated with the proper weather—has not brought them success.

On top of this, they have come to shore only to find their dock crowded with strangers who have gathered to hear their preacher-friend from Nazareth go on and on about the "lilies of the field" and other irrelevancies to the real world they are forced to live and strive within.

The next thing Simon knows, Jesus, who, as a preacher might not be the best example of material success, has the temerity to tell Simon, a crackerjack fisherman, to put out into the deep to catch fish that Simon knows are not there.

What could compel this expert fisherman to go back out rather than protest further the uselessness of it all?

Exhaustion? Exasperation? A chance to prove he is right? Or the Holy Spirit. No doubt, some of each of these explanations; and the lines between them (as within our own hearts) is notoriously fuzzy.

However the decision came to be made, there is in such a reaction some level of surrender, and this is something that Jesus can work with. Simon lets go; and before he can "snap" himself back to reality, he experiences—in this little decision to follow—*the mystery of the Gospel.*

Simon, having said "Yes" to Jesus and having experienced the amazing catch of fish, found that this life self-surrender is the beginning, not the end. Luke says, "When they had brought their boats to shore, they left everything and followed him."

—H. King Oehmig

down the nets was in direct contradiction to Simon's experience as a professional fisherman; yet he placed his trust in the word of the Lord.

This was not Simon's first experience of the power of Jesus. Prior to this, Jesus had healed his mother-in-law of a high fever (Lk. 4:38-39). This story is also told in Matthew 8:14-17 and Mark 1:29-31; but only Luke places the healing before the call of Simon, James, and John.

The fact that Simon, James, and John "left everything" (v. 11) to follow Jesus introduces a recurring theme in Luke's Gospel. Here possessions are shown to be of no concern in the context of God's service. This anticipates the sharing of possessions in the community of Jerusalem in Acts 2 and 4.

Accepting God's call also entails carrying out the tasks of that call. While Simon Peter was to fish for people and Isaiah was to bear forth God's word—Paul was to proclaim the Gospel message.

The core of this message is found in verses 3-4 of today's passage from 1 Corinthians 15. The Resurrection is the heart of this message, and proof of this Resurrection lies in the fact of *Christ's appearances to many*, including Paul himself—even though he had not experienced the earthly ministry of Jesus.

Paul also describes himself as unworthy of his call, since he had persecuted the followers of Jesus. But through God's grace, Christ was revealed to Paul so that he could proclaim the Gospel. This message was freely given in order that others might believe. That grace had so overflowed for Paul that his mission exceeded that of all the others.

POINTS TO PONDER

1. First imagine that you are a member of the crowd that has gathered to hear Jesus teach. How would you describe the events as you observe them from the shore? Now imagine that you are either Simon Peter, James, or John. What are you thinking and feeling as the events unfold?

2. As you look at the actions of Simon Peter, how would you explain his initial response to the bountiful catch of fish (Lk. 5:8)? Why do you think he felt such a sense of his own sin? What do we learn about Simon Peter here? What is the example he sets for us in this story?

3. What do we learn about Jesus and his mission from this passage as well?

4. We read that Peter, James, and John left everything in order to follow Jesus (v. 11). How is the call to Peter, James, and John to follow Jesus a call to us today as well? What do you need to leave behind in order to follow Jesus?

5. Our readings for today focus on God's call, which follows a pattern of commission, objection, reassurance, and sign. How do you see this pattern at work in these passages and in your own life?

BLESSINGS AND WOES

Jeremiah 17:5-10; Psalm 1; 1 Corinthians 15:12-20; Luke 6:17-26

Psalm 1 tells us that *those who* delight in the law of the Lord will prosper, while the wicked will perish. We can choose God's life-giving way, or we can lose life altogether.

In a similar manner, the Prophet Jeremiah speaks of those who are blessed and those who are cursed. Jeremiah lived during the tumultuous era of the Exile. In today's reading, the prophet chastises Judah's leaders who rely on human resources to prevail against the Babylonians, rather than trusting in the Lord. As a result of this misplaced trust, Jerusalem was captured, the temple looted, and the people marched off to exile in a strange land.

Thus "those who trust in mere mortals and make mere flesh their strength, whose hearts turn away from the Lord" (17:5) will experience the fate of dry and lifeless shrubs in the parched wilderness of the desert. In contrast, those who trust in the Lord will be blessed. Even in times of drought, they need not fear and will continue to be fruitful.

Jeremiah goes on to say that the human heart is devious and perverse; its motives answer to no logic and it is seduced to trust in self and human means. The Lord alone can probe the human heart and comprehend who we are. This is the reason that God's judgment is just; for the Lord takes into account not only the *results* of human actions, but the *intention* behind them (cf 1 Sam. 16:7).

Jesus' Beatitudes also present the contrast between two different ways of living. In the verses immediately preceding today's reading (Lk. 6:12-16), Jesus had spent the night in prayer on the mountain in order to discern which of the many disciples who followed him were to be chosen as Apostles. The call of the twelve Apostles also symbolizes the twelve tribes and a reconstituted Israel.

After naming the Twelve, Jesus came down from the mountain with them to stand on a "level place," where a large crowd awaited him (v. 17). The multitude had come to touch Jesus, in hopes of healing from disease and release from the control of unclean spirits (v. 19).

After attending to the needs of the crowd, Jesus proclaims the way of life in God's Kingdom. His words contrast life in the present with life in God's future.

This Sermon on the Plain (6:17-49) is similar to Matthew's much longer Sermon on the Mount (Mt. 5-7). Both are reminiscent of Moses' giving of the Law to the people at Sinai (Ex. 19:20—23:33). But while Matthew compares Jesus to Moses as a lawgiver, Luke shows Jesus as prophet.

Both sermons include the Beatitudes; but whereas Matthew has nine blessings (Mt. 5:1-11), Luke has four, along with four parallel woes: poor/rich; hungry/full; weep/laugh; and rejection/acceptance.

Luke's Beatitudes put more emphasis on ethical and social concerns, while Matthew has a more spiritual focus. The word translated as *blessing* is used in the sense of a pronouncement

PRAYER FOR THE DAY

O Lord our God, accept the prayers of your people; and because we are powerless without you, enable us by your grace to keep your commandments, and to please you in will and deed. *Amen.*

of the Lord's favor. To be blessed or happy is to entrust one's life to the Lord, and results from following God's ways.

Jesus begins with the declaration: "Blessed are you who are poor, for yours is the kingdom of God" (v. 20), meaning those who are economically deprived or marginalized by society. Jesus came "to bring good news to the poor" (Lk. 4:18); and he later defined his mission as proclaiming the "good news of the kingdom of God" (Lk. 4:43).

In contrast, Jesus proclaims "woe to you who are rich" (v. 24)—those who put their trust in wealth and possessions instead of God. The promise to the poor is the Kingdom of God, which is everlasting—while the wealth and power of the rich are transitory.

"Blessed are you who are hungry now, for you will be filled" (v. 21a). Like the poor, the hungry have the promise of future abundance; whereas those who are full now will be hungry later (v. 25a). The promises of these first two Beatitudes echo the words of the Magnificat, in which the Lord has "filled the hungry with good things, and sent the rich away empty" (Lk. 1:53).

"Blessed are you who weep now, for you will laugh" (v. 21b). This is the only place in the New Testament where the word *laugh* appears, as the joy of being in the Kingdom of God. However, those who trust in themselves only will find their laughter turning to weeping and mourning (v. 25b). In the case of the "woes," the connotation of laughter is that of a fool who puts trust in the wrong things.

"Blessed are you when people hate you" (v. 22a). Those who are hated, reviled, excluded, and defamed for their allegiance to the Son of Man should rejoice, for they will be rewarded in heaven.

ON REFLECTION

Joan Chittister offers two parables for the Christian life of blessedness in her book How Shall We Live? *(Benetvision, 2006). One is from the Sufi masters and one from the monastics of the desert. She comments that these may "tell us most about what it means to live an illuminated life in hard times."*

In the first, the Sufis tell about a spiritual elder who asked the disciples to name what was most important in life: wisdom or action?

The disciples were unanimous in their opinions: "It's action, of course," they said. "After all, of what use is wisdom that does not show itself in action?"

"Well, perhaps," the master said, "but of what use is action that proceeds from an unenlightened heart?"

In the second story from the desert monastics, Abba Poemen says of Abba John that he had prayed to God to take his passions away from him so that he might become free from care. "And, in fact," Abba John reported to him, "I now find myself in total peace, without an enemy."

But Abba Poemen said to him, "Really? Well, in that case, go and beg God to stir up warfare within you again, for it is by warfare that the soul makes progress."

And after that when warfare came Abba John no longer prayed that it might be taken away. Now he simply prayed: "Lord, give me the strength for the fight."

—H. King Oehmig

Jesus and his followers would suffer as the prophets had. But Jesus warns of the woe "when all speak well of you" (v. 26), for flatterers are like false prophets who tell people what they want to hear.

The Beatitudes are examples of Luke's divine reversals that contrast the present with the future. By juxtaposing the way of those who will experience blessings (the faithful) with those who will experience woes (the unfaithful), Jesus points to a final judgment and reversal of fortunes. All hardships of the present life will disappear in God's Kingdom.

The Apostle Paul's words, in his letter to the Corinthians, reflect the future promises of the Beatitudes—as he refutes the arguments of those who would deny the Resurrection.

Since Christ was raised from the dead, those who believe in him will also be raised. If God raised *anyone*, specifically Christ, then God was capable of raising *everyone*.

If the proclamation of Christ's Resurrection was a lie, there could be no fulfillment beyond this life for anyone. "If Christ has not been raised, your faith is futile and you are still in your sins" (15:17). Thus, if our hope in Christ were limited to this present life, there would be no hope at all—no faith, no forgiveness, and no salvation.

"But in fact Christ has been raised from the dead, the first fruits of those who have died" (v. 20). Christ's Resurrection is *the first*—assuring that this gift will be granted to all.

POINTS TO PONDER

1. In the Gospel passage's opening verses (Lk. 6:18-19), why did people seek out Jesus? Why do you think he healed their physical and spiritual maladies before he taught them?

2. What does it mean to be "blessed" as the word is used in this passage? What do you think Jesus means in saying, "Woe to you"?

3. Who are the recipients of blessings, and why are they blessed? To whom does Jesus issue warnings, and why?

4. Compare the blessings and woes of the Gospel passage with those in the Old Testament reading (Jer. 17:5-10), as well as to the "righteous" and "wicked" in Psalm 1.

5. Also read the Beatitudes in Matthew's Gospel (Mt. 5:1-11). What further insights do you have as you compare the two accounts? How have you felt blessed in your own life?

THE GOSPEL OF LOVE

Genesis 45:3-11, 15; Psalm 37:1-12, 41-42; 1 Corinthians 15:35-38, 42-50; Luke 6:27-38

Psalm 37 today reminds us of God's sovereignty. We are not to be envious of wrongdoers. Verse 12 surely was in Jesus' mind when he proclaimed—in today's Gospel—that we are to be patient, merciful, and loving even to enemies. The theme of trust in God pervades the whole of the Psalm: *the Lord will uphold the righteous.*

The pronouncements in today's Gospel call us to forsake any hardness of heart and open ourselves to living in God's love. The text continues Luke's version of the preaching of Jesus, with sayings parallel to those in Matthew's Sermon on the Mount (Mt. 5:38-48).

These wise sayings have become familiar to us as "Love your enemies"; "Turn the other cheek"; "Do to others as you would have them do to you"; and "Judge not and you shall not be judged."

The only way that life in this world can be made tolerable is if at least *some* of us will act toward others as we would wish them to reciprocate toward us; to offer the second chance—and the third and the fourth. By such behavior we hope to be faithful children of the Most High. Yet all of these can be hard sayings, and we often fail to act on them. It is human nature to seek one's own gain, and prosperity for one's own family.

But Jesus requires more of us. We might translate his words as: "What sort of goodwill is it for you to love those who love you? Or to do favors to those from whom you expect a return? Sinners do that much." It indicates no great goodness to follow the path of reward and benefit.

Surely Joseph, in our Old Testament text, who was used of God to save his brothers from dying in the famine (Gen. 45:3-11, 15), did not owe them a thing when they came begging for food. But his heart was moved by compassion and a sense of God's larger purposes for all of their lives. He saw beyond the immediate situation to what might be.

God leads us in these paths, as the model for compassion. The Lord is forgiving instead of judging, and generous when there is no obvious cause to be so. Thus we are called to manifest a likeness to our Heavenly Father, who has graciously adopted us to become children of God. This is our calling and our destiny.

Even sinners are likely to respond in kind when goodness is showed to them. The point of being disciples of Jesus is that we are to initiate acts of kindness before any good has been done for us. When we take the initiative, we extend God's care and point to the Divine goodness.

Just as Jesus died for us when he knew we were sinners (Rom. 5:8), so we also are compelled to generosity toward others. And when we are paid with ingratitude, we are to do yet more generous deeds, sometimes even to the same people who have hurt us.

We are to be merciful because God has shown such undeserved mercy to us (v. 36). We are to give, not because we hope to get a

PRAYER FOR THE DAY

O God, we pray, send your Holy Spirit into our hearts, our souls, our bodies, that we may experience the true bond of peace that unites us forever in you, through Jesus Christ our Lord. *Amen.*

return—even though, in the course of things, that may happen. Good may naturally be returned for good.

However, it is not for the hope of reward that we are to act in this way—but *so that we may be true children of God our Father in heaven.*

Our Epistle in 1 Corinthians 15 explains that Jesus' Resurrection is a model for our hope, a pattern for *our* lives as well. The existence of the physical body hints of the reality of what the spiritual body will someday be—like a full grown plant that rises from a seed.

"So it is with the resurrection of the dead. What is sown is perishable, what is raised is imperishable" (15:42). What we will one day be, we cannot yet imagine.

We begin to grasp the reality of this hope, however, as we contemplate the Risen Jesus. The good news for us is that we, made one with Christ, may look to him as our strength and our redemption, now and forever.

ON REFLECTION

In her work Women Who Run with the Wolves *(New York: Random House, 1992), Clarissa Pinkola Estes shares a striking story about "the way of the old African kings" called "One Stick—Two Stick." It is a fitting illustration about community.*

In the story, an old man who is dying calls his people to his side. He gives a short sturdy stick to each of his many offspring, wives, and relatives.

"Break the stick," he instructs them. With some effort, they all snap their sticks in half. "This is how it is when a soul is alone without anyone. The soul can be easily broken."

The old man next gives each of his kin another stick, and says, "This is how I would like you to live after I pass. Put your sticks together in bundles of twos and threes. Now break these bundles in half."

No one could break the sticks when there were two or more in a bundle.

The old man smiled. "We are strong when we stand with another soul. When we are with another, we cannot be broken."

As M. Scott Peck, M. D., cautions in The Road Less Traveled: *"Whenever we confront someone, we are in essence saying, 'You are wrong; I am right.'" Such an action always carries with it an implied arrogance. I know what is best for you; you don't. Do things my way, and you will be OK.*

Done insensitively, as it is with most parents, teachers, and spouses in their day-to-day affairs, this mode of confrontation creates enmity. Done with humility—with a clear view of one's own corruption and fallibility—such a confrontation can be the start of healing.

—H. King Oehmig

POINTS TO PONDER

1. How are God's purposes for Israel worked out in the story of Joseph as recorded in Genesis? How do you perceive that God is working in your own life?

2. According to the Psalm, how are those who put their trust in God to conduct their lives? What are the benefits that will be enjoyed by the righteous?

3. What is the difference between the physical body and the spiritual body as explained by Paul in his letter to the Corinthians? What does this passage contribute to your understanding of the Resurrection?

4. What kind of life does Jesus expect his followers to live as expressed in the Gospel reading? How do his words relate to those of today's Psalm?

5. How can we as individuals faithfully follow these teachings when the world around us often holds to an opposite set of standards? What changes are you challenged to make as you reflect on today's readings?

FOLLOWING IN JESUS' WAY

Sirach 27:4-7 or Isaiah 55:10-13; Psalm 92:1-4, 11-14; 1 Corinthians 15:51-58; Luke 6:39-49

Our Lesson from Sirach teaches that the true nature of our character will be revealed by what we become, as "fruit discloses the cultivation of a tree" (27:6).

In Isaiah 55 the image of growth continues, and we are promised that God's Word will not return empty, but will accomplish its Divine purpose in the world. And we can choose to become part of this process of the planting and reaping of God's harvest.

Just as the prophets looked for a changed heart to be given to God's people, so Jesus in the Gospel called for *repentance*, a change in direction. Only in this way can hearts be turned toward God.

From the collection of Jesus' pronouncements on what it means to be a disciple, both Luke and Matthew selected those that would enhance their accounts of the Lord's ministry. Many of them are familiar to us as the essence of Christian wisdom.

The two Gospel writers chose many of the same sayings; but Luke placed them in various sections of his Gospel, while Matthew grouped most of them to form what we know as the "Sermon on the Mount," including the "Beatitudes."

Luke also put a number of the sayings together in his chapter 6:20-49 to form a discourse that Luke 6:17 says was spoken *after* Jesus had come down to stand in the plain. Both Luke's sermon and that of Matthew find their conclusion in the same illustration.

The section of Luke's discourse assigned for today begins with a pointed question directed against the religious teachers of the nation. "Can the blind lead the blind?" Will not both persons fall into a pit?

Following this, we encounter a warning that the disciple cannot expect a better reception than Jesus himself has received. Indeed, one should be grateful for the same treatment. The disciple cannot be above the teacher. But those who are fully qualified will be like the teacher (v. 40).

Next there comes a warning against the judgmental arrogance that would condemn another for a minor fault while refusing to recognize a more serious defect in oneself. It is here likened to a person who is troubled by a small speck in his neighbor's eye, while he has a log hanging out of his own—clearly an exaggeration, but one that graphically makes its point, as such metaphors do. It is a memorable image and an often-repeated example.

A similar comparison between ordered and disordered lives is made in the statement that a healthy tree produces good fruit, while a diseased tree brings forth damaged goods. From this, verse 45 concludes that a person whose heart is sound produces what is good, while a wrong-oriented person can bring about only evil. Each naturally produces according to its own nature.

PRAYER FOR THE DAY

Loving Father, we pray that you will deliver us from a lack of faith, so that nothing in this mortal life may overshadow the light of your immortal love, which you have manifested to us in your Son, Jesus Christ our Lord. *Amen.*

One can't expect figs to be gathered from among thorns, or grapes to be found on a worthless bramble. Our "fruit" indicates what we are within. "The good person out of the good treasure of the heart" is going to produce good in the lives of others, because we can only give what is within us and what we have to give.

The discourse concludes with a picture of actual construction: the comparison between houses built with a firm foundation and those with no real basis to build on. Clearly this illustrates how lives themselves are to be built.

Those without foundation may come to Jesus and cry, "Lord, Lord"—but those are empty words when the people who mouth them do not proceed to follow the Lord's commands. They achieve nothing.

In contrast, the person who builds on the "rock" of Jesus will know stability and be grounded in the One who is the Sure Foundation. Jesus himself is the basis of our belief and our actions in the Christian life.

In Paul's words in 1 Corinthians 15:54, nothing can overcome us when we are in Christ: "Death has been swallowed up in victory." God in Christ will save us even from this last enemy, for the Spirit gives life.

Therefore our Psalm for today, 92, is a call for us to worship and give thanks for God's bringing us "home" and planting us as mature "trees" in the house of the Lord forever (v. 13).

ON REFLECTION

Leo Tolstoy includes this parable of "The Three Hermits," in his Twenty-three Tales *(1886):*

A bishop on a voyage saw a fisherman pointing. "What are you pointing at?" he asked. "An island where three hermits live," he answered.

The bishop could make out nothing but water shimmering in the sun. Eventually, he saw the island and asked to visit it for a few hours.

He found three old men holding hands. One was small and always smiling. The second was taller and strong, kindly and cheerful. The third was tall and stern.

"How do you serve God?" the bishop asked. "What are you doing to save your souls?"

"We don't know how to serve God," one answered. "We only serve and support each other," said another.

"The only prayer we know is 'Three are ye, three are we, have mercy on us,'" said the third.

The bishop smiled and spent the rest of the day trying to teach them the prayer, "Our Father."

The bishop returned to his ship and sailed away. When it was dark, he sat at the stern gazing at the sea where the island had disappeared.

Suddenly, he saw something white and shining on the bright path that the moon cast on the water.

The light rapidly got nearer, until he could see it was the three hermits gliding on the water.

When the hermits reached the ship, all three spoke with one voice. "We can remember nothing of the prayer you taught us. Teach it again!" they implored him.

The bishop crossed himself. "Your own prayer will reach the Lord, men of God," he said. "It is not for me to teach you. Pray for us sinners!"

POINTS TO PONDER

1. In the opening verses of Psalm 92, the Psalmist declares that it is a good thing to give thanks to the Lord. For what does the Psalmist give thanks? What special thanksgivings do you offer to God for your life?

2. What is the mystery that Paul explores in his letter to the Corinthians? In light of this mystery, how are we to live our own lives?

3. In the Gospel passage, Jesus uses images of a blind person, a speck in a neighbor's eye, and a man who builds a house. What points does Jesus make through the use of these metaphors? How are they supported by the Old Testament texts today?

4. What insights do these passages offer us as we seek to live in right relation with God and those around us?

5. What concrete steps will you take to begin to practice these difficult Gospel teachings?

THE MANIFESTATION OF CHRIST

Exodus 34:29-35; Psalm 99; 2 Corinthians 3:12—4:2; Luke 9:28-36 (37-43)

The Transfiguration connects us to Jesus' Baptism at the beginning of the Epiphany season *and* prepares us for the approaching Lenten season.

As we anticipate the journey of Lent, we have before us this vision of Christ's glory, which will be fully revealed in the miracle of Easter. Matthew, Mark, and Luke all give an account of this experience of mystery and awe (Mk. 9:2-10; Mt. 17:1-9; Lk. 9:28-36); but it is not recorded by the fourth Gospel writer.

The Gospel passage begins with a reference to "sayings" that had occurred eight days earlier: Peter's confession of Jesus as "the Messiah of God" (9:20); followed by Jesus' first prediction of his Passion (vv. 21-22); and then his teaching on the true cost of discipleship (vv. 23-27). This marks a key point in the ministry of Jesus as he turns toward Jerusalem and the events that are to take place there.

Luke's story, unlike that of the other two accounts, is set within the context of prayer (9:28). Luke often depicts Jesus in prayer (3:21; 5:16; 6:12; 9:18); but this time he takes Peter, James, and John up the mountain with him. While he is praying, the appearance of his face changes, and his clothes become dazzling white (v. 29). Then Moses and Elijah appear and talk with Jesus about his coming "departure" (literally, "exodus") or death in Jerusalem.

Moses and Elijah have had their own mountain experiences of the Divine (Ex. 24:13-18; 1 Ki. 19:8-13); and tradition said that the reappearance of these two prophets would be a sign of the coming of the Messianic age.

In another detail peculiar to Luke, we read that Peter and the others were "weighed down with sleep" (v. 32a). Similarly, these three men will fall asleep while Jesus prays on the Mount of Olives the night before his crucifixion (22:45-46). Nonetheless, they witness Moses and Elijah appearing with Jesus.

Peter, "not knowing what he said" (v. 33b), proposes that they erect dwellings to preserve the site. The temporary shelters would be similar to those constructed at the harvest Feast of Booths, one of the three Jerusalem pilgrim festivals.

Peter's response was misguided, as it is impossible to capture such an extraordinary event by erecting a physical memorial. In addition, building three similar dwellings would incorrectly have indicated that Moses and Elijah were equal to Jesus.

At this point, the disciples were terrified, as they were overshadowed by a cloud (cf Ex. 13:21; 24:15-18; Dan. 7:13). Their terror came from a realization that they were in the presence of the Divine.

Then a voice came from the cloud saying, "This is my Son, my Chosen; listen to him!" (v. 35). However, while the words were spoken only to Jesus at his Baptism (3:22), this time they are heard also by Peter, James, and John. Jesus is not only the *Beloved* of God but the *Chosen* of God; and they are to *listen to him*. After the

PRAYER FOR THE DAY

Almighty God, who revealed the glory of your only-begotten Son on the holy mountain, give us strength to bear our own cross, as we are being changed into his likeness from glory to glory. *Amen.*

voice has spoken, Jesus stands alone. He is not just another prophet. He is God's Son, whom the disciples are to hear and obey.

Luke tells us that the Apostles "kept silent and in those days told no one any of the things they had seen" (v. 36). They are obedient to the command of Jesus in 9:21 not to tell anyone. It was not until the events concerning his Passion had taken place that they could begin to understand what they had witnessed.

In the optional portion of the Gospel text, as Jesus comes down from the mountain on the next day, he is met by a large crowd. A man calls out for Jesus to heal his only son, who is possessed by a spirit that causes him to shriek and foam at the mouth. The man had asked the disciples to heal the boy of this affliction, but they were unable to do so. After decrying the lack of faith even in those who have been with him, Jesus heals the boy, and "all were astounded at the greatness of God" (v. 43a). This incident shows the disciples' lack of power and the need for continued teaching from Jesus.

The Transfiguration of Jesus also recalls the experience of Moses on Mt. Sinai. After he came down from the Mount bearing the tablets of the Law, the people were afraid because "the skin of his face shone" (Ex. 34:29). When he

ON REFLECTION

Rudolf Otto in his classic work The Idea of the Holy (1917) offers a profound study in which he asserts that something happens when humans are confronted with unveiled Holiness. Otto speaks of this experience of God as a numinous event, in which a person encounters the mysterium tremendum et fascinans. When Otto refers to the mysterium, he points to something much more than that which is uncomprehended or unexplained, something slightly out of the ordinary.

Rather, he intends by this term the experience of a Reality that is "wholly other," beyond human fabrication and conceptual control. Such an encounter surpasses all human measurability; it is Holy, it is Other.

The tremendum of the Holy evokes utter astonishment and fear from the one who experiences it. But this fear is not so much terror as it is compelling reverence. It is holy awe. Furthermore, in the midst of this overpowering Presence, the person comes to a profound sense of stark creatureliness, as one's tawdry human nature is juxtaposed to the inexhaustible majesty of God.

Yet in the midst of the holy awe, there is what Otto terms the fascinans: fascination and wonder. The person is simultaneously repelled and drawn close—eerily entranced and captivated by the Mystery.

To decide for the Kingdom of God, and solidly to entrust oneself to it, is to participate in the realm of the Spirit and to express its holy will in the world. It is not only to be invaded by the decisive Reality of existence, but, as Jesus was on the mountain, to be transfigured by its essence.

A. M. Allchin has written in The World Is a Wedding (Oxford Univ. Press, 1978): "By the transformation of the heart, through the realization of God's presence at the center of man's being, it becomes possible to see that 'heaven and earth are full of God's glory.' We discover our kinship with the material creatures; we see all things marked with the name of Jesus."

—H. King Oehmig

spoke directly with God, the reflection of God's glory remained on his face. To encounter the Divine face to face meant death, for who could bear to see the awesome majesty of God? Thus the people were afraid to come near him.

Moses gave assurance of safety to the Israelites so that they would come near to hear the words God had given to him. Once he realized the source of their fear, Moses covered his face with a veil. He removed the veil when he spoke with God and when he communicated the Word of God to the people.

The Psalm for today, Psalm 99, gives expression to the holiness and awesome power of the Lord that Moses and the people experienced. The Lord, the Holy One, the "lover of justice" (v. 4) is to be exalted and worshiped above all others. God had spoken to their ancestors, Moses, Aaron, and Samuel, out of the cloud. They kept God's decrees and received the Divine protection and mercy. Thus the people were to respond by worshiping at God's holy mountain.

Using the experience of Moses and the veil, Paul reflects in 2 Corinthians on the difference between the old and new Covenants. Paul declares that the ministry of Jesus, which made us right with the Father, was more glorious than the ministry of Moses—which led to condemnation for those who failed to keep the Law in its entirety.

Moses' veil was designed to keep the people of Israel from gazing upon a glory that later would be set aside. Now a metaphorical veil prevents those who heard readings of the old Covenant from perceiving its full meaning. In Christ that veil has been set aside.

In 3:17, Paul declares that "the Lord is the Spirit, and where the Spirit of the Lord is, there is freedom." As we grow into freedom through Christ, the splendor of God's purposes can be revealed in us gradually, in a way that we can bear. Thus we are being transformed through our earthly journey as we are changed into his likeness from glory to glory.

POINTS TO PONDER

1. In your own words, describe what happened in today's Gospel passage. What do you think Peter, James, and John might have thought and felt at this time?

2. This passage describes a powerful experience of the presence of God. When have you felt God's presence most strongly in your own life?

3. What do you think was the significance of this event for the disciples who were eyewitnesses? How do you think the disciples were themselves transformed as they witnessed this event?

4. Refer to the Old Testament passage for today in Exodus 34:29-35. What do you notice as you compare the transfiguration stories of Moses and Jesus?

5. Also read today's Epistle in 2 Corinthians 3:12—4:2. How are we being transformed by *God's love for us* and by *our love for others?*

TEMPTED BY THE DEVIL

Deuteronomy 26:1-11; Psalm 91:1-2, 9-16; Romans 10:8b-13; Luke 4:1-13

On this first Sunday in Lent we read of Jesus being tempted in the wilderness. Matthew, Mark, and Luke all tell us that Jesus was intentionally led into the desert, where he faced temptation by the devil.

The prayer that Jesus taught his disciples includes the phrase, "lead us not into temptation, but deliver us from evil." As one who was tempted himself, Jesus was well acquainted with what it meant to face such trials. His forty days in the wilderness recall the fasts of Moses (Ex. 34:28) and Elijah (1 Ki. 19:8), as well as the desert wandering of Israel (Dt. 8:2-6).

In commemorating this, the Church sets aside a period of forty days as a time of self-examination and repentance for us to prepare for Easter. Thus, the Lectionary for the First Sunday in Lent always includes one of the accounts of Jesus in the wilderness.

Luke tells us that Jesus was filled with the Holy Spirit after his Baptism in the Jordan. As the Beloved Son, he understood that he was to bring God's revelation to its climax. But now his task was to determine how to fulfill this vocation. Thus the Spirit leads him into the wilderness for a time of vigil and preparation.

During this time, Jesus fasted: "He ate nothing at all during those days, and when they were over, he was famished" (Lk. 4:2b). Fasting was understood as a way of opening oneself to receive God's guidance. But his hunger also left him vulnerable to the first temptation offered by the devil.

Thus, the devil here challenges Jesus to turn stones into bread. Such bread would not only satisfy Jesus' own immediate hunger, but would also relieve the starvation of the world.

Jesus then replies with a reference from Deuteronomy 8:3 that "One does not live by bread alone" (v. 4). Food alone will not supply what the world needs for a meaningful life. Jesus' vocation must go deeper than providing food for everyone. Misery and oppression still exist even where there is no shortage of food.

The devil then holds out the promise of authority over "all the kingdoms of the world" (v. 5). If Jesus will worship him, he tells him, "It will all be yours" (v. 7). Jesus refuses by paraphrasing Deuteronomy 6:13: "Worship the Lord your God, and serve only him" (v. 8).

Finally, the devil takes Jesus to Jerusalem for the most difficult test. At the very top of the temple, he suggests that if Jesus is truly the Son of God, he could leap down, and angels would save him from harm (vv. 10-11). Here the devil demonstrates his own knowledge of Scripture by misusing words from Psalm 91:11-12. Jesus replies from Deuteronomy 6:16, "Do not put the Lord your God to the test" (v. 12). We are called to trust God's promises, not to exploit them or try to force God to act on them.

Thus we can see that being chosen by God does not provide immunity from experiencing trials and temptation. Jesus' temptations played a significant role in his ministry. Here Jesus rejected the seductive lure of social, religious, and political power in favor of uncompromising obedience to God the Father.

However, in verse 13, Luke makes it clear that the temptations are over, but only for

PRAYER FOR THE DAY

O God, just as Jesus was led by the Spirit to be tempted of Satan in the wilderness, come to us in our own temptations, and deliver us for your purposes, to live and serve you, through Jesus Christ our Lord. *Amen.*

a time. The devil would return to thwart the deeper purposes of God when, in Luke 22:3, we read that "Satan entered into Judas called Iscariot."

Of course, there is more in Psalm 91 than the verses taken out of context by the devil. The Psalm begins with the promise that those who put trust in the Lord will be delivered from danger, and "no evil shall befall you, no scourge come near your tent" (v. 10). God's angels will bear the faithful up, enabling them to trample their enemies. The Lord will answer their prayers and grant them long life and salvation.

The Apostle Paul also speaks of temptation, the idea that we can earn salvation and put God under obligation to ourselves. When there is an established set of rules, a person may expect credit for obeying them. As indicated in Romans 10:5, Moses himself proposed that it could be so. But no one can climb to heaven to

ON REFLECTION

Micha Popper, in his work, Hypnotic Leadership: Leaders, Followers, and the Loss of Self *(Westport: Praeger, 2001), delves into the nature of leadership, especially "twisted" leadership. It seems fitting on the first Sunday in Lent, as we read of the Lord's temptation by Satan in the wilderness, to examine the nature of the leadership we follow.*

Popper begins by saying that leadership needs three components to start and to keep it going. It needs a spark, the leader himself or herself. Next, fire needs fuel—that is, followers. And then it needs oxygen to feed the flames—the circumstances in which the leader and followers find themselves. And leadership, like fire, Popper points out, can be warming and pleasant and an essential aid to human well-being—or it can blaze up and destroy.

As to the latter effect, he cites sick leadership flames that have turned into conflagrations— such as the leadership of the Rev. Jim Jones and the debacle of Jonestown in the 1970s.

In 1978, this "leadership" blazed out of control. Jones stood on a small platform in front of hundreds of adoring believers. In a trembling voice, he proclaimed: "You'll never be loved again like I love you." A few hours later, 911 followers, including children, had poisoned themselves to death.

Next, Popper cites the "spark" provided by the leadership of Charles Manson. Manson, you recall, was the leader of the murderous "Manson Family," most well known for slaughtering a number of people at a party in Los Angeles in the late 1960s.

Spark. Fuel. Oxygen. In the desert, Jesus must decide what kind of Messiah-leader he is to be. Will he be a Divine or demonic leader? That is his question of discernment, and that is his struggle with the devil.

The "fuel," both Jesus and Satan knew, was expansive. As Jesus would later tell the disciples: "The harvest is plentiful." This "harvest" of people would love and adore him, follow and obey him—if he could turn stones into bread. Filling empty stomachs would be his way to manipulate them into allegiance, and then they would be his.

The "oxygen" of poverty would never go away. Even Jesus himself said, "For you always have the poor with you" (Mk. 14:7). The "oxygen" of loneliness and emptiness and powerlessness in a world that seemed to be indifferent to human suffering would forever feed his flame.

Over these forty days and nights, we would do well to contemplate what kind of "spark" we follow, what kind of "fuel" we are, and what kind of "oxygen" we are—or are not—supplying to the flame of Jesus.

—H. King Oehmig

bring the climax of revelation down to us. Nor is the Anointed One to be sought in the depths. Instead, Paul cites Deuteronomy 30:14 to say that God's Word is readily available, even on our lips and in our heart.

The Word that is near to us is the word of faith that proclaims *Jesus as Lord* with total trust that God has raised him from the dead. It is this faith and not our accomplishments that secure salvation. Verse 12 adds that salvation by God's grace applies as much to the Gentile as to the Jew. The Risen Messiah is Lord equally of both.

To call upon the name of the Lord is to be assured of salvation; and no one who believes in God's Messiah will be put to shame.

The Lesson from Deuteronomy 26 calls upon God's people to give thanks for Divine blessings and deliverance. In this excerpt from the farewell address of Moses to the people, he reminds them of God's mighty acts on their behalf. He also warns them of the temptations that will be brought about by new experiences in Canaan.

To show that they do remember and celebrate, they must bring an offering to God's sanctuary from the first of every harvest they gather. This offering of first fruits is to acknowledge that the land God's people possess and the bounty it yields are *God's gifts*.

Verses 5-10 are a confession of faith in the form of a recitation of the people's history. The Israelites have come to the end of their time of trial and wandering in the wilderness. Thus they bring their gifts and bow down to God in thanksgiving.

As we begin this season of Lent, may we use this time to look deep within our own hearts and seek God's guidance to resist the temptations that beset us.

Jesus is our example—and nowhere more clearly than in his overcoming the temptation to cheapen his vocation through the seizing of transitory power. Instead, he chose another sort of Kingdom—the one that is eternal.

POINTS TO PONDER

1. After his Baptism, Jesus spent 40 days alone in the wilderness. How do you think he might have felt, both physically and spiritually, during this time? What was the significance of this event for Jesus himself, as well as for us, as we read about it today?

2. Examine the three temptations that the devil presented to Jesus. Exactly what did Jesus refuse to do and why? Relate these temptations to contemporary issues as well as to the specific temptations in your own life.

3. Look at the responses of Jesus to the devil in Luke 4:4, 8, and 12. What do these answers tell us about the ministry of Jesus as well as our own responsibilities as his disciples? What is the significance of the final verse in this passage?

4. As you reflect on today's Gospel passage, what is the nature of evil as revealed in this incident? How are we to recognize and resist evil?

5. What have we learned about the humanity of Jesus, as well as of his relationship with God? What is the most important meaning of the Lenten season for you? How will you use this time to prepare for Easter?

_____

_____

_____

_____

COUNTED AS RIGHTEOUS

Genesis 15:1-12, 17-18; Psalm 27; Philippians 3:17—4:1; Luke 13:31-35

The texts for today focus on what it means to live in a faithful covenant relationship with God.

We begin with the Old Testament reading, which marks a dramatic turning point in the Abraham saga. The first verse of Genesis 15 is set in the context of a vision—a deep mystical encounter with the Divine in which the "word of the Lord came to Abram." The event takes place after Abram's initial call from God to go to a new land, and the promise that God would make of him a great nation (Gen. 12:1-3).

The Lord tells him not to be afraid—i. e., not to be anxious about the future, as God is Abram's shield or protector. Then Abram is informed that "your reward will be very great." Abram asks the Lord what that reward will be, since he and his wife Sarai continue to be childless. In 12:7 and 13:16, God made the promise that Abram's line would continue; but now it would seem that the offspring of one of his slaves would be his heir. However, God assures Abram with a sign, telling him that his descendants would be in number as the stars of the heavens.

God had not coerced Abram or offered any new promises; and in the face of seeming impossibility, Abram put his whole trust in the Lord and *believed*. Abram does not question how this is to happen, but accepts it as so. And "the Lord reckoned it to him as righteousness" (15:6b). In Romans 4:1-15 and Galatians 3:6-9, Paul urges his converts to follow Abraham's example of *justification by faith*.

In Genesis, the Lord goes on to speak again of the promise of the land (v. 7); but Abram questions how he will know that he *does* indeed possess the land. For although Abram has substantial wealth, he is still a wanderer. The Lord's response is to seal the promise with a covenant ritual in which Abram is to bring a specified number of sacrificial animals. All of these are to be cut in two, except for two birds that are to be left intact.

As night came, a "deep sleep fell upon Abram, and a deep and terrifying darkness descended upon him" (v. 12). In this description of an ancient ceremony, "a smoking pot and a flaming torch passed between these pieces" (v. 17). When two parties pass between the halves of such sacrificial animals, they thus pledge loyalty to one another. This is to symbolize God and Abram as partners in the covenant.

However, this is a one-sided covenant on God's part, with nothing required of Abram. Later on, Abraham will establish a covenant with God in which circumcision is required as a sign of compliance (Gen. 17:1-14). But on this day, God promises to give the land "from the river of Egypt to the ... river Euphrates" (v. 18) to Abram's descendants, based solely on Abram's trust and faith.

Psalm 27 eloquently expresses the faith in the Lord that was exemplified by Abram:

PRAYER FOR THE DAY

O Lord, we confess that we have not obeyed your commandments or walked in your ways, and we need your forgiveness. Bring us again with penitent hearts and renewed faith to cling closely to the unchangeable truth of your Word, Jesus Christ your Son. *Amen.*

"The Lord is my light and my salvation; whom shall I fear?" The Psalmist's trust in God as a stronghold secures him against persecution or war. He longs to dwell in the house of the Lord, beholding God's beauty. The final verse is an answer to the petitions of the Psalmist, who is encouraged to be strong and "wait for the Lord!"

Just as Abram and the Psalmist demonstrate trust and confidence in the Lord, Paul urges his converts at Philippi to "stand firm in the Lord" (4:1), as he gives them an example of Christian life that is counter to the world's values. He urges them to follow his example by giving up material or "earthly things" (3:19); for otherwise their end will be destruction.

The true Christian's citizenship is in heaven, where Christ's saving actions will transform what they are now into the likeness of Christ himself. Creative change, if it is to happen at all, must be a change in us—and this can only occur through *God's power in Christ* (v. 21).

ON REFLECTION

Maybe the Jerusalem of Jesus' day looked more like Garrison Keillor's Lake Wobegon than we thought. Remember the characterization from The Prairie Home Companion—*that Lake Wobegon was "where all the women are strong, all the men are good looking, and all the children are above average."*

Keillor's description on the radio show could almost make the Saturday evening listener see the happy faces in warm, loving homes, breathe in the fresh air, and bask in the light of an American utopia.

Maybe Jerusalem was too much like Lake Wobegon—and it made it hard for the people to hear the Gospel. The primitive testimony seems to be clear with multiple attestations: Jesus meant the most to those who needed him the most.

And Jerusalem did not seem to need Jesus in the least. "How often have I desired to gather your children together as a hen gathers her brood under her wings," Jesus laments, "and you were not willing!" (Lk. 13:34). How many times did he show up offering the Abba experience to the Jerusalemites, times perhaps not mentioned in the Gospels? On how many different occasions did Jesus try to heal their sick, and offer release to their captives—only to be ignored or turned away?

Finally, at that Passover which was to be his last, when they acted as though they did need him, Jesus rode into the City of God on the foal of an ass. Then they threw palm branches in front of him, cheering, "Blessed is he who comes in the name of the Lord!" Maybe things had changed ...

But, within a week, the evidence was clear—they did not need Jesus or his message, thank you very much. Jesus revealed no indication of being the reincarnation of "David" come to deliver Israel from foreign occupation. He showed no prowess as a Warrior-King come to return Israel to preeminence among the nations; he only spoke of a Kingdom "not of this world."

Their rejection of him would set in motion the terrible events of the Passion.

How will we see Jesus, here in the Gospel and in our lives, and what will be our response as the weeks of Lent continue?

—H. King Oehmig

Paul's affection for this community shines through as he tearfully urges his brothers and sisters to remain steady in their life in Christ.

Jesus also talks about the choices one must make in order to follow him. The Gospel of Luke, at its midpoint, shows Jesus continuing on his journey to Jerusalem. Here again we are reminded of the covenant God made with Abraham and the consequences to those who have forgotten that covenant. Being heirs of Abraham does not automatically make one an inheritor of God's Kingdom.

Jesus is preaching, teaching, and healing as he continues his journey to Jerusalem. We read that some seemingly friendly Pharisees came to warn Jesus that Herod sought to kill him. Jesus acknowledged the Pharisees' warning, yet he had no real fear of Herod. Jesus knew that a prophet must perish in Jerusalem and nowhere else. Referring to Herod as "that fox" (13:32), he told the Pharisees to tell Herod of the work of healing and casting out demons that he had yet to accomplish.

The remaining verses in the passage comprise the poignant lament of Jesus over Jerusalem. Jesus loves the city for all that it has been and all that it could be. He is able to see beyond the evil destructiveness of the city's power holders to the worth of the people of Jerusalem. He bewails the city's history of repudiating God's messengers, the prophets. In verse 34b, Jesus' maternal and forgiving concern for the city is expressed: "How often have I desired to gather your children together as a hen gathers her brood under her wings, and you were not willing!"

If there had been a positive response to him, the coming tragedy could have been averted. But the rejection of the ministry of Jesus has rendered God's house desolate. Its glory cannot return until it truly blesses "the one who comes in the name of the Lord" (v. 35b).

POINTS TO PONDER

1. According to the Gospel passage, what will be required to be saved or to enter the Kingdom of God? In particular, what is meant in Luke 13:30 about the first being last and the last first?

2. Discuss your own understanding of the Kingdom of God. What do Jesus' words in verses 24-30 add to your understanding?

3. As you read Jesus' lament over Jerusalem in verses 34-35, what was the significance of this city for Jesus? What aspects of the mission and character of Jesus are revealed in this passage, especially in his reply to Herod and his words concerning Jerusalem?

4. Jesus uses several vivid images in this passage. Imagine what it would be like to: strive to enter through a narrow door (v. 24); be left knocking at a closed door (v. 25); be a chick huddled under a mother hen's wing (v. 34)? What does Jesus convey through the use of these word pictures?

5. What warnings are there for us in the Gospel passage? What gives us hope here? Also read the Old Testament and Epistle Lessons for today. What further insights do these passages contribute concerning a life of faithful discipleship, especially as we move toward the miracle of Easter?

_____

_____

_____

GOD'S LOVING FAITHFULNESS

Exodus 3:1-15; Psalm 63:1-8; 1 Corinthians 10:1-13; Luke 13:1-9

The Old Testament readings during Lent reveal some aspects of God's *covenantal relationship* with Israel. God's promise to Abraham to give him numerous descendants has now been fulfilled.

The ever-increasing numbers of Israelites now residing in Egypt became a threat to the Egyptians, who in turn enslaved them. In their distress, the Israelites cried out to God for deliverance. God remembered the Divine covenant with the patriarchs and "took notice of them" (Ex. 2:25).

In today's passage, Moses is called to be God's agent in the liberation of Israel. After killing an Egyptian, Moses had fled from Egypt to the desert of Midian, where he married and started a new life. Moses was tending his father-in-law's sheep in the wilderness near Mt. Horeb when his attention was caught by a bush that was burning but was not consumed. As Moses stood before the bush, the Lord called to him to remove his sandals as a sign of respect, as he was standing on holy ground.

Moses was filled with awe and hid his face. God had seen the oppression of the Israelites, and had come to deliver them from their oppression. Furthermore, Moses would be the one to go to Pharaoh and lead God's people out of bondage in Egypt (v. 10) into a new and prosperous land.

Moses immediately protested that he was not the one for such a vocation; but God assured him that "I will be with you" (v. 12). Moses continued to object by saying that no one would believe that he acted for God; he did not even know God's name. The name God gives him is variously translated as "I AM WHO I AM" (v. 14) or I SHALL BE WHAT I SHALL BE. This was to be God's name forever—for "all generations" (v. 15b).

This name conveyed a sense of Being in which God would be in relationship with the Israelites and would be faithful to them. God remembered the promises made to Israel, beginning with Abraham, and would act through and with Moses to bring about Israel's deliverance.

Paul knew the Exodus story and wanted his converts to know the story as a part of Christ's message. God had adopted the people of the Exodus. The cloud that led their journey and the sea through which they passed were a baptism into a new life (1 Cor. 10:1-2). The manna that came down from heaven and the water that flowed from the rock were their spiritual food and drink, and somehow conveyed the same Divine life that Christians enjoyed—for "the rock was Christ" (v. 4).

Even though these blessings could be seen and touched and tasted, the Israelites' response was unsatisfactory. Paul warns the Corinthians against idolatry (v. 7) by citing the example of the celebration around the golden calf (Ex. 32). Others indulged in sexual immorality, with dire consequences (Num. 25). Paul interpreted

PRAYER FOR THE DAY

Heavenly Father, we do not have the power within ourselves to protect ourselves, inwardly or outwardly. Defend us, we pray, from all dangers in this mortal life to both body and soul, through Jesus Christ our Lord. *Amen.*

the words of the people because of their lack of water (Num. 21:5) as a test of Christ himself, when many died from serpent bites (v. 6). Amid continual complaining about the hardships of the Exodus, still others perished by pestilence (Num. 14:11-12, 16).

These events are also a warning for those in Paul's time. He counseled his converts in Corinth that they too might fall if they did not resist temptation. He assured them that God is faithful. When temptation comes, God's grace is also present to ensure our endurance (1 Cor. 10:13a).

While Paul's call for repentance was based on examples from the past, the warning of the Gospel was based on current experience. It was a commonly held belief that illness and

misfortune were God's punishment for sin. Several of the prophets had tried to explain that suffering does not come by the will of God. But the idea of such punishment persisted, and an example of suffering was presented to Jesus.

Jesus was reminded of an incident in which a number of Galileans were brutally slaughtered by Pontius Pilate's soldiers while they were presenting their sacrifices. In this horrific act, the blood of the victims was mingled with that of the sacrificial animals. Jesus told them that the sin here was not that of the Galileans, but Pilate's cruelty.

Jesus countered this example with another account of undeserved disaster: eighteen people who had died when the tower of Siloam fell on them. Before the tower fell, there was nothing

ON REFLECTION

The parable of the barren fig tree in today's Gospel serves as an evocative illustration of being stuck in unfruitfulness—in "quiet desperation." The unproductive tree had not been bearing fruit because it was clearly rooted in unyielding soil. Perhaps for us this is the soil of material security. Or it is the dirt of family or emotional ties. Or it is the humus of reputation, whether religious or secular.

But the fact remains, there is a memorable image here of seriously depleted ground. Whatever nutrients were once present are there no longer. This is unmistakably worn-out turf, unconductive to growth.

In human terms, the stark image of the withering fig tree suggests a person disconnected to his or her own soul, someone living off the "outer world"—which is incapable of fostering the appropriate inner growth.

We see in this compact parable a person living detached from the fertile soil of the Gospel and the wholeness that only life in the Spirit can bring. In this state, the tree is useless and will eventually wind up as firewood. But this is not the purpose that the owner of the vineyard had intended for the fig tree; he desired its fecundity.

However, nothing changes until the vineyard lord expresses his discontent. If he had not gotten angry with the situation—calling for the fig tree to be cut down—the gardener could well have let this stale situation continue for another three years.

The parable says that there are limits to this wastefulness, and it is for our sake that there is a deadline, since rarely do any of us change without the impinging of consequences.

Seen in theological terms, judgment is God's grace. This grace says that life is too precious to be squandered by living apart from Christ.

—H. King Oehmig

to indicate that they had been unusual sinners.

In the light of these examples, Jesus took up the task of the prophets to correct a false belief. There was no reason to suppose that either group of unfortunates was more sinful than any others. Yet their fate was to be a warning to the group then present (Lk. 13:3, 5). As Jesus looked at the world, it was ripe for judgment. He saw his own ministry as offering enlightenment: the opportunity to receive the good news of the Kingdom. Such acceptance would empower people to recognize their own wrong and guide them to turn away from it.

Jesus illustrated this point with a parable that is not included in the other Gospels. There was a fig tree in a favorable location that should have been producing, but was not. Although fig trees bear fruit annually, this tree had not flourished for three years; so the man who had planted it ordered the gardener to cut it down.

But this is a story of Divine compassion, and the gardener pleads for one more chance. With a trench to give the roots more moisture, along with extra fertilizer, the tree would produce. If after a year, the tree still fails to bear fruit, the gardener will agree to cut it down. The Lord will give us a second, third, and even a fourth chance; but for the fig tree, there is a definite limit. If it still fails to produce, even the gardener who cares for it will finally agree to its removal. While God's patience is infinite, we are still accountable for what we do.

Today's Psalm expresses a profound longing for the presence of God, whose love is better than life itself. God provides the soul with nurture like a rich feast. In response, the Psalmist will joyfully worship the Lord and meditate on God's blessings through the night.

The Lord is ever faithful, providing aid and protection; thus, "My soul clings to you; your right hand upholds me" (63:8).

POINTS TO PONDER

1. In the Gospel passage, some of Jesus' followers were struggling with the issue of the correlation between sin and suffering (Lk. 13:1-5). How did Jesus address their concerns? How do we continue to confront this issue today?

2. What do you think Jesus means in verse 3, and again in verse 5, when he calls for his listeners to repent? How would you define the word "repent"? What must one do to truly repent?

3. Read the parable of the fig tree in verses 6-9 and consider the following questions: What kind of "fruit" is expected from us as followers of Jesus? How are God's judgment and mercy exemplified here? How would you define judgment and mercy?

4. The fig tree was to be nurtured by digging a trench around it and adding fertilizer. How are we nurtured for God's service? What are the sources of this nurture? What changes are necessary in your life to foster your own growth and productivity?

5. Read the Old Testament text for today in Exodus 3:1-15. What are some of the characteristics of an encounter with the Divine in the story of Moses and the burning bush? When have you felt yourself in the presence of God—when have *you* stood on holy ground?

THE LOST IS FOUND

Joshua 5:9-12; Psalm 32; 2 Corinthians 5:16-21; Luke 15:1-3, 11b-32

Paul's call to his converts in Corinth to be ambassadors for God's "ministry of reconciliation" sets the theme for today's readings. The Gospel passage itself is the culmination of three parables in Luke 15 that focus on reconciliation, forgiveness, and the joy of finding what was lost. The stories were told in response to the grumbling of the Pharisees and scribes because Jesus ate with sinners (v. 1).

That Jesus welcomes such people, and is even willing to eat with them, appears to the Pharisees as guilt by association. These parables of grace are the answer to that judgment.

This narrative parable is unique to Luke, and has several layers of meaning. First we see the younger son, who demands to be given his share of his father's inheritance before he has attained the maturity to use it wisely. As the younger son, he would receive one third of his father's assets. He immediately leaves home and goes to a distant country, where he squanders his money in "dissolute living" (v. 13).

When a famine strikes, he has to resort to the most demeaning of occupations for a Jew: herding pigs. His actions have alienated him from his family, country, and religious heritage; and now he faces starvation as well.

Yet the young man is not totally lost, and he "comes to himself" (v. 17a). He remembers that his father's field hands are better off than he is now. He has forfeited his claim as son; but if he can get home, he can ask his father to at least let him become a hired hand. In verses 18-19, the young man repents and confesses his sins against God and his father before turning homeward.

But the father is watching eagerly for the possibility that his wayward son may return.

As soon as he sees him coming in the distance, he is filled with compassion. He runs out and puts his arms around him and kisses him (v. 20). The kiss is a sign of forgiveness, which is granted even before the son repeats his earlier confession (v. 21).

Disregarding his son's words, the father orders new clothes for the boy, and plans an extravagant celebration. The one who was lost has been found! The actions of the father reflect the words of Jesus in verses 7 and 10, in which he proclaims the joy in heaven over one sinner who repents. Here we see that God's love is unconditional and reaches out to the sinner even before he repents.

Now the focus of the story turns to the older brother, who hears the sounds of celebration as he comes home from working in the fields. He is angry when he learns the reason for the festivities, and he refuses to join in the celebration.

As he did with his younger son, the father goes out to welcome him, and then pleads with him to come in. But the older son bitterly asks why such a party was never given for him. After all, he has served his father well as an obedient son; yet "this son of yours" who wasted his inheritance is treated as an honored guest.

PRAYER FOR THE DAY

Our Father, who sent your blessed Son Jesus Christ to be the true Light of the world, grant us always to live in his Light, as he lives in us, with you and the Holy Spirit, one God, now and forever. *Amen.*

The father insists that "You are always with me, and all that is mine is yours" (v. 31b). The father has not needed to receive him back. They might never have seen the younger brother again, and now there is a chance to make life right for him. However, he does not rebuke his older son for his resentment, but declares his love for him as well.

The two parts of the story are linked by the phrase "He was lost and has been found" (vv. 24, 32). The one who was dead to his family is alive again. This is truly cause for celebration.

All of this adds up to a new way of life—a "new creation"—as Paul proclaims in his second letter to the Corinthians. Just as the father's love reconciled him with his estranged son, so are we reconciled to God through Christ, who never stops loving us (5:18a).

The trouble has always been that we wouldn't turn to God because of our failure to respond to God's love and guidance. As Paul makes clear, we don't have to make up for this. Jesus has lived totally without sin and thus claimed the world's sin as his own. Therefore we can become right by God's action.

Yet we can't think of this in human terms. Even the people who had known Christ as a human being could not think of him in that way any longer. When we are adopted as children of God, we are a new people and "everything

ON REFLECTION

Although it isn't guaranteed by any means, suffering can be a great teacher.

In one of the most famous sermons of all time—"You Are Accepted"—Paul Tillich, writing, no doubt, out of his own experience, said: "Grace strikes us when we are in great pain and restlessness. It strikes us when we walk through the dark valley of a meaningless and empty life. It is as if a voice were saying, 'You are accepted ... by that which you do not know. Do not ask for the name now. ... Do not try to do anything now: perhaps later you will do much. Simply accept the fact that you are accepted.'"

When the squandering, improvident prodigal in today's Gosepl walks hump-shouldered past the swimming pool and up the last leg of the driveway, he does a double-take. He sees his father on the porch scanning the horizon with his binoculars. He is not bird-watching, either. He is "boy-watching," hoping beyond hope that his son might return. The boy sees him leap to his feet and race like an Olympic sprinter toward him. The boy prays that he will get his speech right, that it will have its intended effect: to vitiate his father's righteous indignation and convince him to take him back as a hireling.

But just what you would not expect happens. The boy is swept off his feet, covered in a bear hug of whiskers and tears and primordial shouts of disbelief and joy by his father. Still convinced he must atone for his reckless insensitivity, the boy falls to his knees, beats his breast, and begins to confess something on the order of, "I am not worthy so much as to gather up the crumbs under your table." But the confession flies over his father's head. He doesn't even hear it. "Quickly," the father commands his servants, "bring out a robe—the best one—and put it on him; put a ring on his finger and sandals on his feet. And get the fatted calf, and kill it, and let us eat and celebrate; for this son of mine was dead and is alive again; he was lost and is found!" And the merrymaking begins.

—H. King Oehmig

has become new!" (v. 17b). As a new people, we have been given the "ministry of reconciliation" (v. 18b). We are called to be *ambassadors for Christ* to lead others to peace.

There was also a sense of reconciliation as the Israelites finally entered the Promised Land under the leadership of Joshua. As they came to the Jordan River, the priests carrying the Ark of the Covenant stepped into the water. Then the flow from upstream halted while the water downstream flowed away, so that all the people could cross. Now that they were safely on the other side, the disgrace of slavery in Egypt was taken away.

Thus, Joshua took twelve large stones from the riverbed and set them up at the encampment near Gilgal as a memorial of the miracle that had made the crossing possible. The stones were also to be a reminder of the Red Sea crossing and "so that all the peoples of the earth may know that the hand of the Lord is mighty, and so that you may fear the Lord your God forever" (4:24).

Now there was no longer any need for the manna that had sustained the people through their wilderness journey. They could eat of the produce of their own land and celebrate the Passover without the haste of their first celebration.

Psalm 32 is a prayer of thanksgiving; it affirms that *when we do not hide our sin from God, we can discover the blessing of true forgiveness.* The Psalmist acknowledges the healing power of confession (vv. 3-5), and urges the faithful to offer their prayers to the Lord. God is a *strong hiding place* and will deliver us from trouble. While the tribulations of the wicked are great, God will instruct the righteous and surround them with steadfast love.

POINTS TO PONDER

1. As you read this familiar parable, try to identify with the thoughts and feelings of each of the three main characters (father, elder son, and younger son) at the following points in the story: When the younger son asks for his inheritance and leaves; the period of the younger son's absence; the day the younger son returns home; during the celebration for the younger son; when the older son learns of his brother's return; the conversation between the older son and his father.

2. What do you think the relationship among the main characters might have been like before and after these events? What different attitudes toward life are exemplified by the three principal characters? In what way do you identify with each of these individuals?

3. In Luke 15:24, and again in verse 32, what do you think the father means when he says that his son was dead and is now alive?

4. What do we learn from this parable about the love of God and the ministry of Jesus?

5. Read the Epistle for today in 2 Corinthians 5:16-21. In light of the Gospel parable, what do you think is meant by the "ministry of reconciliation"? How are we called as individuals and as the Church to carry out this ministry in the world?

_____

_____

_____

_____

MARY'S GIFT

Isaiah 43:16-21; Psalm 126; Philippians 3:4b-14; John 12:1-8

All four of the Gospel writers present an account of a woman anointing Jesus: Mark 14:3-9; Matthew 26:6-13; Luke 7:36-38; and John 12:1-8. However, there are a number of differences in the specific details among the four stories—including where and when the anointing took place, and who the woman was.

Luke tells of an unnamed woman at the home of Simon the Pharisee, referred to as a sinner, who bathed his feet with her tears and ointment, and then dried them with her hair. When those present condemned the woman for her actions, Jesus praised her faith and forgave her sins.

The accounts recorded by Mark and Matthew take place in Bethany at the home of Simon the leper after Jesus has entered Jerusalem. Again the woman is not named, and she pours her ointment on the head of Jesus instead of his feet. She is rebuked by the disciples for wasting the costly ointment; whereupon Jesus comes to her defense and praises her service to him. Both accounts end with the words, "Truly I tell you, wherever the good news is proclaimed in the whole world, what she has done will be told in remembrance of her."

In the context of John's Gospel, the anointing occurs in Bethany six days before the Passover, and the woman who does the anointing is Mary, the sister of Martha and Lazarus. After the raising of Lazarus from the dead (11:28-43), the Jewish leaders were committed to having Jesus put to death, and he had gone into hiding to avoid arrest (11:54).

The setting of John's story, a meal at the home of Lazarus, served by his sister Martha, is reminiscent of another meal with the same family in Luke's Gospel (10:38-42). At the dinner, "Mary took a pound of costly perfume made of pure nard, anointed Jesus' feet, and wiped them with her hair" (Jn. 12:3). The fragrance of the expensive perfume enveloped the whole house so that everyone present could enjoy it.

The disciple Judas Iscariot, who was about to betray Jesus, protested at the waste of the perfume, which cost as much as the equivalent of a year's wages. The ointment could have been sold and the money given to the poor. In the other accounts of the anointing, those who protest the waste of the ointment are identified as "the disciples" (Mt. 26:8) or "some" who were there (Mk. 14:4). Only John specifically names Judas. But Jesus rebuked Judas by saying, "Leave her alone" (v. 7), and praised Mary for her act of generosity and compassion toward him.

The anointing itself is an act of loving extravagance on the part of Mary, and is also a prophetic act anticipating the anointing of Jesus at his death and burial. His body would be anointed after the crucifixion by Joseph of Arimathea and Nicodemus (19:38-42); but whereas that anointing would be carried out in secret, Mary openly proclaims her love for Jesus for all to see while he still lives.

PRAYER FOR THE DAY

O God, we need the blessed guidance of your will. Help us to love what you command and desire what you give, so that, within this ever-changing world, our hearts may remain fixed on you, though Jesus Christ our Lord. *Amen.*

The fact that she anoints Jesus' feet foreshadows Jesus washing the feet of his own disciples at the Last Supper (13:1-20) as an example of servant ministry. Mary does for Jesus what he will do for others later.

Jesus' words in verse 8 that "You always have the poor with you" is not meant to dismiss those in need, but recalls Deuteronomy 15:11, which calls for opening "your hand to the poor and needy neighbor in your land."

The anointing by Mary also anticipates the Resurrection of Jesus, which will change the world forever. In times past, the Second Isaiah envisioned a future in which God would do a new thing and rescue Israel from exile in Babylon. Isaiah 43:16-17 recalls the first Exodus, when the Lord made a road through the sea and destroyed the chariots of Egypt.

But the people were to forget the old things; there would be a *new* Exodus even greater than the first (v. 19). The Lord would make a road through the wilderness, and would provide "rivers in the desert." The people's way would be safe from predatory beasts so that they could return home and declare God's praise.

Psalm 126 takes up the proclamation of a restoration that seems *like a dream*. The Lord has renewed the fortunes of Zion, and this has been noticed by other nations. Those who had once sown with tears now "reap with shouts of joy" (v. 5) as they come home carrying their sheaves.

Paul too writes of a new thing that God has done through the Resurrection of Jesus Christ. Because of the surpassing value of knowing Christ, everything else pales—including

ON REFLECTION

There once was a devoted priest who wished to have a vision of both heaven and hell, and God gave way to his pleading. The priest found himself before a door that bore no name. He trembled as he saw that it opened into a large room where all was prepared for a feast.

There was a table, and at its center, a great dish of steaming food was set. The smell and the aroma tantalized the appetite. Diners sat around the table with great spoons in their hands. Yet, to the priest's surprise, they were miserable—gaunt with hunger.

They tried desperately to feed themselves, but gave up—cursing God—for the spoons that God had provided were so long that they could not reach their mouths.

So these pitiable self-feeders starved while a feast lay before them. The priest had seen enough, so the door to this room closed before his eyes.

Next, the priest found himself standing before another door that appeared the same as the previous one. He began to despair, as the pain from viewing the first room was overwhelming, and he did not want to see that scenario again.

Again, the door opened, and it led to a room just like the first. Nothing had changed. There was a table at the center of the room covered with a cornucopia of steaming, delicious food. Around it were the same people. But there were no cries of anguish, and no one appeared gaunt and starving, even though they, too, had the same elongated spoons.

Nothing had changed, yet everything had changed. With the same long spoons these people reached to each other's mouths, and fed one another. And their joy was overflowing.

—H. King Oehmig

his Jewish heritage as a member of the tribe of Benjamin and his status as a Pharisee. For Jesus' sake he was willing to withstand the loss of all these things, which he now sees as "rubbish" (Phil. 3:8b). To know the Messiah as Lord, to trust in God's work through Jesus by sharing his sufferings—this was the assurance of salvation.

Before his conversion, Paul had possessed a sort of righteousness that he had "won" for himself by performance of defined duties. Now he understood that this was as nothing. In its place he claimed a righteousness that was to-

tally God's gift. This was granted to him on the basis of his trust in God's redeeming act of raising Jesus from the dead. In that act, Paul saw forgiveness, adoption, and newness of life for believers.

So Paul hoped to know for himself the power of Christ's Resurrection. It would require participation in Christ's sufferings—even being conformed to Christ in death. Paul does not claim that he has already reached that status, but he continues to grow into his call in Christ by leaving behind anything that would hinder his progress (vv. 13-14).

POINTS TO PONDER

1. What do you think is the significance of Mary's anointing of Jesus' feet in this passage?

2. What does Jesus ask of us in terms of identification with his ministry in the world? What must we surrender in order to be one with him?

3. How does Mary's action anticipate the death and Resurrection of Jesus that is coming to pass shortly? How will you prepare for the end of this Lenten season and the coming joy of Easter?

4. How can we show our love for Jesus openly, as Mary did, by our actions in the world?

5. What is the prize of which Paul speaks in the Epistle for today? What steps can we take to begin to reach for that goal, and what will we need to leave behind in the process?

JESUS' PASSION

Isaiah 50:4-9a; Psalm 31:9-16; Philippians 2:5-11; Luke 22:14—23:56

L *iturgy of the Palms.* "Blessed is the king who comes in the name of the Lord!" (Lk. 19:38). So begins the drama of Holy Week. As Jesus rides a colt from the Mount of Olives toward Jerusalem, people gather along the way and spread their garments on the road before him in an ancient expression of honor and respect. The acclamation by the multitudes reflects their belief that Jesus is the bearer of the Messianic Kingdom because of his deeds of power (Lk. 19:37b).

When some Pharisees who witness the entourage tell Jesus that he should restrain his followers, Jesus replies that it would be virtually impossible. If they were silenced, even the stones would shout, for the redemption of Israel and of the world is drawing near. The words of Psalm 118 could well be the words that those stones would shout in exuberant joy and thanksgiving for God's steadfast and everlasting love.

Liturgy of the Passion. The mood of joyous exaltation now shifts, as the account of the Passion begins with Jesus sharing the Passover meal with his Apostles. In the context of this meal, Jesus teaches his disciples what it means to be a servant. As the Apostles argue over who is to be the greatest, Jesus reminds them that "I am among you as one who serves" (Lk. 22:27). For Jesus, being a servant will mean suffering, betrayal, public humiliation, and death, but it also brings the promise of God's Kingdom (22:29).

Jesus' words and actions are reflected in the Third Servant Song of Isaiah, which describes the suffering of God's servant. In obedience, the servant is subjected to insults and injury, and is surrounded by adversaries; yet he

continues to be faithful because he knows that God is with him.

Psalm 31, also a cry of one who suffers, echoes the themes of Isaiah. The writer is broken and in despair, rejected by those around him; yet he maintains a steadfast trust and faith in God, who will provide deliverance: "Let your face shine upon your servant; save me in your steadfast love" (v. 16).

Before going to the Mount of Olives to pray, Jesus prepared his disciples for the coming events. He warned them of the trials to come and foretold the betrayal of Peter. As he prayed, he asked God to "remove this cup from me; yet, not my will but yours be done" (Lk. 22:42).

In the garden, Jesus was arrested by the temple police after being betrayed by Judas. In an attempt to protect Jesus, one of his followers cut off the ear of the High Priest's slave, and Jesus healed the man. Jesus was then taken to the High Priest's house, where he was mocked and beaten. His response as to whether or not he was the Son of God (22:70-71) provided the excuse to take Jesus before Pilate. Peter watched the proceedings from the courtyard; but by the time the cock crowed, he had, as Jesus predicted,

PRAYER FOR THE DAY

Everlasting God, in your great love you sent your Son, our Savior Jesus Christ, to take our nature, to suffer death upon the Cross, giving us the example of his great humility. Have mercy on us, we pray, in this life: that we may walk in the way of his suffering, and share in his marvelous Resurrection, for your honor and glory. *Amen.*

denied his master three times. "And he went out and wept bitterly" (22:62).

More than the other Gospels, Luke describes the accusations against Jesus in political terms. When told that Jesus condemns the payment of taxes to the Romans and claims to be Messiah and king, Pilate sees such charges in terms of Zealot activism. Yet, when asked, Jesus makes no claim to be king (23:3).

Pilate found no basis for a case against Jesus, and when informed that Jesus was a Galilean, had him turned over to Herod's jurisdiction. Herod found Jesus uncooperative as he stood silently before his accusers, in fulfillment of the role of Second Isaiah's Suffering Servant. Luke's account has Herod returning Jesus to Pilate, cloaked in the mockery of an elegant robe, but with nothing to substantiate the accusations made against him by the Jewish leaders.

Since his effort to transfer responsibility to Herod had failed, Pilate sought an alternative method to avoid condemning Jesus. He had him scourged and then offered to dismiss the charges against him as an act of amnesty for the Passover. However, the crowd cried out to Pilate for the release of Barabbas. After some hesitation on Pilate's part, the weak procurator gave in and delivered Jesus to be crucified.

Simon of Cyrene was pressed into service to carry Jesus' cross. Having been surrounded by accusers and mockers, Jesus received sympathy from the women in the crowd. He urged them to weep, not for him, but for themselves and their children.

ON REFLECTION

The mighty and mysterious acts that unfold today and continue over the next two weeks will carry us beyond Jesus the wise teacher or even the miracle worker. They take us straight into the heart of our Paschal faith, into the depths of penitence for sin and liberation from its bondage through Jesus' sacrifice for us.

Jesus, though he was "in the form of God," would empty himself, taking the "form of a slave" (Phil. 2:7), and be counted among the lawless. Thus he would do for the world what the world could not do for itself: free it from the tyranny of evil and violence toward God's anointed, and all God's people.

John Dear has written in Jesus the Rebel:

"Jesus spends his brief life walking against the on-rushing crowd, heading against the wide road to destruction, and walking the narrow path of life. For him, the narrow gate, the narrow path to life, is the way of nonviolence. He refuses to kill, to support killing, to pay for killing, to be silent in the face of killing, and to be comfortable in a world of killing. Filled with life, Jesus teaches and practices nonviolence.

"He possesses not a trace of destruction or violence. How does the culture of death and destruction respond to such luminous, subversive nonviolence? It labels him 'possessed' and does what it only knows how to do: It kills him. But Jesus is raised to life by the God of nonviolence. His choice is affirmed—and he insists that we take that narrow path to life as well."

Kathy Coffey sums it up aptly and simply: "We know the inevitable end, yet walk this way with song. With each step into story the story permeates us. This annual trudge to Calvary... "

—H. King Oehmig

As Jesus was nailed to the cross, he prayed to the Father for the forgiveness of his executioners (23:34). Luke also tells about the two men who were crucified with Jesus. One of the men mocked Jesus, while the other one recognized in him a righteousness that would be vindicated by God (23:43).

Luke tells of how the soldiers played dice for the clothing of Jesus, of how he was hailed derisively as "King of the Jews," and of the darkness at noon and the rending of the curtain in the temple. But Jesus did not die with a feeling of abandonment. His final words in Luke's account are: "Father, into your hands I commend my spirit" (23:46a).

As the letter to the Philippians reminds us, Jesus lived fully in the created world. In becoming man, he poured himself into the likeness of a slave, and in that human nature obeyed the Father's will by suffering and dying on the cross. He willingly endured a shameful end: Nothing was more shameful than a crucifixion. No Roman citizen was sentenced to such a humiliating and ignominious death.

Jesus reached the final depth of humility in his self-sacrifice for the healing of others (2:6-7). Yet this was only the beginning, for God exalted the Redeemer, at whose name every knee should bow. Thus, to the glory of God the Father, every tongue should confess that Jesus Christ is Lord!

_____

_____

_____

_____

POINTS TO PONDER

1. As you read the passage designated for the Liturgy of the Palms in Luke 19:28-40, describe what you think it would have been like to be present as one of Jesus' followers on this occasion.

2. In the Passion account, verses 1-25 of Luke 23 describe the trial and sentencing of Jesus. What are the specific charges brought against him, and how does Jesus respond? In verse 5, Jesus' accusers charge that he "stirs up the people." How did Jesus stir up the people of his own time? How does he continue to stir us up today?

3. Pay particular attention to the actions of Pilate and Herod. How do you explain their reluctance to take responsibility to execute Jesus? Why do you think they "became friends with each other" (23:12) on this day?

4. As Jesus was led away to be crucified (v. 26), Simon of Cyrene carried his cross. Try to put yourself in Simon's place. How do you think he might have felt as he walked to Calvary?

5. As you consider Luke's account of the crucifixion in verses 32-46, reflect on: Jesus' conversation with two criminals crucified with him; the centurion's confession; the darkness that covered the land; the tearing of the temple curtain; and the reaction of those who witnessed this event. What else captures your attention as you read this passage? Pay particular attention to the words of Jesus from the cross in verses 34, 43, and 46. What do we learn about Jesus' ministry to us, in this, his ultimate sacrifice?

THE DAY OF RESURRECTION

Acts 10:34-43; Psalm 118:1-2, 14-24; 1 Corinthians 15:19-26; Luke 24:1-12

As the central event of Christianity, the Resurrection of Jesus Christ is the glorious manifestation of the victory of God's love. Hope has prevailed over death and despair, and Christ has brought the promise of everlasting life to the world.

Although all of the Gospels include an account of the Easter story, there are a number of variations in the details (Mk. 16:1-8; Mt. 28:1-8; Jn. 20:1-18). However, in all of the narratives the women are the first to arrive at the tomb and realize that Jesus' body is missing. They are the first proclaimers of the miracle of Easter. Mary Magdalene is mentioned in all four Gospels; and in John's Gospel she is the only woman at the empty tomb and the first person to see the Risen Lord.

In the Palestinian culture of the time, it was the task of the women to prepare the bodies of the dead for burial. When Jesus was taken down from the cross, the Sabbath was about to begin. Because of the prohibitions against work on this day, there had not been time for Mary Magdalene, Joanna, Mary the mother of James, and the other women to complete this final service for Jesus. Thus they came at dawn on Sunday morning to the tomb where Joseph of Arimathea had placed the Lord's body.

When the women arrived, they found the stone enclosing the tomb rolled aside. Matthew's account at this point is very dramatic, with an earthquake and an angel appearing to roll back the stone (Mt. 28:2).

When the women stepped inside the tomb, they saw that the body was missing. Luke tells us that they were "perplexed about this" (24:4). As they stood, puzzled, "two men in dazzling clothes" appeared beside them. The women were terrified and turned their faces to the ground. The appearance of the two figures is similar to those present at the Transfiguration (Lk. 9:30) and the Ascension (Acts 1:10). Later on the two men would be identified as a "vision of angels" (Lk. 24:23).

They asked the women why they were seeking "the living among the dead?"—for "He is not here, but has risen" (v. 5). The men went on to remind the women of the Lord's prediction of his Passion while they were in Galilee (Lk. 9:22), in which he told his disciples that he would be "handed over to sinners, and be crucified, and on the third day rise again" (v. 7). Thus, reminded of Jesus' words, the women returned and reported what they had seen and heard "to the eleven and to all the rest" (v. 9).

Luke, through the unfolding of his Gospel, has emphasized Jesus' role as a prophet. Here it is the remembrance of Jesus' own prophetic words that provide the answer to the puzzle of the empty tomb. It is through remembering his prophecies that he would die and rise again that the women come to believe, and thus they tell the others. Here Jesus' death, burial, and

PRAYER FOR THE DAY

Heavenly Father, who through your only-begotten Son Jesus Christ overcame death and opened to us the gate of everlasting life: we praise you with joy and thanksgiving on this day of the Lord's Resurrection, with honor and blessing now and evermore! *Amen.*

Resurrection are in fulfillment not only of Scripture but of his own prophecies.

Throughout Jesus' ministry and again at the cross (Lk. 23:49), Luke shows that these women have been faithful followers, and now they are the first to bear witness to the Resurrection. Luke goes on to say in verses 11-12 that the disciples didn't believe the women, but thought this "an idle tale" (v. 11). Earlier they did not understand when Jesus himself told them that he must suffer and die (Lk. 9:45).

However, Peter ran back to the tomb and went inside to see for himself. There he saw the linen cloths and was "amazed at what had happened" (v. 12).

As the reading from Acts demonstrates, the followers of Jesus had further experiences that prompted them to proclaim the good news of forgiveness and eternal life. Faith in Jesus Christ as the Risen Lord grew out of the transforming power of the communities who heard the story of the Easter experience and passed it on. Peter summarizes the Gospel message before the household of the Gentile centurion Cornelius.

Peter begins by acknowledging that Jesus came for all people. "God shows no partiality" (10:34), and all who demonstrate trust and reverence are acceptable in God's sight. Jesus began God's proclamation of peace to Israel, but the message was for everyone. Empowered

ON REFLECTION

The gift of the Resurrection is clearly unconnected to the faithfulness of the disciples of Jesus. Their faith, in fact, had been nonexistent at the time he had needed them the most. The million-dollar gift "buried in their backyard" was the Resurrection, which had come to them out of pure gift-love from God. And it claimed three things to be foundationally true for the rest of the disciples' lives and ministries.

1). In meeting the Risen Lord, they came to know more than that Jesus was merely alive. He was much more than a death-defying anomaly. He was the embodiment of the Kingdom of God, the New Reality, and in contact with Jesus, they tasted of its reality in the here-and-now.

2). In meeting the Risen Lord, they came to understand that he indeed was "Lord and Christ." The Resurrection of Jesus was God's vindication of his life and ministry, confirming that what he had said and done were not the works of a magician or of a false prophet, but were indeed the authoritative expression of Abba.

3). In meeting the Risen Lord, the disciples came to know that Resurrection meant much more than conquering the individual problem of surviving death. It revealed the defeat of the power of evil—so that nothing can ultimately separate us from the love of Christ (Rom. 8:31-39). Jesus Christ is Lord. The Risen Jesus is truly "Christ our Passover," the One who carries the believer over the abyss of death and raises us all to the Promised Land of God's eternal domain.

The Resurrection of the body, the Risen Jesus teaches us, means that we do not belong finally to this world, but to God alone. Alleluia!

—H. King Oehmig

by the Holy Spirit, Jesus went about doing good and healing those who were oppressed by the devil.

However, the world failed to see the good of Jesus' ministry, and its leaders mobilized against him. He was crucified, but God overcame Jesus' enemies by raising him from the dead on the third day. He then appeared to those chosen by God to be witnesses of the Resurrection.

Those who saw the Risen Christ have been called to tell others that through Christ their sins will be forgiven. All of this, Peter affirmed, could be supported by the prophetic words of Scripture.

For the Apostle Paul, the primary reason for praise and thanksgiving to God is the fact that Jesus the Messiah has been raised from the dead. This proves God's love and power on behalf of all who come to faith. Christ's death was the sacrifice offered for our release from sin, and his Resurrection made clear that the sacrifice was effective.

In 1 Corinthians 15, Paul explains that Christ's Resurrection is the first fruits, the guarantee that we also shall be raised (v. 20). Since death came through one individual, Adam, the resurrection of the dead will also come through an individual—Christ himself.

Likewise, if human rebellion as represented by Adam enslaved us all to death, *human obedience*—in the person of *the conquering Christ*—will return to claim us as his own. Thus Paul's words bring assurance that all things are in God's hands, and Jesus reigns!

Thus we go forth in joy to proclaim the message of Christ's Resurrection. *Alleluia!* Christ is risen. The Lord is risen indeed. *Alleluia!*

POINTS TO PONDER

1. As you read the Gospel passage, try to imagine that you are one of the women who went to the tomb. How would you describe your thoughts and feelings as the events unfold? Contrast how you felt as you approached the tomb with how you felt as you returned to tell the other disciples.

2. When the women returned from the tomb, how do you think they would have explained to the others what had just happened? How do we tell the story of what happened on Easter to others *today*?

3. Also refer to the other readings for today in Acts 10:34-43 and 1 Corinthians 15:19-26. What do these passages tell us about what it means to live as followers of Jesus after Easter?

4. During the Eucharist we proclaim that: "Christ has died. Christ is risen. Christ will come again." As you read these words on this Easter Sunday, what added significance do they have for you?

5. Death on a cross was not only a horrible way to die, it was also a means of execution reserved for the worst criminals. What other paradoxes are found in the Easter story? How are we as individuals, as well as the world, changed by the events of Easter?

FAITH WITHOUT PROOF

Acts 5:27-32; Psalm 118:14-29; Revelation 1:4-8; John 20:19-31

The Lectionary readings for the Easter season proclaim the Resurrection and define its life-giving consequences for the world. The first readings are from the Acts of the Apostles, and describe the response of the emerging Christian community. In Year C, the second readings are from the Book of Revelation, expressing the hope of a new heaven and new earth through God's final victory over death.

For all three years of the Lectionary cycle, today's section of John's Gospel is read on the second Sunday of Easter. This passage describes two appearances of the Risen Lord before the disciples.

On the evening of Easter day, the frightened disciples are gathered behind locked doors. Jesus had been brought before Pilate on a charge of sedition, and his followers had reason to think that they might be accused as well, because of their association with him.

In John's account, Peter had already found the Lord's tomb empty, and Mary Magdalene had told the disciples that she had seen Jesus alive. But none of them had given credence to a bodily resurrection, and they were not ready to believe Mary's report.

As the passage begins, it is late on the day of the Resurrection. The Risen Christ is no longer restricted by the physical limitations that others know. Thus he simply appears within the locked room and greets the disciples with the words, "Peace be with you" (20:19). He shows them the wounds on his hands and side, and as he repeats the phrase again, the disciples rejoice as they recognize him.

However, these familiar words are much more than just a customary greeting. They are words of forgiveness, as he reconciles to himself the followers who had abandoned him at the cross. In this action, we see the pattern of forgiveness and reconciliation that is necessary in a community of faith.

Then Jesus entrusts them with a mission: "As the Father has sent me, so I send you" (v. 21). This is the heart of John's Gospel. Just as the Son has revealed the Father, now the disciples are to reveal the Son to the world. But the disciples cannot accomplish this on their own. Thus the Lord gives them the power they will need. He breathes on them, as in the beginning God had breathed life into Adam (Gen. 2:7). Just as Adam represented new life, the disciples signify a new community that will testify to a new era of eternal life in Jesus Christ.

Jesus adds a further charge and an empowerment: "If you forgive the sins of any, they are forgiven them" (v. 23). Likewise, they have the authority to "retain the sins of any," since some would refuse reconciliation a number of times before yielding to it.

One week later, the disciples again are gathered. Already they are observing the first day of the week as a celebration of the Lord's

PRAYER FOR THE DAY

Almighty God, who through the mystery of Jesus' Passion gave to us the new covenant of reconciliation: may we who have been reborn into the fellowship of Christ's Body continue to show forth in our lives what we profess by faith, through Jesus Christ our Lord. *Amen.*

Resurrection. This time Thomas, who had been absent the week before, is present. When told of the Lord's previous appearance, Thomas had stated the need to see for himself the physical proof of the wounds of Jesus. When Jesus appears among them again, he offers to Thomas the proof he had demanded. But it is no longer needed, as Thomas recognizes Jesus with the words, "My Lord and my God!" (v. 28).

It is not necessary for Jesus to breathe upon Thomas; through the representative acceptance by the others, Thomas has already received the Holy Spirit. There remains only the need to declare the blessedness of those who have come to true faith without the need for sight as proof (v. 29b).

As the Apostles proclaimed the Resurrection, they, too, performed great deeds among the people. Their actions caught the attention of the Sadducees, who found it threatening that such power was not under their control. Thus the High Priest had the disciples arrested and imprisoned. But they escaped when an angel of the Lord opened the prison doors (Acts 5:17-25).

Peter and the other Apostles were brought before a council convened by the High Priest because they continued to teach in the name of Jesus despite orders not to do so. They replied that they would obey God and not human authority. And afterward they continued to teach in the temple (5:42). Such threats have no power over those filled with the Holy Spirit.

ON REFLECTION

An Hasidic tale is told of an old rabbi of great wisdom whose fame had spread far beyond his own congregation to the villages and rabbis on the other side of the mountain. One day, suddenly, he died. So the young rabbis were bereft. Now they said, "What are we going to do when our people look to us for guidance? Without the old master where are we going to get the answers to the great questions of life?"

They decided among themselves to pray and fast until the old man's holiness and wisdom would be infused into one of them. And sure enough, one night in a dream, the old man appeared to one of the younger rabbis.

"Master," the young teacher said, "it's so good that you've returned to us. You see, with you gone, the people are now looking to us for answers to the great questions of life, and we're still unsure. For instance, Master, they're demanding to know—on the other side, of what account are the sins of youth?"

And the old man said, "The sins of youth? Why, on the other side, the sins of youth are of no account whatsoever."

And the young rabbi said, "On the other side, the sins of youth are of no account whatsoever? Then what has it all been about? On the other side, what sin is punished if not the sins of youth?"

And the old man answered very slowly but very clearly, "On the other side, that sin which is punished with constant and unending severity is the sin of false piety" (from Tales of the Hasidim*).*

Thomas hadn't been first to affirm the new reality. But he was no fool. He saw Jesus standing before him, and he believed. The only words possible in that moment were, "My Lord and my God!"

—H. King Oehmig

In the brief sermon in verses 30-32, the Apostles proclaim the essential teachings of the Good News. The crucified Jesus was raised up and exalted by God as Leader and Savior, to bring forgiveness to those who repent of their sins. They themselves were witnesses to these things, as was God's Holy Spirit, who dwells with those who obey God.

Later, the Christian mystic who gave us the Book of Revelation offers another vision of the exalted Christ. Written to offer encouragement to the faithful in a time of persecution, John's prophecies proclaim that God will ultimately triumph.

The opening verses identify the book as a prediction or revelation of eminent events delivered by an angel to John, who testifies to the Word of God. A blessing is offered to those who read, hear, and heed what he has written. Although the prophecy is addressed to seven specific churches in the Roman province of Asia (1:11), these communities can represent all of the churches.

John proclaims that God's nature is eternal and unchanging (v. 4); and Jesus is God's "faithful witness," the first-begotten from death and ruler of the kings of the earth, who has freed us from sin with his blood (v. 5). Like the figure of the Son of Man in Daniel 7:13-14, this exalted Jesus was to come with the clouds. Every eye would see him, and in particular those who had nailed him to the cross. Thus the Lord God declares, "I am the Alpha and the Omega ... who is and who was and who is to come ... " (v. 8).

The Psalmist also testifies to the strength of the Lord who brings salvation and eternal life: "I shall not die, but I shall live and recount the deeds of the Lord" (v. 17). The one who was rejected "has become the chief cornerstone" (v. 22). Thus we give praise and thanksgiving for the steadfast love of the Lord, which endures forever.

POINTS TO PONDER

1. Imagine the scene as the disciples are gathered together on the evening of the Resurrection (Jn. 20:19-23). What do you think the atmosphere in the room might have been before and after Jesus appeared?

2. What commission does Jesus give the disciples at this time? How does he empower them for this ministry? How are we called to carry out this same mission in the Church today? How are we empowered for this ministry?

3. In verses 24-25, Thomas demands proof that the other disciples have seen Jesus, and then he too meets the Risen Christ. What do you think compelled Thomas to proclaim Jesus as Lord (v. 28)? How do you know that Jesus is Lord? How do you resolve your own doubts on difficult issues of faith?

4. As you reflect on the actions of Thomas in this passage, what is the example that Thomas sets for us today?

5. In this Gospel passage, Thomas and the other disciples see the Risen Christ within the community of believers. How does your faith community help you to grow in maturity and live out your life in Christ more fully?

_____

_____

_____

_____

"FEED MY SHEEP"

Acts 9:1-6 (7-20); Psalm 30; Revelation 5:11-14; John 21:1-19

The appearances of the Risen Christ in the readings for today provide opportunities for new and renewed faith.

Although John tells us in 21:14 that this account was of the *third* time Jesus appeared to his disciples, it seems like a first appearance, since they did not initially recognize him. (The other appearances are found in Jn. 20:19 and 20:26.)

Here seven of the disciples are gathered by the Sea of Tiberias (or Galilee). When Peter announces that he is going fishing, the others join him. However, after an entire night of work, they have not caught anything.

At daybreak an unidentified man appears on the beach and calls out to them, asking if they have caught anything. When they reply that they have not, he tells them to cast their net on the right side of the boat, where they will find some fish.

They still have not recognized the figure on the shore as Jesus, and there is no reason they should obey. But they have nothing to lose, so they cast their net in the direction Jesus has told them. The net fills at once, and becomes so heavy that the men are unable to haul the catch aboard.

But then at once the so-called "beloved disciple" exclaims, "It is the Lord!" (v. 7). He is also the one who first believed at the empty tomb on Easter morning (Jn. 20:8).

Peter immediately puts on his clothes and swims to shore. The other disciples follow in the boat that is now laden with fish.

When they come ashore, they see that Jesus has already started a fire and is preparing fish and bread, manifesting God's continued provision for the community. Jesus then invites the disciples to add to the meal some of the fish they have caught. As their meal is baking, the fishermen sort and count their fish, and find 153. Despite the huge catch, the net is not damaged.

When they finish eating, Jesus turns to Peter and says, "Simon son of John, do you love me more that these?" (v. 16). Three times Jesus asks the question, and three times Peter answers in the affirmative. Peter is hurt by the fact that Jesus continues to ask the same question. This threefold pattern not only recalls Peter's three denials of Jesus before the crucifixion, but also gives added emphasis to the charge given to Peter.

Jesus gives Peter a threefold commission to feed and tend his sheep. He is really talking about the nature of service to others and the cost of discipleship. The Good Shepherd is willing to lay down his life for the sheep (Jn. 10:11, 17-18); and in 21:18-19, Jesus describes the death that will come to Peter. In verse 19b, Jesus calls Peter to "Follow me."

This time was not the final Resurrection appearance of Jesus; and as the experience of Saul of Tarsus attests, such appearances were not limited to the followers of Jesus.

PRAYER FOR THE DAY

O God, whose blessed Son made himself known to his disciples in the breaking of bread: open the eyes of our hearts that we truly may know him and experience his redeeming work, now and forever. *Amen.*

Saul, who was to become Paul, was one who took great pride in his ancestral heritage and practices (Phil. 3:5). He initially persecuted those who followed Jesus because he saw their faith as an offense against Judaism (Acts 8:3). But after his conversion experience, this zeal was channeled into bringing others to Christ.

Paul's "conversion" was a call from God similar to those of the Old Testament prophets. Acts records three separate accounts of Paul's experience (9:1-19; 22:4-16; 26:9-18); while Paul recounts his own version in Galatians 1:13-14.

Like other Jews, Paul anticipated the coming of God's Messiah, and his encounter with the Resurrected Jesus is a turning point, as he is charged with a new mission.

"Breathing threats and murder against the disciples of the Lord" (Acts 9:1), Paul secured the support of Caiaphas the High Priest to arrest members of the Christian community in Damascus and bring them to Jerusalem.

On the journey, Paul had a supernatural experience with lights from heaven and the voice of Jesus calling, "Saul, Saul, why do you persecute me?" (v. 4). When Paul asked who

ON REFLECTION

The Risen Jesus is not a wraith, not an hallucination, not the projection of the disciples' wish-fulfillment. He is totally himself—and more. He stands on the shore, and speaks to the disciples across the water. He instructs them where to catch fish. He builds a fire and cooks fish and roasts bread—and then he eats a meal with his friends.

There is nothing like real life to bring us up to speed—that is, if anything can. Although this was a pre-Kodak moment, with no camera phones available—the experience of this picnic with their beloved Master was seared on the memories of the disciples.

We aren't so fortunate. Though we have this stirring account, we are readers, while they were participants.

Anthony de Mello writes of the preciousness of disclosure *in his book* One Minute Wisdom:

The discussion among the disciples once centered on the usefulness of reading. Some thought it was a waste of time, others disagreed.

When the Master was appealed to, he said, "Have you ever read one of those texts in which the notes scrawled in the margin by a reader prove to be as illuminating as the text itself?"

The disciples nodded in agreement.

"Life," said the Master, "is one such text."

The Resurrection often manifests itself to us in the way that it happened to the disciples—that is, in their hour of disappointment, difficulty, and doubt, when they have "caught nothing."

When we have given up on our own attempts at self-salvation and making it on our own, the Resurrection breaks into our lives with its transforming power. We need only to be ready to receive—to enter into love, without counting the cost.

—H. King Oehmig

was speaking, Jesus identified himself and ordered Paul to go to Damascus to be told what to do next. Paul's fellow travelers were stunned because they heard a voice but saw no one, and Paul himself was stricken blind. He was led to Jerusalem, where for the next three days he waited sightless in the dark—like Jonah in the belly of the great fish or Jesus in the grave.

The Lord then appeared in a vision to a faithful disciple named Ananias, and told him to go to Paul. Because of Paul's fearful reputation, Ananias was reluctant to go—until the Lord told him that Paul had been chosen to be the Apostle to the Gentiles (v. 15).

Ananias went to Paul and laid hands on him, calling him "Brother Saul," saying that Jesus had sent him so that Paul's sight might be restored, and so that he could receive the Holy Spirit (v. 17). Immediately Paul was able to see again, as "something like scales fell from his eyes" (v. 18). He was then baptized and soon thereafter began to proclaim in the synagogue that *Jesus is the Son of God.*

John of Patmos, in his vision of heaven, depicts the Risen Christ as a slain sacrificial ram. In Hebrew tradition the sheep was considered the primary animal to be used for sacrificial purposes. This was properly to be a yearling ram, or in some special circumstances, a fully-grown ram with developed horns.

The living creatures that support God's throne, and the elders who surround it, worship the victorious Lamb (5:11-14). Their song proclaims that the slain Lamb's blood has ransomed for God a Kingdom, a royal priesthood. The Lamb is worthy of all power and wisdom and honor and blessing. *Amen!*

Psalm 30 also offers a song of praise and thanksgiving for the God who has "brought up my soul from Sheol, restored me to life from among those gone down to the Pit" (v. 3). It is a pledge to give praise continually to the God who rescues and restores life—now and forevermore.

POINTS TO PONDER

1. As you read the Gospel passage, how would you describe the main characters and their actions? Why do you think Simon Peter suggested that they go fishing?

2. What is the picture of Jesus that is presented here? What do we learn about the relationship between Jesus and his disciples?

3. How did the disciples finally know that the man on the beach was Jesus?

4. In John 21:10, Jesus asks the disciples to bring some of the fish they have just caught to add to the breakfast he was preparing for them. Why does Jesus ask us also to contribute today as we do his work in the world?

5. Read the passage from Acts 9:1-6 (7-20), also assigned for today. What stands out for you in this story of the conversion of Paul? In what ways can you identify with his experience? What is the example he sets for us here?

OUR GOOD SHEPHERD

Acts 9:36-43; Psalm 23; Revelation 7:9-17; John 10:22-30

Scripture frequently uses the metaphor of shepherd and sheep to describe the relationship between the faithful and God. Easter 4 is often referred to as Good Shepherd Sunday, as we turn to John chapter 10.

It is the winter Feast of the Dedication or Hanukkah, a time which commemorates the rededication of the temple in 164 B. C., after it had been defiled when Antiochus Epiphanes made sacrifices to Zeus on the altar (1 Macc. 4:36-59). Jesus is walking in the portico of Solomon at the temple, when he is asked whether or not he is the long-awaited Messiah (Jn. 10:24).

Jesus' presence at the temple presented a challenge to some of the Jews, and John's Gospel describes confrontations between Jesus and the religious leaders much earlier in his ministry than do the other Gospel writers. Since there were those who already thought of Jesus as the Messiah, they demanded that he resolve this issue. If Jesus affirms this claim, his enemies could develop tactics to refute him.

Jesus replies by saying that his life and teachings have already provided all the evidence anyone could ask. Everything that Jesus has done has been in the name of the God the Jews claim as their own, yet they do not believe him. His works have been performed faithfully, and therefore they give witness to Jesus who has performed them. To ask for any further statement is to refuse to accept the evidence.

Jesus goes on to tell his listeners that they are not able to believe because they are not his "sheep" (v. 26). His sheep listen to his voice and give heed to his words and teachings. Jesus recognizes them for his own, and they follow him. Each shepherd has a distinctive call that his own sheep recognize, and that makes possible the separation of herds after a night of sharing a common sheepfold.

The Lord's care for "his own," however, goes beyond that of a shepherd for a flock. He provides more than green pastures and still waters from which they eat and drink. *Jesus offers them eternal life.* His sheep will never perish or be snatched out of his hand (v. 28) because they have been given to him by the Father. Therefore, no power can separate them from God (cf Rom. 8:35-39).

All of this is leading the hearers to understand—or to reject—that there exists an inseparable union between Jesus the Son and God the Father. *They are one reality* (v. 30). This is true not only in a metaphysical sense, but also in the moral dimension of love and obedience. Whoever has seen or heard Jesus has also seen and heard God. Thus in hearing his voice and following where he leads, the disciples of Jesus partake in the sacred essence of the Holy Trinity.

PRAYER FOR THE DAY

We praise you, Risen Lord, the good shepherd of your people, who knows us each by name. Guide and correct us by your Holy Spirit, that your people, prone to err and stray like lost sheep, might be brought into the sheepfold of the Father, where true joys are to be found in glory everlasting. *Amen.*

However, as Jesus finishes speaking, the crowd wants to stone him for blasphemy. Again he calls for them to look at the evidence of the work he has done and declares his unity with the Father (v. 38). But in order to avoid arrest, he must leave Jerusalem.

The familiar words of Psalm 23 epitomize our understanding of the relationship between the Good Shepherd and his sheep. When we affirm that "The Lord is my Shepherd" (v. 1), we acknowledge our dependence upon God. Just as sheep, especially in an arid country such as Palestine, must be led to green pastures and still waters, so the trusting believer accepts the Lord's guidance and direction along right pathways.

And as sheep must rely on the shepherd who has shown care for them, even when he leads them through a dangerous, foreboding landscape to *reach* the green pastures and still waters—so the Lord's disciples will fear no harm when called upon to endure toil and danger in obedience to God's call. As sheep learn to see protection in rod and staff, we also find refreshment in God's anointing, and in a cup that overflows with grace and love.

Thus we come to know that the goodness and mercy of God are forever with us, even when we cannot perceive goodness and mercy; and we know ourselves as heirs of the place that the Lord has prepared for us.

The Revelation to John gives us another image of the shepherd. As the seer looks around him, he sees a great multitude that no one can count. They come from all tribes, nations, and languages as they stand before the throne

ON REFLECTION

The divinity of Jesus shines through his activity.

In Baptism, we and Christ are one; and just as the world would know the Father by the works of the Son, so shall the world know the Son by our works in his name. Or they will not know the Son because of the lack of works or fumbled works we do.

Rowan Williams has written in Where God Happens *(Shambhala, 2006): "Saint Anthony of the Desert says that gaining the brother and sister and winning God are linked. It is not getting them signed up to something or getting them on your side. It is opening doors for them to healing and to wholeness. Insofar as you open such doors for another, you gain God, in the sense that you become a place where God happens for somebody else. … God comes to life for somebody else in a life-giving way, not because you are good or wonderful, but because that is what God has done. So, if we can shift our preoccupations, anxiety, and selfishness out of the way to put someone in touch with the possibility of God's healing, to that extent we are ourselves in touch with God's healing. So, if you gain your brother or sister, you gain God."*

That Jesus and the Father are one emanates not initially from the first word processor of a fourth-century Greek theologian at Nicea—but in the lives of unsophisticated, broken people who need someone to heal them and who find that Jesus delivers far beyond anything they have known before.

We are called to offer to the world Jesus as the Good Shepherd, the Beautiful One—in all his attractive radiance. All our acts of ministry for him and about him are really a presentation of who he is. This is the most substantive testimony to his messiahship that anyone can offer.

—H. King Oehmig

of the Lamb, wearing white robes and waving palm branches. The white robes signify their deliverance from tribulation, and the palms their victory over trials.

The visions of Revelation proclaim what Jesus' Resurrection means in heaven. The saved are a countless multitude; access to Jesus, the Lamb of God, cannot be restricted to any single group. In joy they proclaim the reality of their salvation (7:10). The angels who surround the throne and the living creatures who support it all join in praise of the nature of God (v. 12).

This work was composed in a time of intense persecution, so it portrays the saved as those who have washed their robes in the blood of the Lamb who was slain for their redemption. Now they are forever in his presence, freed from hunger and thirst to worship God day and night in the temple.

The Lamb who is at the center of the throne is their shepherd. He will guide them and lead them to the water of life, and "God will wipe away every tear from their eyes" (v. 17).

Whereas the Book of Revelation speaks of the general resurrection to come, the passage from Acts for today tells of one particular resurrection that demonstrated that God's promises were already in the process of true fulfillment.

The raising of Tabitha, or Dorcas, is very similar to the raising of the daughter of Jairus in Luke 8:49-56. We are told that Tabitha was a faithful disciple who was "devoted to good works and acts of charity" (Acts 9:36). When she became ill and died, an urgent request was sent to Peter to come immediately. There was much weeping and despair as Peter was shown the clothing she had made for others.

Peter then ordered everyone to leave the room as he prayed over her. When he said, "Tabitha, get up" (v. 40), she opened her eyes and sat up. When she was shown to be alive again, many others came to believe in God's power that had raised Jesus from the dead.

POINTS TO PONDER

1. In verse 24 of today's Gospel passage in John 10, the Jews ask Jesus to tell them plainly whether or not he is the Messiah. How would you characterize Jesus' reply to them? Why do you think they refuse to believe that Jesus is the Messiah?

2. Why do you think there are those who continue to have difficulty believing that Jesus is the Son of God? How would you explain to someone else why you believe that Jesus is the Messiah?

3. In this passage, Jesus describes his sheep. As you read verses 27-29, consider the following questions: How would you characterize the sheep? How does one become a member of Jesus' flock? What is it like to be one of Jesus' sheep? What sets Jesus' sheep apart from those that are not of his flock?

4. What is the relationship between Jesus and his sheep? How would you describe Jesus as our Shepherd? In verse 30, Jesus says, "The Father and I are one." What implications does this statement have for our own relationship with Jesus?

5. In what way would you describe your relationship with Jesus and with God the Father? How are these relationships nurtured? As you look at the other Lessons for today, what do you learn about God's care for us?

_____

_____

NEW LIFE FOR ALL PEOPLE

Acts 11:1-18; Psalm 148; Revelation 21:1-6; John 13:31-35

In today's readings we see that the benefits of Christ's sacrifice of love extend *to all people*, as Jesus commands us to glorify God through our mutual love.

Set immediately after Judas has departed from the Last Supper, the sayings of Jesus in the Gospel passage for today begin his "farewell discourse" from a tradition that is peculiar to John. Here Jesus addresses three issues—and the disciples will have to resolve all three in order to survive after the crucifixion and continue Jesus' mission.

First, the disciples must learn to recognize—even in the Lord's humiliation—the vindication of his total ministry. They must also come to think of Jesus as living forever in the presence of the Father. Finally, they must maintain unity among themselves that is more than duty or common interest. Their solidarity must make the love of God that they have experienced through Jesus *an internal reality.*

Jesus begins to teach them by declaring that "Now the Son of Man has been glorified" (13:31). The earthly life of Jesus was one of humility. Born in a stable, he grew up in the home of a carpenter in Nazareth.

His preferred company was the poor, the disinherited, and the marginalized. After Jesus was executed with two bandits, a guard was placed at his tomb to prevent any honor being paid to him in death.

We read in Philippians 2:8 that God has highly exalted Jesus because he "humbled himself and became obedient to the point of death—even death on a cross." Thus his sacrificial death for the redemption of the world can be spoken of as the *glorification* of the Son of Man. And, in turn, God is glorified in him.

Jesus also declares that his followers cannot come where he is going. If we think of this only as the Lord's returning to the Father, there are other words that also must be considered. There is a promise that Peter, who cannot follow Jesus now, will be enabled to follow him later. There is the assurance that, in the many lodging places of his Father's house, Jesus is going to prepare a place (Jn. 14:1-6).

So Jesus is not telling the disciples that they can never come into the presence of God as he does. Martyrdom is possible, and Peter and the others will come to it. However, there is one journey along which no one can ever follow Jesus, and that is to his sacrifice on the cross.

Jesus leaves his followers with the one command: they are to love one another as he has loved them. This entails more than loving our neighbors and respecting the rights and needs of others. The way Jesus loved his disciples was to lay down his life. This special kind of love that is to build up the Christian community

PRAYER FOR THE DAY

Come, Holy Spirit, and pour upon us your continual wisdom, that we may know Jesus to be the way, the truth, and the life, the One who leads us to the Kingdom of God. Give us grace so to follow your path day by day, that our believing may result in doing, and become a means of grace for all to whom we are sent, through Jesus Christ our Lord. *Amen.*

reflects the mutual love that exists between Father and Son (cf Jn. 15:12-15).

The existence of such sacrificial love among Christians is the distinguishing characteristic of the people gathered in the name of Jesus. It means to care for fellow disciples even before we care for ourselves. Thus the commandment Jesus gives the disciples is not "new" in the sense that the command to love had never been given (cf Lev. 19:18). It is "new" because this commandment to love is rooted in the unique sacrifice of Jesus.

In the Acts passage in the story of Peter's dream, we see an example of how far this love is to extend. The implications of this dream would mark a major shift in the early development of the Christian community.

Peter is criticized by the "circumcised believers" (11:2) in Jerusalem for associating with Gentiles. Not only had Peter visited the homes of Gentiles, he had eaten with them and baptized them (Acts 10). By eating with Gentiles, Peter was disregarding ritual purity laws, identifying himself with Gentile idolatry, and compromising the messianic claims of his community.

Peter tells of his dream in which a large sheet full of animals came down from heaven. A voice commanded Peter to eat, but he refused because some of the animals were considered unclean. But a voice proclaimed, "What God has made clean, you must not call profane" (v. 9). Peter then went to the house of the Gentile Cornelius and preached, recalling the words of

ON REFLECTION

The New Testament way of describing the power of Christianity is a simple one. It originates not so much in sociological constructs, or in similar class patterns, or in inventive ecclesiastical structures—it wasn't that Constantine liked Christianity because it offered "a good way to run a railroad."

No, the "revitalizing" power of the Gospel came directly from the mouth of Jesus just after his last supper with his disciples: "I give you a new commandment, that you love one another. Just as I have loved you, you also should love one another. By this everyone will know that you are my disciples, if you have love for one another" (Jn. 13:34-35).

Dietrich Bonhoeffer, in his famous work, The Cost of Discipleship, *captured the essence of revitalizing* agape:

"All that a follower of Jesus has to do is to make sure that his obedience, following, and love are entirely spontaneous and unpremeditated. If you do good, you must not let your left hand know what your right hand is doing—you must be quite unconscious of it. Otherwise, you are simply displaying your own virtue, and not that which has its source in Jesus Christ.

"The genuine work of love is always a hidden work. ... If we want to know our own goodness and love, it has already ceased to be love. ... This voluntary blindness in the Christian is his certainty, and the fact that his life is hidden from his sight is the ground of his assurance."

Looked at in one light, this kind of loving is a huge order—humanly impossible. But approached as life lived through the breath of the Spirit, enjoying the fragrance of God's love showered down to us daily in innumerable ways—it is simply abiding.

—H. King Oehmig

Jesus when he promised baptism with the Holy Spirit.

Just as the Apostles had experienced the Holy Spirit, so had these Gentiles; therefore, how could he oppose God by denying them baptism in the name of Jesus Christ? Peter's testimony silenced his critics, who praised God and acknowledged that the Gentiles were also recipients of "the repentance that leads to life" (v. 18).

Peter reveals a transformation in his own understanding of the teachings of Jesus that *God's gift of salvation is offered for all* (v. 17). However, the controversy over the status of Gentile believers in the messianic community would persist until it reached final settlement at the Council of Jerusalem (Acts 15).

The passage from Revelation expands even further on the inclusive vision of God's Kingdom. In the heavenly city of the New Jerusalem, all things are transformed—the old heaven and earth have passed away. The holy city itself is adorned in joyous expectation, like a bride awaiting her husband.

In this world, there will be no more death, grief, crying, or pain. God is present to "wipe every tear from their eyes" (21:4), for in this new community the barriers between God and humanity have been eliminated.

We can know that what the seer has witnessed to is true, because the Lord God is the beginning and end of all things. The old world has passed away, and through Christ a new era has begun—a "new heaven and a new earth" (v. 1).

Psalm 148 gives voice to the joy of this new life. In this hymn of praise, all of creation glorifies God—from the inhabitants of the heavens to the deep sea monsters and all the creatures of the earth. All of humanity, from kings and princes to the old and young alike, are to *glorify the Lord.*

POINTS TO PONDER

1. As used in the Gospel passage, "to glorify" means to reveal the essence of. How does the ministry of Jesus, and especially his coming death, glorify God? How can we glorify God through our own actions? Discuss this in terms of the Church in general and yourself in particular.

2. What does Jesus mean in John 13:33 when he says that his disciples cannot follow him where he is going?

3. In verses 34-35, Jesus gives his disciples a "new commandment." Why does Jesus call the commandment to love one another a new commandment?

4. What is the nature of Christ's love for us? What does it really mean for us to love others as Christ loves us? Give specific examples of how we can demonstrate this love in our lives. When have you been a recipient of this love?

5. In verse 35, Jesus says that his followers will be known by their love for one another. How does the Church live out the truth that God's love is for all people? How are you personally challenged by these words?

THE HELPER

Acts 16:9-15; Psalm 67; Revelation 21:10, 22—22:5; John 14:23-29

In today's Gospel reading, Jesus' promise of the Advocate, the Holy Spirit, serves to prepare us for the coming of Pentecost.

The "Farewell Discourse" in John 14 continues with Jesus stating that he is "going to the Father" (v. 28). But before his "hour" comes, he teaches the disciples how they are to relate to God in their total lives. Fundamentally, it is a relationship of love. But any genuine love demands self-giving; and this self-giving on the disciples' part springs from obedience to the self-giving Lord.

God the Father loves them already; but it is in the keeping of Jesus' commandments that they will come to know of the Father's love—not as a proposition to which they give assent, but as an intimate, personal experience. Therefore, Jesus can promise that Father and Son will come together and stay to make their dwelling with the disciples forever.

There is, in this mutual relationship of love, no separation of believers from God or Jesus; hence it is a present experience of salvation.

Those who do not love Jesus will not keep his words; they cannot do so. Yet it is not a human teaching that they refuse. The word with which Jesus addresses his listeners is not his own. It originates in the Father; thus, to disregard it is to reject the truth of the Father.

Not only can Father and Son dwell with the disciples, but the Divine presence will be received as a "Paraclete"—"one called alongside to help." The Paraclete has been defined as counselor, helper, advocate, comforter, and guide, and is all of these and more. But here it means *the presence of Christ continuing with his beloved after his Ascension,* fulfilling and bring-

ing to perfection the work begun during his ministry on earth.

Later in the discourse, the Paraclete will be described as the "Spirit of truth." At times, the Spirit of God would descend upon the prophets, inspiring them to speak the truth of the Lord. But now that Jesus had come, the work of the Spirit became even more clearly defined and associated with Jesus as the fulfillment of all the prophets.

This Paraclete will teach all things, yet none of this will be new or discordant with God's revealed will in the past. The Spirit will bring to remembrance what Jesus taught, and previously uncomprehended truths will be made alive for the disciples. Because of the Spirit's ongoing presence, the disciples will be made bold to proclaim Jesus Christ.

Jesus assures his followers that with the gift of the Paraclete they will also experience the peace of God that cannot be overcome or extinguished (Jn. 16:33).

Jesus also pledges that his imminent departure will not mean the end of fellowship with

PRAYER FOR THE DAY

O gracious God, in whom we live and move and have our being, so clothe your people in your love, that we may desire what you command, so that through the abiding presence of the Spirit of Truth we may know the Resurrected Lord, and the power of the new creation, through Jesus Christ our Savior. *Amen.*

his disciples. He must depart, but it will be in order to return to them in a yet more enabling way. The disciples are not, therefore, to think of his departure with grief. In love for him, they are to rejoice because, even through his suffering, *Jesus is going to the Father.* Thus he will carry out the Father's plan for redemption.

The words of Jesus in verse 28b are not meant to imply the subordination of Jesus to the Father, but rather that, in his earthly life, Jesus is necessarily subject to human limitations. In returning to the Father, the Son will be set free from these limitations and united with the Father. Therefore the disciples should rejoice, since the Risen Jesus will be equally present to them wherever and whenever they call upon his name.

In the passage from Acts, we can see the Spirit at work as Paul continues to spread the news of the Risen Lord. Paul has had a vision in which a man pleads for him to come to Macedonia. He heeds the vision as a genuine call from God, and travels to the Roman colony of Philippi, one of the major cities of Macedonia.

On the Sabbath, Paul speaks to a group of women gathered by the river, including a woman named Lydia, a "worshiper of God" and a "dealer in purple cloth" (16:14a). As one who worshiped God, she might have been either a devout Jew or perhaps a Gentile "God fearer."

She was very receptive to Paul's message: "The Lord opened her heart" (v. 14b). Thus Lydia and her household were baptized in a manner reminiscent of the baptism Peter performed in the household of Cornelius in Acts 10. Just as Cornelius was the first Gentile convert in Acts, Lydia was the first European convert.

Following her baptism, Lydia prevailed upon Paul to accept her hospitality. As a merchant of purple cloth, Lydia was a wealthy woman, and

ON REFLECTION

Our unity in Christ is not to be based on a fragile, undifferentiated peace—a cheap grace—but on the Spirit's active presence, enabling the community to put away "all bitterness and wrath and anger and wrangling and slander, together with all malice, and be kind to one another, tenderhearted, forgiving one another, as God in Christ has forgiven you" (Eph. 4:31-32).

C. S. Lewis wrote in Mere Christianity *that Christians have often disputed as to whether what leads the Christian home is good actions, or faith in Christ. One could ask the same question of maintaining strong Christian community. Lewis answers, "I have no right really to speak on such a difficult question, but it does seem to me like asking which blade in a pair of scissors is most necessary."*

Wayne Teasdale has written in The Mystic Hours:

"The world is divided enough by religions, culture, languages, ethnicities, tribes and nations. Even more profound are divisions between the haves and have nots, the educated and the uneducated, those whose hearts are open and those whose hearts are closed. These crushing divisions work to isolate people and rob the world of peace. The challenge is to realize our essential interdependence, our fundamental need for one another. The key to social peace and community, indeed the key to the spiritual life, is remembrance: of God, ourselves, one another. Only when we remember our inescapable relatedness to one another will peace become a reality."

Christian community is a grace of the Spirit.

—H. King Oehmig

her patronage would have been important to Paul's ministry in Philippi. She is an example of how key women provided financial resources for the emerging Christian community.

The all-embracing love of God is also manifested in the vision of heaven found in the passage from Revelation. The holy city of Jerusalem is itself a temple that needs neither sun nor moon. All the glory that ever was is there, and the city knows no darkness. Nothing false or corrupting can find a place in this glorious scene.

A life-giving river flows from God's throne and nourishes the tree of life. This tree produces twelve kinds of fruit, and its leaves are for the healing of the nations. All pain and woes are to end through God's design.

The city is the dwelling place of the Lamb, which precludes the presence of evil or desecration. This is also a place of ongoing worship and praise by the redeemed. They will see the face of the Lamb, and his name will be written upon their foreheads (v. 4b). This is the true mark of belonging—of being heirs of Christ, exalted to reign with him forever and ever.

For the Psalmist, the presence of God's Spirit to all the peoples and nations of the world becomes a source of blessing and praise (67:3). The opening verse echoes the Aaronic blessing from Numbers 6:25, and continues by asking that God's ways be known and reverenced throughout the earth. *May God continue to bless us; let all the ends of the earth revere the Lord* (v. 7).

POINTS TO PONDER

1. According to John 14:23-24, how are we to show our love for Christ? How do you attempt to carry out this command in your daily life?

2. What do you think Jesus means when he says that "we will ... make our home with them" (v. 23b)? In what ways have you seen evidence of the indwelling presence of God in your life and in the lives of those around you?

3. What is the relationship between Jesus and the Father as expressed here? How are we too invited into this relationship?

4. What are the qualities of the Holy Spirit as Jesus describes the Spirit here? What will the Spirit teach us? Jesus also speaks of the peace with which he leaves us (v. 27). When have you experienced this peace in your own life? How can we make this peace a reality in the world around us?

5. In verse 27b, Jesus tells his disciples not to be afraid or troubled. What did this mean for the disciples at that time? What are the things that frighten and trouble you the most today? How does the presence of the Holy Spirit provide reassurance and comfort in your need?

UNITED IN THE FATHER

Acts 16:16-34; Psalm 97; Revelation 22:12-14, 16-17, 20-21; John 17:20-26

Our Gospel continues what is called Jesus' "High Priestly Prayer." The prayer itself begins as *petition*—for Jesus himself to glorify the Father as he faces death on the cross (Jn. 17:1-5). Next the prayer offers *intercession*, as Jesus prays for his immediate disciples to be protected and unified in the Father's name (vv. 6-19).

In verses 20-26, the Lord's intercession expands from those with him on that final night to include disciples who have remained in Galilee or elsewhere—and to encompass future disciples as well. It is a prayer that *all of us may be one* as we praise the unity of God the Father and the Son.

Jesus says that the glory that God the Father has given to him, he gives to the disciples as God's children. Because that glory is now theirs, the disciples may enjoy the same unity that the Father and Son possess.

Verse 23 expands upon this to say that Jesus is present in his disciples just as God is present in Jesus himself, so that their unity may be complete. The Father loves these adopted children in the same way as the eternal Son is loved.

Verse 24 adds another request for the disciples of all generations. They have been given to Jesus by the Father; thus Jesus pleads that they may be with him forever, able to perceive the glory that is his and that he has given to them—even if they cannot truly recognize it in themselves.

That gift from the Father to the Son demonstrates the love between them that has existed from before the foundation of the world. The prayer concludes with the declaration that, although the world has not recognized its Creator, Jesus has known and understood the Father completely. Furthermore, he has made the name and nature of God fully known to those who have recognized that he is sent by God.

Thus this love, which is another way of describing mutual knowledge of Father and Son, can be present in all the disciples, as the Redeemer himself is present (v. 26).

The revelation that Jesus has imparted to the disciples will continue to be developed, from glory to greater glory. Yet even now, the disciples are aware that Jesus has been sent by God. As their knowledge is enlarged, the disciples' perception of the Father's love and of the Lord's presence with them will grow and will finally reach completion in the larger life Jesus has prepared for them (Jn. 14:2-3).

On this Seventh Sunday of Easter, as we stand between our observance of the Ascension and the Day of Pentecost, we as members of God's family can gladly claim solidarity with these disciples. As Jesus prays for them he also intercedes for us.

PRAYER FOR THE DAY

Glorious God, of majesty unbounded, you have exalted your only Son Jesus Christ to reign over all: send us your Holy Spirit, the Lord and Giver of Life, that we may not remain comfortless, and that we may be strengthened daily to do your will, with a whole-hearted commitment and with a single-minded conviction. *Amen.*

The concluding chapter of Revelation looks for the glorious return of the exalted Redeemer who is the beginning of creation and its end. The righteous, those who "wash their robes" (22:14), are counted as the *blessed ones* who will have the right to enter the city by the gates and partake of the tree of life. In Revelation 7:14, the ones who have come out of the great tribulation have washed their robes white in the blood of the Lamb.

In 22:16, Jesus declares that he has sent this testimony to the churches: Jesus, who is the "descendant of David, the bright morning star." The Spirit who indwells the disciples and the Church itself as the Bride of Christ invites all who thirst after God to come. For the promise is that "Surely I am coming soon" (v. 20).

In the passage from Acts, we read that as Paul and his companions were going to a place of prayer, they met a slave girl who had a "spirit of divination" (16:16). Her owners made money from her fortunetelling. For several days she followed them about, shouting "These men are slaves of the Most High God, who proclaim to you a way of salvation" (v. 17).

When Paul finally exorcised the spirit from the girl in the name of Jesus, her owners were outraged at their loss of income and dragged Paul

ON REFLECTION

The spiritual reality that the Ascension of Jesus raised for his followers was that others would come to believe in Jesus because of their witness. With Jesus' return to the "right hand" of the Father, he would no longer be walking the dusty roads of Galilee or Judea, proclaiming the arrival of the Kingdom, bringing listeners to faith through parables, or healing the sick. That time had passed. The "baton" of "being fishers of people" had been handed to the disciples.

Central to their success was the factor of unity. The poignant prayer of Jesus the High Priest in today's Gospel demonstrates how deep was the concern of the departing Master for his beloved. The Divine intimacy between Jesus and Abba God, the glory of their mutual indwelling, is petitioned for the disciples in their unity with one another and in their ministry.

There are many ways in which this unity is expressed. The Christian community is sometimes referred to as the "blessed company of all faithful people" (BCP, p. 339)—who believe that Jesus is the Christ and have faith in his name (Jn. 20:31).

Another image is Paul's "Body of Christ" (1 Cor. 12:12-31), which highlights the organic unity among diversity present in the community.

Then there is the "communion of the Holy Spirit" (2 Cor. 13:13; cf 1 Cor. 1:9)—an identity arising from the understanding that the Church is a creation of the Spirit (Jn. 20:22), and that possessing the Spirit is essential to being Christian (Rom. 8:9; 1 Jn. 4:13).

We can also be called the "community of hope"—a description implying that life in the Church gives only a foretaste of the glorious fellowship at the end time, the final hope of completion in Christ (1 Jn. 3:2; Rom. 8:23).

A popular metaphor for the Church today is the "family of God." We are God's children through water and the Spirit in baptism.

Yes, we are all of the above, by God's grace.

—H. King Oehmig

and his companion Silas before the magistrates. They sought to discredit all that Paul and his fellow missionaries were accomplishing.

The crowd joined in the verbal attack, which soon led to violence. Paul and Silas were flogged, thrown into jail, and had their feet fastened in stocks.

In the middle of the night, as Paul and Silas were praying and singing, there was a violent earthquake that shook the foundations of the prison. All the locked doors were opened and the prisoners' chains released. When the jailer awakened and saw what had happened, he was ready to kill himself because he knew he would be held liable if the prisoners escaped. When Paul reassured him that all the prisoners were still there, the jailer fell down in gratitude. He recognized that Paul was an agent of a God far greater than anything he had known, and asked what he must do to be saved.

Paul responded by saying, "Believe on the Lord Jesus" (v. 31). Then he and Silas "spoke the word of the Lord" (v. 32) to the man. After tending the wounds of Paul and Silas, the jailer was baptized along with his household.

Psalm 97 gives expression to the joy we feel for God's gift of salvation: "The Lord is King! Let the earth rejoice; let the many coastlands be glad!" (v. 1). With Divine power, God guards the lives of the faithful, rescuing them from the wicked. The "light dawns" (v. 11) for the righteous, and joy is the reward of all believers. Thus on this Sunday after the Ascension we affirm the Lord as our King. *Rejoice in the Lord, O you righteous, and give thanks to God's holy name!*

POINTS TO PONDER

1. In John 17:22-24, what is the glory that we have received through Jesus Christ?

2. Jesus speaks here of the oneness that his believers share with him and with God the Father. How have you personally experienced this oneness?

3. Jesus prays here for the unity of his followers. How do you think we can more effectively work toward achieving this unity in the Church today? What will be the fruit of this oneness, as well as some of the obstacles we might face (as the Apostle Paul faced, Acts 16:16f) in attaining this unity of spirit?

4. In the Gospel passage, Jesus prays for us today who are his believers. How would you characterize his prayer for us? How does it make you feel to realize that 2,000 years ago, Jesus prayed for you?

5. What are we as the Body of Christ called to do in response to this prayer of Jesus?

_____

_____

_____

_____

_____

_____

_____

THE COMING OF THE SPIRIT

Acts 2:1-21; Psalm 104:25-35, 37b; Romans 8:14-17; John 14:8-17 (25-27)

For forty days after the Resurrection, Jesus appeared to his disciples at various times and places. But after he ascended to the Father, the disciples were once again left alone. As faithful Jews, they had gathered in Jerusalem for the Feast of Weeks, or Pentecost, as it was known to Greek-speaking Jews (the festival occurred fifty days after Passover). This joyful celebration was originally an agricultural festival in which the first fruits of the grain harvest were offered; but by the first century, it also commemorated the giving of the Law to Moses at Sinai.

While the disciples were together, they were suddenly overwhelmed by an awesome rushing blast of wind, as visible tongues of fire settled on each of them. No one among them was left without a share of God's gift (Acts 2:3-4). They were immediately filled with the Holy Spirit, not just for performing specific tasks as were the judges and prophets of old, but for *all their lives*, just as Jesus had been filled at his Baptism.

They immediately burst forth in words of praise, in languages that the disciples themselves did not know but that were recognized by Jewish pilgrims at the festival. The crowds who observed the disciples were "amazed and astonished" (v. 7) to hear these Galileans proclaiming "God's deeds of power" (v. 11) in their own tongues. Thus the prophecy of Joel was fulfilled (2:28-29), as God poured out the Divine Spirit upon all flesh.

With the coming of the Holy Spirit, God had released a force to unite the world in peace and love under the lordship of Jesus Christ.

Although Pentecost marks a dramatic event in the life of the emerging Christian community, references to the work of God's Spirit are found throughout Scripture. In the Hebrew Bible, the word *ruach*, which stands for wind, breath, or spirit, is used in the accounts of creation.

Today's Psalm gives praise to God who created and provides sustenance for all. God's Spirit is the source of all life: "When you send forth your spirit, they are created; and you renew the face of the ground" (104:30). Thus we sing our praises to God today for the gift of God's life-giving Spirit.

Paul calls attention to another aspect of this Spirit—the Divine presence of the Risen Christ in us. Through Christ's work of setting us free from the bondage of sin and death, we live no longer in the flesh, but in the Spirit. Indeed, Paul declares that we cannot truly belong to Christ apart from the Holy Spirit (Rom. 8:9b). If we are in the Spirit, we have an indestructible

PRAYER FOR THE DAY

Eternal and loving God, on this day you poured out on your people the gift of the Holy Spirit, so that every race and nation may come to know you as Father, and Jesus Christ as Lord. May the Holy Spirit forever bind us together in perfect love, give us right judgment in all matters, strengthen us to do your will, and finally bring us to our eternal home in Light everlasting. *Amen.*

newness of life. The Divine presence enables us to renounce the "flesh," or that part of us that rebels against doing the will of God.

We are not given this amazing gift in order to return to the slavery of our old ways; we have been set free from our past failures. Thus we become aware, through God's Spirit, of the *adoption* that enables us to truly know God as Father. And it is in relationship to Christ our brother that we find that *even our suffering* may be gathered up as part of our new life in grace.

In the Gospel passage for today, Jesus tells his disciples that they will be able to do even greater things than he has done through the power of the Spirit. Philip has expressed concern about being separated from Jesus and therefore from God; thus Jesus discloses the unique ways in which he will be present in the believing community after his earthly departure.

The way of love will enable the disciples to keep the commandments Jesus has given them (14:15). Furthermore, the presence of Christ

ON REFLECTION

For Luke, the Day of Pentecost "speaking in tongues" that fell on the disciples was less about "ecstatic, unintelligible speech" than about the conferring of the Divine ability to "speak about God's deeds of power" in Jesus Christ. Literally, they embodied the message. As bold Spirit-bearers, they expressed the life of Christ first in Jerusalem, and then to the world.

So what else can we expect besides tongues, after being "grasped" and freed by the power of the Spirit? Continued "tongues" of grace, in all of the wider meanings of the term—literary and devotional, eloquent and instructional? Everyday miracles? Varieties of gifts exploding in new dimensions of healing? Yes.

As Tim Robinson has put it, "Miracles are explainable; it is the explanations that are miraculous."

The wind that roared over the disciples and the tongues as of fire that rested on each one of them marked both an end and a miraculous beginning. Jesus had "sat down" in glory— but not to an idle life of ease. As Paul would maintain, the Spirit of God is the Spirit of the exalted Lord.

The only sure sign of the Holy Spirit was not tongues of fire or rushing wind, or the charismatic gifts, but the presence of holy love (1 Cor. 13). Jesus had told the disciples that not everyone who said to him, "Lord, Lord" will enter the Kingdom of God, but only those who did the will of Abba, a will measured by agape. Prophecy will cease one day. So will tongues. So will deeds of power by faith. So will knowledge, and martyrdom. Only one thing has enduring value: Spirit-infused love.

Thomas Merton in his work, The Wisdom of the Desert *(Sheldon Press, 1974), includes a vignette from the fourth century. It reads:*

"Abbot Lot came to Abbot Joseph and said: 'Father, according as I am able, I keep my little rule, and my little fast, my prayer, meditation and contemplative silence; and according as I am able, I strive to cleanse my heart of thoughts. Now what more should I do?'

"The elder rose up in reply and stretched out his hands into heaven, and his fingers became like ten lamps of fire. And he said, 'Why not be totally changed into fire?'"

—H. King Oehmig

will ever abide with the community through "another Advocate" (v. 16), as the gift of the Father. *Advocate* is a juridical term referring to one called to the defense of an accused.

As a heavenly intercessor, the "Paraclete" would function in a way similar to Moses, who pleaded for the people before God. And the earthly ministry of Jesus for the disciples will be continued through the Advocate.

Jesus' departure, at first a staggering blow to the disciples, will ultimately be for their benefit. It will not be a complete separation; through the work of the Holy Spirit, even without Jesus, the disciples will not be left orphaned.

But the return of the Divine presence will be perceptible only to believers, and not to the outside world. Jesus himself has not been of this world, nor does his Kingdom belong to it. Nevertheless, it is this world which Jesus came to save by taking away its sin. The Advocate, who shall remain with the disciples forever, can be called the "Spirit of truth" (v. 17a).

The Spirit will make possible a continuation of the God-given knowledge begun in Jesus that comes to believers by faith (v. 26). Thus the departure of Jesus should not mean fear, but peace and joy for the disciples, in confidence that they will not be "orphaned," but led into all truth.

POINTS TO PONDER

1. As you read Acts 2:1-21, as well as the Gospel Lesson for today, try to imagine these two very different events and consider: What do you imagine the disciples might have thought and felt when Jesus told them, "Whoever has seen me has seen the Father" (Jn. 14:9)? In contrast, what do you think it was like to be in Jerusalem on the Day of Pentecost?

2. How was the Spirit important on these two different occasions? How were the disciples empowered by the Spirit? What were they called to do as a result of the presence of the Spirit?

3. How do you think the disciples were changed by these events? How were others affected as well?

4. In these two passages the Spirit is described as truth, wind, and fire. What do these images tell us about the Spirit? What other images would you use? What do we learn from these two events about the work of the Spirit?

5. In these biblical passages, the Spirit was promised and then manifested in very tangible ways. How do you see the Holy Spirit working in your own life, in your congregation, and in the world today?

THE HOLY TRINITY

Proverbs 8:1-4, 22-31; Psalm 8; Romans 5:1-5; John 16:12-15

Although the Trinity is not specifically named in Scripture, the basis for the development of the doctrine is found throughout both Testaments.

In simple terms, the Trinity is an expression of how God is known and experienced by humanity. We *can* know God through creation; and in today's passage from Proverbs, Wisdom, or *Sophia*, is personified as a woman similar to the spirit (or "wind from God") of Genesis 1:2. Wisdom was the first of God's creation to take an active part in the creative process, working beside God "like a master worker" (Prov. 8:30).

Almost more than anything else, this passage expresses the joy of creation, in which Wisdom rejoices and delights. There is a tone of playfulness and exuberance here; this gives us a glimpse of a God who gives life to the world, and celebrates with us in our very existence.

Psalm 8 also speaks of the glory of creation, which is described as the work of God's fingers (v. 3a). The hymn goes on to remind us of the unique place of humanity in this created order.

As we gaze upward, we cannot help but feel insignificant in the vast cosmos (vv. 3-4). Yet humankind has been created *next to God*; and God has entrusted us with the responsibility of caring for this magnificent creation.

Jesus, as the only begotten Son who came to us in human flesh, declares the reality of the infinite God in another way. John testified that no one has ever seen God, but as God the Son, Jesus makes God known (1:18). Jesus has been sent by God, whose intention for the created world is reflected in Jesus' actions and attitudes.

The earthly ministry of Jesus had been fulfilled, and here we see him leaving those to whom he had declared the nature of God. Yet as he left them, there remained more for him to declare (16:12).

During his ministry *he* had been their advocate in relation to God. He had brought them comfort and encouragement in the assurance that their sins and their failure could be forgiven and made good. He had been their protector; but now he was to leave them so that *another Advocate* might come to them—a helper who would make the unseen presence of the Father and the Son continually real to them.

This Advocate was to witness to the Lord's own truth of *all that Jesus had done and said*. John's emphasis concerning the work of the Advocate is grounded in the Hebrew Scriptures, in the witness of God's Spirit through the prophets. Yet now the Spirit was to remain present—not just within leaders, on specific occasions, for a definite purpose—but continually, within all faithful believers in Christ (cf Acts 2:11).

This gift of the Advocate was imperative as the exact provision that the disciples' coming work would require. While Jesus was with

PRAYER FOR THE DAY

Holy God, who by your gracious will have given us the confession of a true faith in the glory of the eternal Trinity: keep us steadfast in the Unity of Three Persons that we may forever continue in your service, O Father, the Creator; O Son, the Redeemer; and O Holy Spirit, the Sustainer, one God, now and forever. *Amen.*

them, they were constantly turning to him to meet their problems and needs. Now that they themselves were being sent to carry on his work in the world, they would turn to the Holy Spirit within them to find presence and guidance. In that way, strength would be provided by the love of the triune God who empowered them.

And it was so. They would be dispersed to far-out places, and the Advocate would be with each of them in their individual need. What they once feared to do, they would now find within their power.

Things dimly remembered from the Lord's teaching began to come clear to them. The second Advocate did not bring them anything new (v. 13). Rather the Spirit caused them to understand more fully what Jesus had already given them, and in so doing, gave glory to God.

At the same time, aware as they were of their own limitations, they found that they were accomplishing what they did not have in themselves to achieve. Thus they had to say that it was all due to God within them. *Everything they were given,* they acknowledged, came from God. The fullness of faith and accomplishment was brought to them through the Son, Jesus. And all of it operated in them as the work of the Holy Spirit.

ON REFLECTION

"I love the recklessness of faith. First you leap and then you grow wings," wrote *William Sloane Coffin in* Credo *(Westminster John Knox Press, 2003).*

"There is nothing anti-intellectual in the leap of faith, for faith is not believing without proof but trusting without reservation. Faith is no substitute for thinking. On the contrary, it is what makes good thinking possible. It has what we might call a limbering effect on the mind; by taking us beyond familiar ground, faith ends up giving us much more to think about."

Trinity Sunday, with its ultimately unexplainable Doctrine of the Holy Trinity, certainly takes us beyond the familiar ground of our everyday thinking. Yet our experience of Christian life, within the practice of our faith through the Christian Year, certainly reveals to us—as we're "flying"—how well we are supported in our belief.

The doctrine of the Trinity models for us the character of Christian experience.

The problem the Church faced was in squaring the encounter of "Christian" believers with "God, Lord, and Spirit"—with the unity and singularity of God as expressed in the core of Hebrew monotheism: "Hear, O Israel: The Lord is our God, the Lord alone" (Deut. 6:4). How do you do the math?

It took almost 400 years for the Church to get its head on straight about Trinitarian orthodoxy. So we shouldn't be too hard on ourselves, if, Sunday after Sunday, we rise to our feet after the sermon and experience some puzzlement as we recite the Nicene Creed.

We might not grind our teeth over it, but we may in fact scratch our heads. If so, we are in good company. Christians for two millennia have been doing likewise. One wonders: Has our triune experience in a Triune Reality overcomplicated things—or has it been the simplest way to make sense of a complex experience without denying or minimizing any element of the faith?

Perhaps our best response is to let the joy of Trinitarian reality "breathe" through our worship experience; to let go of rational analogies and even explicit definitions, as we open our hearts to the One-in-Three in whom we live and move and have our being.

—H. King Oehmig

In Paul's letter to the Romans, we see this Spirit at work in the world and in the lives of those who follow Jesus. Our needs are supplied through our relationship with God. This "connection" is an internal reality that gives life as we enter into right relationship or are reconciled with God through Jesus Christ (5:1).

Paul calls upon the Christians of Rome to accept the peace of reconciliation with God that the experience of God's grace or favor makes available. It is through Christ that we obtain access to this grace (v. 2). Paul sees this redeemed state as a cause for rejoicing in the midst of whatever troubles we may experience. He even speaks of "boasting" in our sufferings. Such assurance is possible because of the chain of purposes in verses 3b-5a.

We are challenged to acknowledge the glorious purposes of God as they unfold within our own circumstances. Then, as believers, we can even rejoice because of the troubles themselves. In submitting to the ordeals of this world, the Christian will, in the end, find God's approval. "Hope" refers back to the miraculous sharing of God's own glory (v. 2b). The believer then becomes aware of Divine approval in perceiving the presence of God's Holy Spirit as God's love is poured into our hearts (v. 5).

So, through the disciples' own experience of the Spirit of truth in their lives, as a fulfillment of Jesus' promise, an understanding of God as Trinity came into their consciousness. But the Christian community did not define such a doctrine all at once. It was not until the great councils of the fourth and fifth centuries that a more final explanation was formulated.

In Holy Week we proclaim that Christ died for our sins. At Easter we rejoice that God raised Jesus. Ascension recalls that our Savior is at the right hand of the Father, where he makes intercession for us. Pentecost celebrates that the Spirit who moved in creation, who gave life and soul to humanity, who was involved in every act of Jesus, has been poured out upon the fellowship of disciples, and so also upon us. Thus we affirm that God's Spirit will continue to act in us as we turn in love and obedience to the unity of the Father, Son, and Holy Spirit.

POINTS TO PONDER

1. As Jesus speaks to his disciples in John 16:12, he declares that he has many other things to impart. How does Jesus still teach us through the "Advocate" who continues to operate in our lives?

2. How has the world's understanding of God been changed by the work of the Holy Spirit in the disciples? What is the legacy of their faithfulness that comes down to us today?

3. Another function of the Holy Spirit is stated in verses 13-14. How does the Spirit guide us into all truth?

4. What is your own understanding of the Holy Spirit as the Third Person of the Trinity?

5. Also refer to the other Scripture passages for today, and reflect on how their insights aid our understanding of the Trinity. How can the teachings of Trinity Sunday lead to deeper discipleship in your own life?

_____

_____

Proper 1: See Epiphany 6; Proper 2: See Epiphany 7; Proper 3: See Epiphany 8

TRUE FAITH

1 Kings 18:20-21 (22-29), 30-39; Psalm 96; Galatians 1:1-12; Luke 7:1-10

In our Gospel we read of how a Roman officer, a centurion serving as an administrator in Palestine, came to admire and even to love the people he ruled. He built them a synagogue. He also loved the members of his household—close servants as well as family.

And so, when one such servant was critically ill and judged close to death, the centurion was ready to do anything to see him healed, including the stretching of his own faith.

The centurion had been hearing of an unconventional rabbi who was in Capernaum. This man was said to have brought healing to many people. So he asked the elders of the synagogue to appeal to this Jesus, to have him come and bring healing to his slave.

This they were glad to do. When they came to Jesus and appealed to him earnestly—saying, "He is worthy of this, for he loves our people"—they received Jesus' consent. But Jesus taught and acted as a rabbi. He would have had scruples about entering the house of a Gentile, even such a well-recommended man.

The centurion *had* thought of this, and when Jesus was not far from the house, the centurion sent friends to say to him, "Lord, do not trouble yourself, for I am not worthy to have you come under my roof. … But only speak the word, and let my servant be healed" (Lk. 7:6-7).

Here was a centurion who was used to having soldiers under him at his command. He understood the way the world works and did not set himself up to expect more than Jesus would deliver.

When Jesus heard of this man's words and his humility, he turned to the inevitable crowd that gathered behind him and said, "I tell you, not even in Israel have I found such faith" (v. 9).

And Jesus' word *was* sufficient. When the friends who had been sent to Jesus returned to the house, they were to find that the servant had been completely restored to good health. God had answered and worked through Jesus' ministry of healing.

Jesus was sent first to the chosen people; but as the Apostle Paul would preach in today's Epistle—he was also to be a "light to the Gentiles," the answer to the longing and desperate need of all nations without God.

For Paul, the faith that can bring us salvation must be God's gift. No one can earn it. To try to set up a pattern or performance would tempt people to believe that they were earning it. That was the heart of Paul's message to the Galatians.

The Gospel as Paul preached it proved itself not to be of human origins or any earthly source, but truly the revelation of Jesus Christ for all. Paul was therefore not seeking human

PRAYER FOR THE DAY

Almighty and all-loving God, you call us to be related by faith with you and through love with our neighbor: give us the inspiration not only to worship you, but also to do your will in the image and likeness of Jesus Christ, who, with the Holy Spirit, lives and reigns with you, one God, now and forever. *Amen.*

approval—but rather God's approval. So we cannot aim to please people first, and expect to be considered servants of Christ.

This was the revelation of Jesus Christ, and as such reveals the importance of the *greatness of God's mercy* toward all who seek salvation.

In today's Old Testament passage we read of the Prophet Elijah's triumph in a contest over the prophets of the false god Baal.

Elijah had said to the people: "I, even I only, am left a prophet of the Lord; but Baal's prophets number four hundred fifty. Let two bulls be given to us; let them choose one bull for themselves, cut it in pieces, and lay it on the wood, and put no fire to it; I will prepare the other bull and lay it on the wood, but put no fire to it. Then you call on the name of your god and I will call on the name of the Lord ... " (1 Ki. 18:22-24).

Elijah called on the name of God, and God answered in the fire that consumed the burnt offering, the wood, stones, dust, and even the

ON REFLECTION

A story is told of a man who was so frustrated with the slow pace of his usual bus that he decided to walk home.

On the way, he ran into another man walking.

"Ah, friend!" he cried. "I'm saving a dollar and a half by walking instead of riding in that bus."

"You're a wasteful idiot," the other man immediately replied.

"Why? How could that be?"

"Well," the fellow traveler explained, "having discovered such an important saving as that, why—you could have walked behind a taxi and saved ten times as much!"

There are many angles from which to view the same reality. Jesus' healing of the beloved slave of a Roman officer serving in Capernaum, who was near death, illustrates that his healing power extends beyond his physically "being there."

The centurion had asked the elders of the synagogue to appeal to Jesus to come and heal his servant. This the elders were glad to do, as the centurion was a benefactor of the community and had built a synagogue for them.

But as Jesus approached his house, the centurion sent a message that he was not worthy to have such a one as Jesus enter his home. Yet he knew that Jesus only had to speak the words, and his servant would be healed.

Jesus' response was to praise the centurion for his faith: "I tell you, not even in Israel have I found such faith" (Lk. 7:9). When the elders who had been sent to Jesus returned to the home of the centurion, the slave was fully recovered.

It is not our position in life, our striving, or our cleverness that will get us "there." It is our relationship to Jesus in his compassion and strength.

—H. King Oehmig

water in the trench surrounding the altar (1 Ki. 18:38).

When the people saw this, they fell on their faces and declared, "The Lord indeed is God; the Lord indeed is God" (v. 39).

Psalm 96 calls the whole earth to sing to God a new song. The gods of the nations are no more than idols. The Lord is the Creator to whom all peoples are to ascribe honor and power, glory and majesty.

Today we are privileged to have greater revelation than did the Psalmist in his time; but we can respond in no better way ourselves than to "Praise the Lord!"

POINTS TO PONDER

1. What was the challenge that was posed to the Prophet Elijah in "proving" the greatness of his God?

2. Psalm 96, our Psalm for today, is a hymn of praise. How and why do you offer praise to God on this day? How has God answered you in your petitions for wisdom?

3. In the Epistle, Paul calls the Galatians to be true to the Gospel of Christ and to seek God's approval, and not human approval. What challenges do you encounter as you attempt to follow this standard in your own life?

4. As you read the Gospel passage for today, what kind of man was the centurion? Why do you think he sent for Jesus in the first place? Why was Jesus amazed at this man?

5. What can we learn about the nature of faith from the centurion and from this Gospel event? How has belief in Jesus' transforming power strengthened your own faith?

RAISED TO LIFE

USS Year C Proper 5

1 Kings 17:8-16 (17-24); Psalm 146; Galatians 1:11-24; Luke 7:11-17

Both the Old Testament and our Gospel readings for today tell similar stories in which the dead are brought back to life. Both of the stories center around widows.

In ancient Israel, women whose husbands had died had no inheritance rights and were dependent upon other family members or charity for their very survival. God is depicted as the one who defends widows and their children, and the neglect of widows and orphans incurs Divine wrath. In the early Christian community, provisions were made for the equal distribution of food to widows (Acts 6:1-6).

Nonetheless, simple day-to-day existence of widows and their children could often be precarious.

The story from 1 Kings takes place during the course of a three-year drought in which the Lord prompted Elijah to go to the territory of Sidon, where a widow would provide food for him. When Elijah arrived, he asked the woman to bring him water and bread.

When she revealed that she had only enough oil and flour to prepare a final meal for her son and herself, Elijah told her not to be afraid to prepare the food, and that the meal and oil she had would supply her until the end of the drought. The widow did as Elijah requested, and indeed, the store of meal and oil lasted as Elijah had promised.

By responding to the request of Elijah, the widow had put her own existence as well as that of her son at risk; but her life was transformed as she acted in response to the prophetic request and Divine promise.

However, that promise was put in danger when the widow's son fell ill and died. Now the woman feared that the presence of Elijah had

caused God to remember a past sin of hers that had brought about the death of her child as punishment.

Elijah took the child and laid him on his own bed. As he stretched over the child's body, he prayed to the Lord to "let this child's life come into him again" (v. 21).

The prophet's action in regard to the child represents the Divine power passing through him; but it is the fervent prayer of the man of God, Elijah, that brings the boy to life again.

Jesus and his disciples would have been familiar with this story of Elijah as well as a similar incident in the ministry of Elisha (2 Ki. 4:18-37). Luke's account of the raising of the son of the widow of Nain has several parallels with the Elijah and Elisha stories, and is not found in the other Gospels.

As is often the case in Luke's Gospel, this story is paired with another event—the healing of the centurion's slave (Lk. 7:1-10). When the beloved slave of a Roman officer serving in Capernaum became ill and was near death, the centurion asked the elders of the synagogue to

PRAYER FOR THE DAY

Gracious Lord, whose will is human well-being in its totality, open our hearts and minds to receive your never-failing love, that we may know the healing power of Jesus Christ, and be made well in mind, body, and spirit, in the peace of the Holy Spirit, who lives and reigns with you in glory everlasting. *Amen.*

appeal to Jesus to come and heal his servant. This the elders were glad to do, as the centurion was a benefactor of the community and had built a synagogue for them.

But as Jesus approached his house, the centurion sent a message that he was not worthy to have such a one as Jesus enter his home. Yet he knew that Jesus only had to speak the words, and his servant would be healed. Jesus' response was to praise the centurion for his faith: "I tell you, not even in Israel have I found such faith" (Lk. 7:9). When the elders who had been sent to Jesus returned to the home of the centurion, the slave was fully recovered.

As Jesus continued on his journey, he came to the town of Nain, which is mentioned nowhere else in the New Testament. As he, his disciples, and the crowd with him approached the town, they came upon the funeral procession for a man who was the only son of a widow. For a widow to lose her son meant not only a source of great personal grief and the end of many hopes, but also the loss of material support.

The text tells us here that Jesus had great compassion for her and told her not to weep. In violation of Jewish purity laws (Num. 19:11), Jesus then touched the funeral bier and said, "Young man, I say to you, rise!" (v. 14). The

ON REFLECTION

Here was one like no other—Jesus the Lord of life.

Nyambura Njoroge wrote in The Ecumenical Review *(Oct. 1997): "Like the people in Nain and the women at the empty tomb, all those who listen and turn to Jesus rejoice in hope, for he revealed the divine presence in the world—resurrection. The mourners and the widow were going through a ritual of shared grief on the way to the cemetery, thereafter to go on with their lives. But Jesus interrupts business as usual and brings to birth something new. That is how Jesus deals with suffering. He does not ignore, trivialize or glorify it by telling people to persevere and to hang in there. Instead he confronts the cause of grief, the pain and injustice. He resists suffering, death and systems of injustice. He is a witness to his Father that God has indeed 'looked favorably on his people!' God has turned to the people; and those who witnessed Jesus' presence and his power to bring back life turned to God, rejoiced in hope and acknowledged the fulfillment of God's promise."*

One of the major themes of Luke's Gospel is that Jesus is a prophet who fulfills and exceeds the deeds of those from former times such as Elijah and Elisha. Here we see Luke using the title prophet *to identify Jesus for the first time. Taken together, the healing of the centurion's servant and the raising of the widow of Nain's son mirror the stories of Elisha and Elijah, and are in fulfillment of Jesus' own prophecy in Nazareth (Lk. 4:24-27).*

Donald S. Armentrout has written: "The story is the same for us. Whenever faith is born, Jesus says 'Arise.' 'Arise' from the drowning water of baptism to the beginning of a new life. 'Arise' into a life in the mercy and forgiveness of God. 'Arise' into a life with Jesus in our hearts. 'Arise' and become part of a life that will not cease when your heart stops beating, but will continue on into God's eternity."

—H. King Oehmig

man who was dead sat up and began to speak as Jesus gave him to his mother (cf 1 Ki. 17:23).

In returning the son to his mother, Jesus restored the woman's security and hope for the future. Jesus' compassion for her as he acts on her behalf highlights his identification with the marginalized of the world.

Luke ends the account with the reaction of the crowd as their initial fear gives way to praise of God. Those who witnessed this event recognize that Jesus, the agent of the miracle, is a great prophet. According to tradition, prophecy had ended with Ezra, and its renewal was expected to indicate the approach of God's Messiah. Therefore the people present declare that God has looked favorably on them (v. 16), and the word about Jesus spreads through Judea.

The Epistle for today is the first of a series of readings from Paul's letter to the Galatians. Paul had founded the church in Galatia, but his authority there was being challenged by those who he felt wanted to "pervert the gospel of Christ" (1:7). The letter reveals the tension in the early community over compliance with Jewish law in regard to Gentile converts.

In the reading for today, Paul tells the circumstances of his own call to emphasize that his commission came directly "through a revelation of Jesus Christ" (1:12) and not through any human authority.

Paul had zealously persecuted the church of God in order to preserve the traditions of his Jewish ancestors. However, the Lord had set Paul apart for his apostolic vocation: "to reveal his Son to me, so that I might proclaim him among the Gentiles" (v. 16). Thus Paul has moved from persecuting the church to "proclaiming the faith he once tried to destroy" (v. 23); and through his actions, God is glorified.

POINTS TO PONDER

1. As you read the Old Testament and Gospel passages for today, reflect on the following points: What are the similarities and differences that you notice in the two stories? Imagine that you are either the widow of Zarephath or the widow of Nain. Describe what it might have been like for them as their sons died and then were restored to life.

2. What prompted Elijah in 1 Kings and Jesus in the Gospel to perform these miracles? How would you characterize the responses of those present to the miracles?

3. What do we learn about both Jesus and Elijah from these stories? In particular, what do we learn about Jesus' role as a prophet? What do you think is the significance of these stories of the dead being brought back to life?

4. In the Epistle passage, Paul tells the Galatians what led him to proclaim Jesus as Lord. What events in your life have contributed to your own relationship with Christ? What point does Paul make here about Divine versus human authority?

5. All of today's readings reflect the restorative power of God's presence. How have you felt this presence in your own life?

_____

_____

_____

YOUR FAITH HAS SAVED YOU

1 Kings 21:1-10 (11-14), 15-21a; Psalm 5:1-8; Galatians 2:15-21; Luke 7:36—8:3

As ruler of the Northern Kingdom of Israel (869—850 B. C.), Ahab had been in conflict with the Prophet Elijah for allowing the worship of Canaanite gods introduced by his Phoenician wife Jezebel. Now Ahab's actions with regard to his seizure of land belonging to Naboth the Jezreelite bring Ahab and Elijah together once again.

Naboth had a vineyard adjacent to Ahab's palace, which Ahab wanted and offered to buy. Naboth viewed this land as his inheritance from God and refused Ahab's offer (1 Ki. 21:3). When Ahab sulked over Naboth's refusal, Jezebel took matters into her own hands by arranging to have Naboth falsely accused of cursing God and the king. Thus Naboth was stoned to death for blasphemy, and the rights to his land subsequently went to Ahab.

As Ahab prepared to take possession of the vineyard, the Lord spoke to the Prophet Elijah, who went to Ahab and confronted him with his crime and its consequences. He goes on to vividly describe the fate that awaits Ahab (v. 19b). Not only has Ahab brought about the death of an innocent man, he has abused his power as a ruler. Thus Elijah declares that Ahab and his entire household are to be destroyed (vv. 21-26). However, Ahab repents and the punishment is deferred for now.

Psalm 5 is a plea for God's protection from those, like Ahab, who are guilty of lies and deceit. God does not delight in wickedness, and there is no peace for those who are evil. The Psalmist recognizes the abundance of God's steadfast love (v. 7), and bows down in awe to worship the Lord.

Paul, in his letter to the Galatians, argues that we are brought into a right relationship with God through faith in Christ, and not through obedience to the law. As the Christian movement spread beyond Jerusalem, more and more converts were Gentiles. This led to conflict over whether or not it was necessary for these Gentiles to follow Mosaic law and be circumcised in order to be accepted.

The meeting in Jerusalem in Acts 15 seemed to have resolved the issue by requiring that Gentiles "abstain only from things polluted by idols and from fornication and from whatever has been strangled and from blood" (v. 20). However, as the letter to the Galatians shows, the status of Gentiles in the community was still unclear. The issue addressed here is whether or not Jewish followers of Jesus should eat with Gentile Christians.

Peter had learned in a vision (Acts 10:10-35) that God makes no distinction between believers. But while in Antioch, Peter was criticized by James and others for refraining from table fellowship with Gentiles. Paul openly confronts Peter for abandoning his previous convictions and being afraid to take

PRAYER FOR THE DAY

Gracious God, so incline our hearts to follow where you lead, so fill us with your unfailing power and love, that we may boldly express the Gospel of Jesus Christ: that a great harvest of followers may come through the wisdom and winsomeness of your Holy Spirit, to your glory. *Amen.*

an unpopular stand. The ministry of Jesus and the redemption he had won through the Cross were for everyone. No race or people or heritage could claim precedence in salvation.

Paul goes on to say that "we know that a person is justified not by the works of the law but through faith in Jesus Christ" (v. 16). Only trust in the work of Christ can bring about our salvation. It is now Christ who lives in us, unworthy as we are.

God's grace does not depend upon one's individual observance of Jewish law, and the unity of the Christian community is based solely upon the Gospel of Christ. To make any other claims is to deny the grace of God and to say that Christ's death was for nothing (v. 21).

Today's Gospel gives an example of God's forgiveness rooted in love. This incident of the woman who anoints the feet of Jesus is unique to the Gospel of Luke, but has parallels in Matthew 26:6-13; Mark 14:3-9; and John 12:1-8. Jesus accepts the invitation of Simon the Pharisee to dine with him at his home. While they are eating, a "woman in the city, who was a sinner" (v. 37), sought Jesus out and entered the house. Weeping, she began to bathe his feet

ON REFLECTION

When the "woman of the city" stands behind Jesus with the alabaster jar and begins to weep, and then proceeds to kiss and anoint his feet, this outer action mirrors a deep inner truth.

Her gift is valued and cherished in spite of her sinfulness. This is possible because Jesus, at some point before the episode at the dinner party, must have already conveyed this priceless gift on her: the acceptance and love that everyone longs for.

Acceptance with God; life abundant …

Gail Godwin in her insightful book Heart: A Personal Journey has written:

"The most revolutionary part of Jesus' teaching was that a good inner disposition—a good heart—is more important than following codes for correct external behavior. It's as simple as that, yet the literal-minded and the orthodox sticklers for form keep missing it. Where is this God's kingdom of yours, they keep asking him. What is it like? When is it coming? How should we behave to get in? Give us some rules. And he keeps telling them, it's here, it's all around you but you haven't recognized it, it's inside you, it's spread all over this earth, and the only rules you need worry about are loving God with your whole heart and loving one another as I have loved you."

In Christ's unconditional love, we will experience rejection or apparent defeat—and hence be susceptible to a sense of failure and even of shame. But by his grace we will not need to have our lives dominated by our past history, our unworthiness, or even our sins.

The outcast person's uniqueness is valued and cherished in spite of. Jesus does for the woman what the law could not do: namely, heal the shame that binds her.

—H. King Oehmig

with her tears and dry them with her hair. She then kissed his feet and anointed them with the ointment she had brought.

The Pharisee could not understand why Jesus would allow such behavior, and doubted his legitimacy as a prophet, since he allowed this woman to have such intimate contact with him. Didn't Jesus know that she was a sinner?

Jesus perceived what Simon was thinking (ironically, proof of Simon's own criteria for identifying a prophet), and told Simon a parable (vv. 40-43) about two debtors—one who owed 50 denarii and the other 500. When neither man was able to repay the money owed, their creditor forgave both of them their debts.

Jesus then asked Simon which of the two men would love his benefactor more. Simon replied that he supposed that the one who owed the greater debt would be the more grateful.

Jesus then goes on to explain the point of the story by comparing the woman's extravagant display of love for him to Simon's perfunctory hospitality. Everything Simon had neglected, the woman had more than supplied (vv. 44-46). Her actions showed her acknowledgment of her sin and gratitude for forgiveness; Simon's actions showed a lack of love and forgiveness.

Jesus recognized her faith and her intense love for God. She displayed remorse and an overwhelming love; thus Jesus could say to her: "Your sins are forgiven" (v. 48). Jesus' words here remind us of the peace that comes with God's saving grace: "Your faith has saved you; go in peace" (v. 50).

As Jesus continues his ministry to bring the "good news of the kingdom of God" (8:1), he is accompanied by the twelve Apostles as well as by a number of women he had healed, including Mary Magdalene, Joanna, and Susanna. These women provided financial support for the ministry of Jesus, as well as later being present at Jesus' crucifixion, burial, and Resurrection. The specific naming of the women illustrates once again that the ministry to proclaim God's Kingdom is shared by and open to all.

POINTS TO PONDER

1. Read the Gospel passage from the viewpoint of Simon the Pharisee. How do you explain his attitude and actions toward Jesus and the unnamed woman? What was his understanding of the role of a prophet? How do you think he might have felt as Jesus forgave the woman's sins?

2. Read the story again from the perspective of the unnamed woman. Why do you think she sought out Jesus in the first place? How do you think she might have felt as the events unfolded?

3. What is the effect of the parable in Luke 7:40-43? How does this parable speak to you today?

4. How would you characterize the response of Jesus to Simon in this story? How would you describe his response to the woman? What do we learn about Jesus here?

5. Also refer to the other readings for today. What do we learn from all these passages about forgiveness, repentance, sin, and God's grace?

RELEASED

1 Kings 19:1-4 (5-7), 8-15a; Psalm 42 and 43; Galatians 3:23-29; Luke 8:26-39

Jesus, having been driven off course by the previous night's storm, comes ashore in the country of the Gerasenes "which is opposite Galilee" (8:26). Mark's account (5:20) locates the area of the Decapolis on the eastern shore of the Sea of Galilee. Historically, this was Jewish territory; but at this period of time the region was dominated by Gentile cities.

As Jesus steps onto the shore, a "man of the city who had demons" meets him (v. 27). We are told that the man wore no clothes and lived among the tombs instead of in a house. According to Jewish custom, this man would be considered ritually unclean because he inhabited a graveyard (Num. 9:9).

When the man sees Jesus, the demon inhabiting him recognizes the power of Jesus as the "Son of the Most High God," and begs not to be tormented further (v. 28), as Jesus commands the spirit to be gone (v. 29).

Since the demon already knows the identity of Jesus, Jesus now asks for the demon's name, which is revealed as *Legion*. A Roman legion had 6,000 men, suggesting that this man was possessed by 6,000 demons. They beg Jesus not to order them to go back into "the abyss" or dwelling place of the dead, but rather to let them enter a nearby herd of pigs. When Jesus gives them permission, the demons enter the pigs, and the pigs run into the water to drown.

As unclean animals, pigs were unfit to be eaten by Jews and were therefore considered worthless. Although the demons sought to save themselves by being cast into the swine, they were considered destroyed anyway when the pigs drowned; it was believed that demons could not survive in the water.

When we next see the man, he is fully clothed and "in his right mind" (v. 35), due to Jesus' deliverance. However, the people are very much afraid and disturbed by what they have seen, and they ask Jesus to leave. They feel threatened by further economic blows after loss of the herd of swine, and distrust the power of the exorcism itself. Jesus was not a safe person to have around.

As Jesus prepares to depart, the man who had formerly been possessed begs to come along. However, Jesus directs him to return to his home and tell others what God has done for him; whereupon the man leaves, "proclaiming throughout the city how much *Jesus* had done for him" (v. 39b).

The Old Testament reading is also about the difficulty of overcoming evil forces. After the Prophet Elijah has defeated the priests of Baal at Mt. Carmel (1 Ki. 18:17-40), Jezebel, wife of King Ahab, vows to have him killed. In fear for his life, Elijah flees to the wilderness. Feeling that he has failed in his calling as a prophet of the Lord, he asks to die (19:4b).

When he falls asleep, an angel of the Lord brings him food and drink to nourish him for forty days and forty nights as he journeys to a

PRAYER FOR THE DAY

Gracious and everlasting God, who in Jesus Christ came not to be served but to serve, and to give his life as a ransom for many, so clothe us in your Holy Spirit that when we face adversity or persecution for the sake of the Gospel, we may remain love bearers and faithful servants of your unfailing goodness until the Day of the Lord. *Amen.*

cave on Mt. Horeb (Sinai), the mountain of God. The Lord appears and asks Elijah what he is doing there. Elijah complains that although he has been "very zealous" for the Lord (v. 10), he is now left alone and hiding in fear for his life.

God then instructs Elijah to wait for the Lord to pass by. As Elijah waits, there is a mighty wind, then an earthquake, and then fire—all signs of God's presence. But the Lord is not in any of these mighty displays of the forces of nature. Finally, Elijah experiences a "sound of sheer silence" (v. 12)—or, as in one translation, a "soft, murmuring sound."

Hiding his face in his mantle, he goes to the entrance of the cave, where the Lord repeats the question, "What are you doing here, Elijah?" (v. 13b). Elijah repeats his previous response; whereupon the Lord tells him to "return on your way to the wilderness of Damascus" (v. 15). The Lord then goes on to give Elijah a new commission (v. 15b-18).

Out of the silence, Elijah finally hears God's voice and understands that the Lord works not only in the triumphs of life, such as the victory at Mt. Carmel, but also in times of seeming failure.

ON REFLECTION

The ancient world that Jesus and the disciples occupied was a haunted world filled with spirit beings. The invisible landscape was infested with unseen hosts. There were, of course, angels—on the whole, benevolent beings, usually messengers dedicated to the service of God and humanity.

But there were also evil angels, along with terrible supraterrestrial beings—cosmic powers, as well as agents of Satan—that proliferated in the realm of the unseen. Such devils were believed to work malignant deeds on a vulnerable populace through means as diverse as political institutions, natural disasters, and personal liability: on the lonely traveler, a little child, women in childbirth, and those newly married.

They domiciled in unclean places, lurked in tombs, or howled in the desert. These malicious beings were thought by the ancients to cause certain diseases, particularly those involving a loss of control: epilepsy, delirium, convulsions, hysteria, or nervous disorders. This was not just a Hebrew point of view, but was common belief in the Oriental world.

Today we believe that to experience deliverance from such destructive forces, one must choose—and surrender—to a Source that is more powerful. Sometimes, to overcome the effects of evil in the world, it means submitting to the surgeon's skill or the work of an antibiotic or chemotherapy or psychotherapy or a recovery group or prayer—or a combination of any and all of these things.

Common to each of these treatments, however, is a request for help and the willingness to risk one's life on that choice. Surrender of self is essential. When one turns to God from evil, it entails an admission that my way is not working, and can only lead to destruction; and that only a power greater than myself can release and restore me to God.

Rather than debating the nature of the man's pathology, it would be far better to focus on the cure Jesus offered. As the man was able to throw himself at the feet of Christ, God's power was released. The essence of this text is that God's power manifests itself most dramatically when we surrender ours.

—H. King Oehmig

Psalms 42 and 43 eloquently express the desire to seek God, especially in times of despair or persecution. Although presented as two separate Psalms, the common refrain found in 42:5, 11 and 43:5 suggest that they should be considered as one.

Following the pattern of a lament, 42:1-4 expresses the author's longing to be in the presence of God: "As a deer longs for flowing streams, so my soul longs for you, O God..." (v. 1); with the refrain of verse 5 expressing hope for God's help.

Verses 6-10 comprise the second part of the lament, as the Psalmist recalls God's presence from the past, while enemies continue to raise questions about "Where is your God?" (v. 10b). The second part of the lament also concludes with the refrain in verse 11.

The tone changes in the final section of the Psalm, which is expressed as a prayer in 43:1-4. Now the Psalmist asks God for vindication and defense of his cause: "Send out your light and your truth" (v. 3). Now the supplicant can rejoice and offer praise to God.

This time the refrain (v. 5) is seen as a sign of hope, with an emphasis on the final stanza: "Hope in God" (v. 5b) *as a reality.* The prayer has been answered.

In Paul's letter to the Galatians, Jesus is revealed as the source of faith that renders all prior ways of relating to God as irrelevant. Adherence to the discipline of the law previously defined a right relationship with God; but now dependence upon these rules is no longer necessary, for by faith we become children of God.

The baptism that is the outward and visible sign of our union with Christ through faith is totally independent of race (Jew or Gentile), social class (slave or free), or gender (male or female). Although inherited differences may affect what we do in this world, we are all *one in Christ Jesus* and "Abraham's offspring, heirs according to the promise" (3:29). For this we give grateful thanks.

POINTS TO PONDER

1. As you read today's Gospel passage, consider the following questions: What do we learn about Jesus and his ministry here? How did those around Jesus react to his words and actions? Why do you think they responded as they did?

2. How were lives and understandings transformed through Jesus' ministry in this place? What further questions or issues were raised for you?

3. Why do you think Jesus told the man to go back to his home rather than to follow Jesus?

4. What is the most significant learning that this incident contributes to your own faith journey?

5. Refer the Epistle reading for today in Galatians 3:23-29. Here Paul proclaims the revolutionary notion that all human divisions are as nothing in our life in Christ. What challenges do his words present? How are we called to live out this unity in the world today?

THREE WOULD-BE FOLLOWERS

2 Kings 2:1-2, 6-14; Psalm 77:1-2, 11-20; Galatians 5:1, 13-25; Luke 9:51-62

The Gospel passage today marks the beginning of Luke's travel narrative. Jesus is on a mission: he has "set his face to go to Jerusalem" (9:51), and nothing will deter him from his appointed course. Jesus' life will end with his being "lifted up" in that city; but he will attain glory through rejection, suffering, and ultimately death. In this first stage of the journey, Jesus faces opposition and rejection.

The episode in verses 52-55 is unique to Luke. Since the most direct route for Jesus to take from Galilee to Jerusalem was through the often unfriendly villages of the Samaritans, messengers were sent ahead to prepare the way. But when they arrived, they were not welcomed—nor were any other pilgrims to Jerusalem.

The Samaritans believed that Mt. Gerizim, not Jerusalem, was the center of true worship (Jn. 4:20). There were other major points of theological dissention between Jews and the Samaritans as well, and a long-standing antipathy between the two groups ran deep. However, Luke shows a concern on the part of Jesus to reach out to the Samaritans.

Disciples James and John are offended by the disrespect shown to Jesus, and demonstrate their misunderstanding of Jesus' mission. They feel that the Samaritans should be punished by fire from heaven—similar to the way Elijah brought down fire on his enemies (2 Ki. 1:10). But Jesus does not want to be identified with the actions of Elijah, and rebukes the disciples for considering such a thing. Thus they move on to another village for the night and continue the journey the next day.

The remainder of the passage describes encounters with three individuals that serve to reveal the nature of discipleship. First a man approaches Jesus and declares that he is willing to follow him wherever he goes (v. 57). Jesus replies that, while even birds and animals have a place to live, "the Son of Man has nowhere to lay his head" (v. 58).

Although Jesus did not live as an ascetic, he did renounce worldly security, and his followers would be called to do likewise. This way of Jesus is not for the faint-hearted or those concerned about personal safety and comfort.

In the second encounter (vv. 59-60), Jesus himself issues the invitation to "Follow me," but the man asks for time to bury his father first. Tradition placed a strong emphasis on the obligation to properly bury one's parents. But Jesus' response to "let the dead bury their own dead" (v. 60) implies that those who do not hear the words of Jesus are already spiritually dead. Those who are spiritually alive must heed the call to God's service and proclaim the Kingdom *now!*

In the final encounter (vv. 61-62), a third individual takes the initiative to become a

PRAYER FOR THE DAY
Wonderful and holy God, who has spoken through prophets and disciples to bring people out of darkness and into your all-embracing Light, clothe us with wisdom and boldness from on high to be effective agents of Jesus Christ, so that all people may know the Gospel by the working of the Holy Spirit, who lives and reigns with you, one God, forever and ever. *Amen.*

disciple, but he first asks permission to say good-bye to his family. Jesus compares one with such second thoughts to a person who begins the work of plowing a field and then looks back on what he gave up. In such a case, neither the work nor the family is likely to benefit from a divided spirit.

Once we have accepted God's call, Paul gives us further instructions on how we are to live our lives as disciples. He tells us that "For freedom Christ has set us free" (Gal. 5:1). This freedom calls us to love one another and forsake self-indulgence; indeed, the whole law is summed up in the command to "love your neighbor as yourself" (v. 14).

In this life of service we are to be led by the Spirit, and away from any behavior that would tend to exclude us from the Kingdom of God (vv. 18-21a). Instead we are to pursue the fruits of the Spirit.

Thus, as disciples of Jesus we are to love one another and be guided by the Spirit into "love, joy, peace, patience, kindness, generosity, faithfulness, gentleness, and self-control" (vv. 22-23a). These fruits of the Spirit are gifts from God and are the manifestation of our relationship with Christ Jesus.

The Old Testament passage tells the grand final act in the story of the Prophet Elijah. Elijah's ministry had reached fulfillment: he

ON REFLECTION

Nobody in the Gospels ever got to be a disciple of Jesus by volunteering. You become a true disciple of Jesus on the basis of his call, not simply through deciding to put yourself at his disposal. Somehow our red-blooded, American way of life takes offense at such a realization. Our self-directed nose gets pushed out of joint. We thought we really had something to offer God!

But Jesus declares: "You did not choose me but I chose you" (Jn. 15:16). It is not about our qualifications, or preliminary training, or moral fiber, or I. Q. Whereas entry into rabbinical school was based largely on the initiative of the candidate—with Jesus, it is just the opposite. The initiative always lies with him.

So what are the conditions for discipleship? What does the Lord require of would-be followers? This, simply this. That they be ready to climb to their feet when Jesus says, "Follow me." Without qualification. Without hesitation. Without consulting "better judgment." Without seeking outside advice or input from others. Forget checking with the folks back home. Or consulting the weather. Jesus demands an unconditional and immediate response. The one who hesitates is lost. It's that simple, that complicated.

Join up when Jesus extends the offer. It's a decision all disciples have to make, yet one that can't be forced, or stuffed down anybody's throat. It can't be inherited or manipulated. But it can—and should—be reaffirmed day by day. Even in the briefest, most halting way, each day we are invited to yield ourselves wholeheartedly to the unseen Lord, to follow in trust his leading into situations of service beyond our wildest dreams.

Henri Bergson has written: "Life is the opposite of inertia. At every stage, life has to fight against the undertone of matter—against the lag and slack of things towards relaxation, rest and death. Even our freedom, in the very movements by which it is affirmed, creates the growing habits that will stifle it, if it fails to renew itself by constant effort."

Hold onto the plow, Jesus says. The Kingdom itself is at stake.

—H. King Oehmig

had overthrown the prophets of Baal, anointed successors to the thrones of Israel and Aram, and designated Elisha as his own successor. Now he was to be taken up into heaven, and although he would have chosen to meet the end of his time on earth alone, Elisha would not leave him. So together they went to Bethel, then to Jericho, and finally to the Jordan.

As they came to the river, Elijah rolled up his mantle and used it to strike the water. As with Moses and the Exodus, the water parted, and they crossed to the other side on a dry riverbed.

Now it was time to designate an inheritance for Elisha, who asked for an eldest son's double portion of the prophet's spirit. Although this was an extreme request, Elijah said that it would be granted if Elisha were able to see Elijah taken up. As they continued walking, a fiery chariot of horses appeared and "Elijah ascended in a whirlwind into heaven" (2 Ki. 2:11).

As Elijah disappeared, his mantle fell to the ground, and Elisha picked it up. He returned to the Jordan and struck the water as Elijah had done, with the invocation: "Where is the Lord, the God of Elijah?" (v. 14). Again the waters parted, and the members of the prophetic guild who had been watching recognized that the spirit of Elijah now rested on Elisha. He had indeed received his double portion.

Just as Elijah had been taken up into heaven, he could also return. Thus the tradition developed that the return of Elijah would signify the coming of God's Messiah. And even now at the Passover Seder, a door is left open and a place is set for Elijah in case he should return.

The miraculous ascension of Elijah was an awesome event that inspired faith. The Psalmist also recounts other mighty deeds of the Lord as a source of inspiration in times of despair (77:1-2). No God is as great as our God, who controls the mighty forces of nature and redeems the people. "You are the God who works wonders" (v. 14).

POINTS TO PONDER

1. Verse 51 of today's Gospel passage in Luke 9 marks a turning point in the ministry of Jesus, as he heads for Jerusalem and his inevitable death. What have been some of the major turning points in your own faith journey? How have you felt God working in your life at these critical times?

2. What is the example that Jesus sets when he rebukes his disciples for their desire to take revenge against the inhospitable Samaritans (v. 55)?

3. Look at the responses of Jesus to the three different people who offer to follow him (vv. 57-62), and consider: What is your initial reaction to the response of Jesus to each person? Why does Jesus seem so uncompromising here? Why do you think Jesus turned each of these people away? How do you imagine each of these persons might have felt at being left behind?

4. What was the cost of following Jesus in each person's situation? As potential followers of Jesus, what were their priorities to be?

5. Also refer to the other Lessons for today. What do we learn in these readings about discipleship? What must we do in order to respond to the call of Jesus to "follow me"? How are we liberated by heeding this call?

_____

_____

_____

_____

LABORERS FOR THE KINGDOM

2 Kings 5:1-14; Psalm 30; Galatians 6:(1-6), 7-16; Luke 10:1-11, 16-20

The account in 2 Kings 5 of the healing of the Syrian army commander Naaman is a colorful episode that begins with the faith of an Israelite slave girl. In Scripture, leprosy is more often a general term for a variety of skin diseases, not always Hansen's Disease. Nonetheless, the afflicted were subject to a number of social taboos and religious purification requirements.

The slave girl recognized that Naaman was a decent man, so she told Naaman's wife that there was a great prophet in Israel through whom God worked. If Naaman would go to this prophet, he would surely be healed.

Naaman went to the king of Aram, who wrote a letter to the king of Israel requesting healing for Naaman. Soon Naaman arrived in Israel with a full entourage and elaborate gifts. Upon receiving the letter, the king of Israel was greatly distressed. He viewed the request for healing as an impossible task that could be a provocation from his enemy—until the Prophet Elisha heard of the situation and proposed that God would provide a solution.

When Naaman arrived at the home of Elisha, he was insulted when the prophet himself did not appear. Instead, Elisha sent a messenger who told Naaman to bathe seven times in the Jordan River. Naaman expected a magical ritual from Elisha himself. And surely bathing in one of the rivers of his own country would be more effective.

But as he turned away in anger, his servants persuaded him simply to do as Elisha had commanded. So Naaman carried out the command and was cured "according to the word of the man of God" (v. 14). In Luke 4:27, Jesus refers to the healing of Naaman the Syrian as an example of a non-Israelite who was the recipient of Divine healing, when the lepers of Israel rejected God's saving help.

Psalm 30 is a thanksgiving for deliverance from death, which could certainly reflect the experience of Naaman as he was cured of his disease. The Lord answered the Psalmist's cry for help, so that weeping was turned into joy, and mourning to dancing. For this the Psalmist will give thanks and praise to God forever.

In today's Gospel, Jesus sends out seventy disciples who are to prepare for the Lord's coming through their witness. Earlier, Luke had told of how Jesus had sent out the Twelve (9:1-6) with similar instructions. Mark (6:7-11) and Matthew (9:35—10:16) also record this event; but the sending of the seventy (recalling the seventy elders appointed to assist Moses in Num. 11:16-25) is unique to Luke.

The seventy are sent out two by two as a sort of advance party to the towns that Jesus himself will visit later. He tells them that there is an abundant harvest; but there must be more laborers if the ripeness of the Kingdom is to be taken advantage of.

They are like lambs venturing into the midst of wolves—essentially defenseless. Thus

PRAYER FOR THE DAY

Immortal and holy God, you alone can order our unruly wills and infuse our souls with the law of love: grant that by the indwelling of your Holy Spirit we may know the yoke of the Gospel of Jesus Christ to be the light and source of true rest, that we may fulfill our callings with freshness and gladness of heart, to your honor and glory. *Amen.*

they are sent in pairs for mutual support. Haste demands that they travel light, without purse, bag, or sandals. There is no time for ordinary social discourse along the way.

As they enter a dwelling they are to say, "Peace to this house!" (v. 5). For those who accept this proclamation, the reward will be heavenly peace. And for those who reject it, the peace will return to its source. They are to remain in the same house, not moving to better accommodations. Moreover, they are to do away with any scruples concerning the ritual cleanliness of the food provided.

In those towns where they are accepted, they are to cure the sick and proclaim that "The kingdom of God has come near to you"

(v. 9). But in those towns where they are not welcomed, they are to wipe the dust off of their feet and move on. There was no time to argue with those who were not ready to accept the coming of God's Kingdom.

In verses 13-15, which are not included as a part of today's reading, Jesus pronounces woes upon those towns that don't receive the message. Verse 16 is a reminder that the seventy are acting on behalf of Jesus and God the Father.

When the seventy return, they are filled with joy, and report that even demons are subjected (v. 17). Jesus confirms that their mutual ministry has brought about the defeat of Satan. Jesus' vision of Satan being cast down from heaven (v. 18) represents God's liberating

ON REFLECTION

By going among the needy humanity of their day, the seventy embraced a way of life, an emptiness, an urgency. It is in the places of acute pain in our world today—in international strife, human rights, poverty, racism, and sexism—that the power of Jesus for healing and renewal is most needed. And often the least realized.

Elizabeth-Anne Stewart writes in her book Jesus the Holy Fool *(Sheed and Ward, 1999)—which almost started a riot when she read aloud from it at a convention in South Africa (her title being initially misunderstood):*

"As Holy Fool, Jesus scorns the world's wisdom and lives out of the wisdom of God. God's wisdom, we will see, is also essentially foolish by the world's standards, and so Jesus' folly is not unique to him but expresses the life of the Trinity. Foolishness, then, or to be more precise, Holy Foolishness, is a divine quality. It leads both to the folly of the cross and to the comedy of the resurrection—'comedy' here meaning the restoration of the common good, and God's having the final laugh.

"By imitating Holy Foolishness, Christians can find courage and meaning in their own lives—the boldness to stand outside the social circle of acceptability and to name what is, no matter what the price; the single-mindedness to place the love of God before all else; the daring to take great leaps of faith when everyone else asks, 'Where is the safety net?'

"Jesus the Holy Fool is one who empowers the weak and the vulnerable. He lays the mantle of prophecy upon the voiceless and calls the marginalized to lead others to heroic stands. When the world laughs, ridiculing those who dare march to a different drummer, Jesus the Holy Fool applauds, inviting them to share the circus ring with all the holy clowns of history."

Do we find ourselves standing with him alongside the Twelve—and the seventy—as "holy fools"? If not, why not?

—H. King Oehmig

mercy, which, through the power of Christ, delivers humanity from the effects of evil. However, Jesus tells his followers not to rejoice in the fact that the spirits are subject to their command, but rather because their own names are recorded above.

The mission of the seventy foreshadows the missionary activity of the early Christian community. The need for laborers means that all of Jesus' followers must share in preparing the way of the Lord.

In all of his letters, Paul declares to his converts that their salvation is a gift to them from God. They cannot earn it; but they do not inherit it either. In this concluding chapter of Galatians, Paul sums up the arguments he has developed.

Part of what must be done occurs in relationships within the community. When some are "detected in a transgression" (6:1), others must bear in mind that they are also subject to temptation. Therefore, in a spirit of gentleness, they are to restore fallen sinners within the community and "bear one another's burdens" (v. 2).

Next, because the saving relationship with God has been granted to them without any effort on their part, members of the Christian community must understand that before God *they have no claims* and must evaluate their own actions accordingly. All must take responsibility for their own behavior and should provide support for their instructor (v. 6).

Those who are devoted to God's way shall reap eternal life (vv. 7-8). And believers must not tire of doing what they are called to do, working for the good of all—especially other believers (v. 10).

Symbols such as circumcision no longer have any meaning, and Paul warns against those who would insist upon the circumcision of new converts as a means of boasting of their own success. Paul argues that the only thing in which anyone can take personal pride is the Cross of Jesus Christ.

POINTS TO PONDER

1. In verses 1-11 of the Gospel passage in Luke 10, what is the significance of the very specific instructions that Jesus gives to the seventy? How do you think they might have felt as they set out on their mission?

2. How would you describe what the mission of the seventy was to be? What authority did they have to carry out this mission, and what was the source of this authority?

3. What were the possible risks and dangers of this mission? How were the seventy to respond to a community that welcomed them; and in contrast, to the ones that rejected them?

4. In verse 17, we read about the return of the seventy. How do you think they might have felt at this time? What had they accomplished? What was the true significance of their mission as indicated by Jesus in verse 20?

5. In verses 9 and 11, Jesus says that "the kingdom of God has come near." What do you think Jesus meant by that? What challenges does this passage pose for the mission of the Church? How are you personally inspired by the words of Jesus here and by the mission of the seventy?

_____

_____

_____

_____

WHO IS OUR NEIGHBOR?

Amos 7:1-17; Psalm 82; Colossians 1:1-14; Luke 10:25-37

Today we learn about what it means to live more fully in relationship with God and others, so that we will "bear fruit in every good work" as we grow strong in the knowledge of God (Col. 1:10). But as the Parable of the Good Samaritan shows us, it is not enough to grow in knowledge if we do not move from the realm of the theoretical to the domain of the practical.

In our Gospel reading, the seventy have just returned in high spirits from their missionary travels, and Jesus has blessed them for their understanding (10:23-24)—when a lawyer comes forward "to test Jesus" (v. 25). The lawyer asks questions not for information or understanding, but to "gain advantage" over Jesus.

In the ensuing give and take, the lawyer asks Jesus what he must do to inherit eternal life. Jesus turns the question back to him by asking what he reads in the Law. The lawyer responds with the "summary of the Law" from Deuteronomy 6:5: to love God; and Leviticus 19:18: to love one's neighbor. By combining the two commandments into one, Luke shows them to be of equal importance.

Jesus approves of the lawyer's answer, saying, "Do this, and you will live" (v. 28); but the lawyer continues to press the point as a way to justify or "assert himself" by asking: "And who is my neighbor?" (v. 29). In other words, how shall I recognize the person I am obligated to love? In typical fashion, Jesus unfurls the story of the Good Samaritan to let the hearer decide the answer.

There were several centuries of conflict between Samaritans and Jews (Jn. 4:9), beginning with the Assyrian occupation in 722 B.C. During the time of Ezra and Nehemiah, the Samaritans opposed the rebuilding of the temple in Jerusalem, and centered their worship around the shrine on Mt. Gerizim. Over the centuries other points of dispute over theology and liturgy evolved, which resulted in enmity, distrust, and very limited contact between the two groups.

In the story, a Jewish man traveling between Jerusalem and Jericho was attacked by robbers, who stripped and beat him, leaving him half dead by the roadside. Traveling the road to Jerusalem was a high-risk journey, and thus this incident was not unusual. The first two travelers who happened by were a Jewish priest and a Levite—both privileged members of the religious order. Both men "passed by on the other side" (vv. 31, 32) to avoid ritual contamination from what appeared to be a dead body.

The third traveler who came along was a Samaritan who, "moved with pity" (v. 33), tended the man's wounds and took him to a nearby inn. The next day he left money with the innkeeper for the continued care of the injured man, promising to pay any additional costs on his return journey.

Jesus then asked which of the three travelers was a neighbor to the man who was attacked.

PRAYER FOR THE DAY

O God, holy and mighty One, so incline the hearts of your people of faith to spread your message of healing love that those who do not know you, or love you, may come into the fellowship of grace through Jesus Christ our Lord, who with you and the Holy Spirit lives and reigns, one God, in life everlasting. *Amen.*

When the lawyer replied, "The one who showed him mercy," Jesus told him to "Go and do likewise" (v. 37).

Here we see that our neighbor is anyone who needs help that we have the means to supply. This understanding transcends cultural, social, and religious boundaries. The Samaritan, who would have been considered a heretic by the man he assisted, is in fact an example of Jewish morality. Those expected to show mercy did not. Luke was illustrating the universal nature of the Gospel. The issue is not who is my neighbor, but who is *not* my neighbor.

Amos is the earliest of the 8th-century prophets, which also included Hosea, Isaiah, and Micah. Although he was born in the southern kingdom of Judah, God called him as a prophet to the northern kingdom of Israel. Because of the greed and corruption of the rulers and the failure of the religious leaders to follow God's commands for justice, Amos proclaimed the destruction of Israel and the exile of the people. His prophecies were fulfilled in 722 B.C. when the Assyrians conquered Israel.

Amos had a series of five visions (7:1-3, 4-6, 7-9; 8:1-3; 9:1-4) in which he saw the destruction of Israel. In the first two, the Lord relented (vv. 3, 6), and Israel was spared. However, in the other visions, including the one in our reading for today, the Lord does not relent.

ON REFLECTION

Robert W. Funk has written in Honest to Jesus: Jesus for a New Millennium *(HarperSanFrancisco, 1997):*

"Those who listened to Jesus tell the parable of the Samaritan, as good Judeans, would have expected the third person along that road to be a Judean. The hero of the story would naturally have been one of them. How shocked they must have been when that figure turned out to be a hated Samaritan. At the mention of the Samaritan, Judean listeners would have bristled, rejected the plot, and quit the story, in spite of their initial inclination to give it a sympathetic hearing.

"Those who refused the narrative were those who identified themselves literally with participants in the story. Some Judeans, priests, and levites took themselves literally and so were offended. There were probably no Samaritans present. Had there been, they, too, would have suffered indignity at the thought of giving such profuse assistance to a Judean."

Jesus was not telling stories to please or comfort. Instead, he exhorts: Go on, yourselves, and do the impossible.

"God," the elder said, *"is closer to sinners than to saints."*

"But how can that be?" the eager disciple asked.

The elder explained: *"God in heaven holds each person by a string. When we sin, we cut the string. Then God ties it up again, making a knot—bringing the sinner a little closer. Again and again sins cut the string—and with each knot God keeps drawing the string closer and closer."*

As always, Jesus turns things upside down. The parable of the Good Samaritan retains the ability to shock us, and the potential to shatter the conventional assumptions of the religious-and-politically "correct."

It ought to make us uncomfortable enough to see, taste, feel the pit, identify our neighbor … and maybe get a not-very-assuring, but clearer idea of ourselves as sinners—and how we can move closer to Jesus' way by simply reaching out.

—H. King Oehmig

The Lord showed Amos a plumb line set in the midst of the people of Israel. Because Israel did not measure true and was found to be lacking, the Lord would no longer pass them by; Israel would thus be overthrown.

Verses 10-17 tell of the clash between Amaziah the priest and Amos. First Amaziah complained to King Jeroboam that Amos was conspiring against him by predicting the death of the king and the downfall of Israel (v. 10). The priest urged Amos to take his words of destruction to Judah instead.

Amos answered that he was but a humble herdsman and "a dresser of sycamore trees" (7:14). He was not a member of one of the professional prophetic guilds, yet he had been called to prophesy to Israel. Because Amos was speaking the word of the Lord, silencing him would make no difference in the fall of Israel and Amaziah himself. Israel would be sent into exile because they did not heed the word of the Lord.

The justice of God that Amos declared to the people of Israel is also proclaimed in Psalm 82. God is depicted as ruler of the Divine council, for only then will there be justice for the weak and needy, and protection from the wicked. The other gods "have neither knowledge nor understanding" (v. 5) and will face death like mortals. Thus the Psalmist calls on God to "judge the earth; for all the nations belong to you!" (v. 8).

In Colossians 1:1, Paul identifies himself as "an apostle of Christ Jesus by the will of God." The letter continues with a prayer of thanksgiving in verses 3-12. Paul commends the Colossians for the faith, love, and hope evident in the community. He praises their witness to the Gospel, which they have learned from their faithful leader Epaphras.

Paul goes on to ask God to grant them knowledge, wisdom, and spiritual discernment. He encourages them to lead lives "worthy of the Lord," fully pleasing to God (v. 10). He asks that they may be made strong through the glorious power of the Lord and be "prepared to endure everything with patience" and joy (v. 11). Verses 13-14 express Paul's confidence that they will be able to carry out this mission because of Christ, who brings redemption and the forgiveness of sins.

POINTS TO PONDER

1. As you read the Gospel passage, put yourself in the place of the lawyer. What do you think motivated his original question? What might his reactions have been throughout his exchange with Jesus?

2. The lawyer answered his original question in Luke 10:27 with the words we recognize as the Summary of the Law. How would you define the word *love* as used here? Give specific examples of loving God with one's heart, soul, strength, and mind.

3. Describe this incident from the viewpoint of the man who was robbed and beaten. How do you think his life might have been changed by the experience? How do you think he might have reacted toward the Samaritan? As you identify with the priest and the Levite, ask: What are the excuses we use today that prevent us from helping those in need?

4. Imagine that you are the Samaritan. What do you think motivated him to assist the man who had been robbed? What do we learn about being a good neighbor from the actions of the Samaritan and the innkeeper?

5. In verse 37, Jesus tells us that a neighbor is one who shows *mercy*. How would you define mercy in this context? Who has been a true neighbor to you in your life?

MARTHA AND MARY

Amos 8:1-12; Psalm 52; Colossians 1:15-28; Luke 10:38-42

In the fourth of five visions, the Lord shows the Prophet Amos a basket of summer fruit. In a play on words, the Hebrew word for *fruit* becomes the word for *end*—as God declares that "The end has come upon my people Israel" (8:2).

In the preceding visions, God had foretold the destruction of Israel for its corruption and failure to follow God's commandments. Verses 3-4 describe the death and destruction to come. In particular, the oppression of the poor and needy by greedy and dishonest merchants is denounced: "buying the poor for silver and the needy for a pair of sandals" (v. 6a).

God will not forget such injustice, and the very earth will tremble as a result. There will be earthquakes, darkness, and mourning in the land (vv. 8-10).

There will also be a famine, but this is not to be just a lack of food and water, but a famine "of hearing the words of the Lord" (v. 11). The people will search everywhere for the word of the Lord, "but they shall not find it" (v. 12).

There is a sense of desperate searching as they "run to and fro" (v. 12). Israel had experienced both physical famine and drought before, but now they would also suffer spiritual famine as a pronouncement against them. Only in the face of God's silence would the people understand their need for God's presence.

The final chapter of Amos proclaims the eventual salvation of God's people and the restoration of the kingdom under a Davidic king. Justice will prevail and the land be rebuilt, but only after the destruction of Israel and the exile of its people.

Psalm 52 echoes Amos' words of destruction and judgment against the wicked and corrupt.

The first four verses describe the treachery and deceit of one who loves evil more than good. However, the Lord will bring judgment against those who put their trust in riches and not in God (vv. 5-7). Thus the Psalmist offers thanksgiving: "I trust in the steadfast love of God forever and ever" (v. 8).

In today's Gospel reading, an occasion of hospitality sets the context for teaching on the balance between doing and reflecting. After Jesus' exchange with the lawyer (Lk. 10:25-37), he and his disciples continue on their way to a village, where Jesus is welcomed into the home of a woman named Martha.

While Martha was occupied with providing hospitality for her guest, her sister Mary "sat at the Lord's feet and listened to what he was saying" (v. 39). Exasperated by the lack of assistance from her sister, Martha complained to Jesus that Mary had left her to do all the work by herself. Jesus replied that Martha is "worried and distracted by many things" (v. 41), while only one thing is truly needed. In this, "Mary has chosen the better part" (v. 42).

This incident is unique to Luke, although the sisters Mary and Martha may be the same women mentioned in the Gospel of John (11:1-

PRAYER FOR THE DAY

Come, Lord Jesus, and pour upon us each day your grace to relieve our fears and guide us in the way of peace: that through the power of the Gospel, we may bear good fruit for the welfare of the world, to the glory of your name. *Amen.*

30; 12:1-8). The story has been interpreted in a variety of ways, often to illustrate the tension between the contemplative life (Mary) and the active life (Martha)—faith versus works. It is also often pointed out that Jesus ignored contemporary social taboos here by allowing a woman to sit at his feet as a learner.

Martha, in her attempt to provide Jesus with the best hospitality possible, broke a primary rule by being so consumed with her tasks that she neglected to pay proper attention to her guest. Martha's service on his behalf was not rejected by Jesus; but in this case, Jesus wished primarily *for his word to be heard.*

Martha had received Jesus as prophet, but became so distracted by her duties that she was missing his teaching. In contrast, Mary made the better choice as a good hostess by sitting at Jesus' feet.

The Apostle Paul, writing in his letter to the Colossians, speaks of the importance of reconciliation in Christian life. Colossae was a Gentile city, and its inhabitants were strangers to Israel's God. When knowledge of God's revelation was brought to them, they saw themselves as God's enemies (1:21).

Then Paul's comrades gave them the Good News that God's Son had offered his life as a sacrifice for them in order to secure their forgiveness and renewal. All this was because God loved them, and the Redeemer sought to render them holy and blameless.

Now they had hope, and as long as they continued to trust in the redeeming sacrifice,

ON REFLECTION

What Martha did not realize, back in the kitchen as she was confecting an elaborate dinner—sweat beading her forehead and flour dusting her apron—was that her sister Mary, coolly sitting at the feet of Jesus, was actually being as effortful as she was.

How can that be? She's sitting there, soaking up all those Divine thoughts and never budging from her position to lift a finger. Yet this is work?

But Mary wasn't being lazy—anything but. It's just that Mary's effort was in the form of presence and availability *to Jesus. She could have been (as Martha was) present in the house but unavailable. She could have sat there with thoughts of the casserole running over, or the lamb burning on the grill, or wondering how many disciples had come and how much they would eat. ...*

She could have lingered at the feet of Jesus with her mind still in the kitchen. All that would have made her present *but* unavailable.

Presence and availability are born of focus, or total attention. What is required, therefore, is the setting aside of self. This means the bracketing of our agendas—as wonderful and necessary as we tell ourselves they are—to be present and available to God and one another.

Mary may have been relatively still, in place—but she knew how to focus, and she had centered her being on Jesus and his truth.

A story is told of a gentle nun who was well known for her prayer life. Someone younger came to her and asked her how she had reached the point at which prayer was constant.

"Looking back," she said, "it seems that the prayer has always been deep in my heart. Once it was like an underground spring covered by a great stone. Then one day Jesus came along and removed the stone. The spring has been bubbling up ever since."

—H. King Oehmig

their enmity to God was canceled and they were God's people. This had been the object of Paul's ministry. For all those desiring to continue in that faith, Paul's example could point the way. Here was a man who suffered because he had given himself completely to the community of believers.

But he took joy in those sufferings because they were offered in union with the redeeming sufferings of Christ. So they helped to make the whole community an extension of Christ's redeeming presence in the world.

Thus reconciliation with God becomes *union with the Divine* that is beyond human understanding. It represents a mystery that prior generations could not penetrate; but now this glorious generosity that makes the Redeemer present with us has been revealed to God's people (v. 26). By God's will we are given the hope of coming to glory, of being presented to Christ with our potential fully attained. "It is he whom we proclaim ... so that we may present everyone mature in Christ" (v. 28).

POINTS TO PONDER

1. Read the Gospel passage and imagine that you are Martha. Read it again and put yourself in Mary's place. What different thoughts and feelings do you experience from the perspectives of these two women?

2. With which of these sisters do you identify more easily? How do you think each woman might have felt after Jesus gave his answer to Martha in Luke 10:41-42? What do you think might have been the relationship between these two women?

3. We read that Martha was distracted by her many tasks. What are some of the duties and responsibilities that prevent you from listening to the message of Jesus? What can you do to minimize these distractions?

4. What do you think Jesus means in verse 42 when he says that Mary has chosen the "better part"?

5. Refer to John 11:1-44 and John 12:1-7. What else do we learn about Martha and Mary from these passages? How do they serve as models of discipleship for us today?

"YOUR KINGDOM COME ... "

Hosea 1:2-10; Psalm 85; Colossians 2:6-15 (16-19); Luke 11:1-13

Today's Gospel reading begins with Jesus himself at prayer (Lk. 11:1), which prompts the disciples to ask him to *teach them to pray* as John the Baptist had taught his followers. Jesus' teaching here on prayer is divided into three sections, beginning with the Lord's Prayer in verses 1-4.

Matthew's longer version of the Lord's Prayer (6:9-13) is set within the Sermon on the Mount, and is proposed as a substitute for the wrong kind of prayer in their religious duties (6:5-8). But Luke's version flows naturally from the context of the disciples' request.

The prayer opens with the simple address to God as Father. This concept was already present in Hebrew Scripture (Dt. 32:6; Mal. 2:10), although the most common form of address in the synagogue service was "Our Father, Our King." Thus Jesus does not offer a new idea of God, but rather a unique perspective of familiarity and closeness in contrast to the formal prayers of Palestinian Judaism. Disciples are to approach God in prayer with the same intensity and intimacy as a child comes to his or her human father (cf Rom. 8:15; Gal. 4:6).

Jesus' model prayer expresses confidence in God's holiness and sovereignty. God's holiness sets God apart from all created things, and we ask that the reign of God—God's Kingdom—be established in all the world (Lk. 11:2).

The second part of the prayer (vv. 3, 4) moves the focus from the nature of God to God's relationship with humanity. The first petition asks for subsistence—"our daily bread." The second petition in verse 4a asks for forgiveness of sins. Just as God provides for our physical needs, God can also heal our brokenness. However, we must offer this forgiveness to one another as well. By doing so, we open a new way of being in relationship with others.

The final petition (v. 4b) requests that we not be brought "to the time of trial." Jesus himself was tempted concerning the way he was to fulfill his vocation, and here we ask to be given the grace to withstand the trials and temptations that come to us.

Verses 5-8 offer a parable about persistence in prayer. A man comes knocking at the door of a friend in the middle of the night. He asks for three loaves of bread for a guest who has just arrived. Although the reluctant neighbor initially refuses to get out of bed and get the loaves, he eventually complies—not out of friendship, but because of the petitioner's shameless and repetitive *asking*. Persistence in our prayers strengthens our resolve and enhances our openness to receive the blessings God has to bestow.

The remaining verses in the passage contain further sayings that also focus on persistence in prayer. Verses 9 and 10 say that when we ask, we shall receive. When we seek, we shall find.

PRAYER FOR THE DAY

Gracious and eternal God, we praise you for the mystery of your Being revealed in the Gospel of Jesus Christ: grant us your Holy Spirit so that the eyes of our hearts may be awakened to your unseen but continual Presence. Bless us that we may be faithful witnesses of your holy Kingdom, until it arrives in its completeness on the last day. *Amen.*

And when we keep knocking, the door will be opened. Again, we must be bold enough to ask in the confidence that God will answer.

Jesus then makes his final point by using an analogy of human parents who would not resort to trickery when meeting their children's requests by giving a snake for a fish or a scorpion for an egg. Thus, just as mere humans "know how to give good gifts" (v. 13), we can be confident that God the Father will do even more—by giving "the Holy Spirit to those who ask."

For two weeks, the Old Testament reading is taken from the prophecies of Hosea, who resided in the Northern Kingdom of Israel in the 8th century B. C., after the time of Amos. This was a turbulent period of political unrest in Israel, with the impending invasion of the Assyrians leading to the fall of the Northern Kingdom in 722 B. C. Hosea's prophecies center around the condemnation of Israel for its unfaithfulness to God, worship of the pagan Baals, and political corruption.

ON REFLECTION

The Lord's Prayer. *This simple model of prayer that Jesus gives is followed here by an illustration that stresses another aspect of prayer. That is, insistent, tireless asking. Ask and keep on asking. Seek and keep on seeking. Knock and keep on knocking.*

It is fascinating to note that Jesus does not say to "ask correctly" or "seek properly" or "knock judiciously"—but, like the journeyer at midnight, to beat the door down with importunity. Just ask, seek, and knock. God can take care of whatever. The Divine switchboard will not get overloaded or short-circuited.

In the short illustration that comes next, Jesus (tongue firmly planted in cheek) points out that God is not about to fling you a copperhead when you ask for a trout, or serve you a scorpion when you ask for scrambled eggs, any more than a fallen human father would give his own child such an insulting treatment.

Papa-God can be trusted to give each of us whatever we need. Let the prayers pour out freely, and set out the bushel barrels ready to receive—because that is how God works.

As Michaela Bruzzese writes in Sojourners *(July-Aug. 2001):*

"In Luke, the God to whom Jesus prays is described like a parent, imagery that was not new in Judaism ... Luke portrays the disciples asking Jesus for instruction, highlighting the teacher-disciple relationship that dominates his writings. The prayer that Jesus teaches is beautiful in its simplicity, emphasizing dependence on God, the parent-like relationship with God, and the need to extend mercy to others as we would like it extended to us.

"Since this is before Jesus' death and the celebration of the Eucharist, the disciples could not have understood the profound meaning of bread in the prayer. For contemporary Christians, however, Jesus' prayer reveals the humble, day-to-day presence of God. The Christ is at once redeemer of the world and the most common and humble substance in our lives. ... It is hour by hour that we construct the kingdom, in small and large acts of mercy and solidarity. With this daily bread, we too become food for the world; with this body, we too can become a source of life to others."

—H. King Oehmig

Hosea personifies the infidelity of Israel through his marriage to the promiscuous Gomer. Israel had succumbed to the practices of the local pagan cults, which included ritual prostitution to insure the fertility of the land. Hosea was commanded by God to take one of the cult prostitutes as his wife and to have children with her. Whether the children Gomer bore were actually Hosea's is not made clear, but the names God commanded him to give them were symbolic of God's judgment against Israel.

The first was a son to be called Jezreel, whose name recalled a massacre in the valley of that name and was a prediction of God's destruction of Israel's royal house. Next came a daughter to be named Lo-ruhamah as a sign that the Lord would no longer have pity or compassion for Israel, but would save Judah. The third child was a son named Lo-ammi to show that the Lord would no longer be the God of Israel.

But the passage ends with a note of hope for the future, as the Lord goes on to say that the number of the children of Israel shall be as the sand of the sea, in accordance with the promises made to Abraham (Gen. 22:17). There will be a time when Israel and Judah will be reunited, and again called "Children of the living God" (Hos. 1:11).

Psalm 85 speaks to the promises of Hosea 1:10-11. The Lord has "restored the fortunes of Jacob" (v. 1) and forgiven the iniquity of the people. Thus love and faithfulness, righteousness and peace will come together to make a pathway for God.

Paul's words to the Colossians continue his Christological teachings, which are the basis of the Christian manner of life. In accepting Christ as our Lord, we establish our life in Christ and our faith is strengthened. But we must see to it that such faith is not displaced by any misguided, humanly derived tradition, for only Jesus Christ guides us in the way of truth. When we are in Christ we have a "spiritual circumcision" (2:11), which eliminates the need for physical circumcision.

We now live in the spiritual reality of baptism, and are alive and forgiven, as our sins have been nailed to the cross with Christ (v. 14). Jesus has despoiled the hostile powers and claimed us for himself, disarming all other rulers and authorities and triumphing over all. Paul goes on to say that neither the observance of dietary laws nor calendar feasts is needed in a right relationship with God. Still less should worship be offered to any mediator other than Christ, our Head.

POINTS TO PONDER

1. Prayer is the focus of the Lessons for today. As you read Luke's version of the Lord's Prayer in Luke 11:1-4, consider the following questions: What does it mean to you to address God as Father? What is our relationship with God and others as defined here? How is this prayer a model for Christian living?

2. What special role does this prayer have in the life of the Church as well as in your own spiritual life?

3. What else do we learn about prayer from the parable in verses 5-8? In verses 9-13, Jesus gives further teaching about prayer. Describe the functions of *asking, seeking,* and *knocking* in our prayer life. How is the Holy Spirit involved (v. 13)?

4. Also read the other Lessons for today. What do we learn from them about our relationship with God?

5. What insights have you gained about prayer from your discussion today? In particular, what have you discovered about the Lord's Prayer? What steps can you take to further enrich your prayer life?

THE SOURCE OF FULFILLMENT

Hosea 11:1-11; Psalm 107:1-9, 43; Colossians 3:1-11; Luke 12:13-21

The Prophet Hosea, in his writings, laments over the infidelity of Israel, demonstrated by their worshiping pagan gods and forsaking the Lord.

The passage today begins: "When Israel was a child, I loved him, and out of Egypt I called my son" (11:1). Israel was called to be God's people, and through God's love the nation was delivered out of bondage in Egypt.

Using the imagery of a parent caring for a child, Hosea describes God's love for Israel (vv. 3-4). God taught them to walk, held them, healed them, fed them, and "led them with cords of human kindness, with bands of love" (v. 4).

But despite God's loving care, Israel continued to worship foreign gods. "My people are bent on turning away from me" (v. 7). The tone of the writing changes dramatically in verses 5-7, which describe the consequences of Israel's faithlessness.

The nation will be swept up in war and destruction: "The sword rages in their cities ... " (v. 6). They call to the Lord, but God "does not raise them up at all" (v. 7).

Once again the tone changes in verses 8-10, as God's compassion for Israel overrides anger (v. 8). God will not allow Israel to perish like the cities of Admah and Zeboiim, which were destroyed with Sodom and Gomorrah (Dt. 29:23).

God does not act as do mortals (cf Is. 55:8). God is "the Holy One in your midst" (v. 9) who acts in boundless love and forgiveness.

The promise of redemption is held out in verses 10-11, as God calls Israel home again. The roar of the lion would normally instill fear, but here it is a signal of the Lord's invitation.

Despite their faithlessness and continual turning to false gods, the Lord will remain faithful and redeem Israel.

Hosea's own experience of the unfailing love of God is echoed in Psalm 107. The Psalmist calls all those who have been rescued from trouble to give thanks for the steadfast love of the Lord.

They come from all the corners of the world, as the Lord answers their cries and leads them to safety. God satisfies their hunger and thirst with all good things.

The Gospel passage also draws attention to God's grace and love by distinguishing between the life consumed by the acquiring of possessions and the one that is "rich toward God."

Here a man addresses Jesus as "teacher," and asks him to act as an arbitrator in a dispute over a family inheritance. It was a common practice to ask a rabbi or religious man to act as a judge on issues of what constitutes right conduct. Then, as now, disputes about inheritances could tie up property for indefinite periods of

PRAYER FOR THE DAY

May your unending compassion, Holy God, be poured out on your people. Grant that this food that never perishes may nourish and sustain the proclamation of the Gospel of Jesus Christ. May all peoples of the earth be fed through the grace and mercy of your Holy Spirit, through you and our Lord Jesus Christ, one God, in glory everlasting. *Amen.*

time and cause long-lasting conflict among the parties involved.

Here the man says to Jesus, "Teacher, tell my brother to divide the family inheritance with me" (Lk. 12:13). However, the man's motivation in addressing Jesus was prompted by self-interest and not by an inquiry into the proper workings of the law. Jesus refuses to become involved in such a dispute (v. 14); his commission from the Father far exceeds the scope of resolving how a particular family's property should be divided.

Jesus now turns to the gathered crowd with a strong warning to "Take care!" (v. 15) and to be on guard against the dangers of greed and coveting possessions. He continues by illustrating his point with a parable found only in Luke's Gospel.

There was a rich man who possessed land that produced so abundantly that the man was confronted with the problem of trying to find a place to store all of his crops. In verses 17-19, the man ponders his options and decides to tear down his existing barns and build bigger ones to store all his grain and goods. Thus, with safely stored provisions to last for many years, he can "relax, eat, drink, be merry" (v. 19). A similar sentiment is found in Isaiah 22:13: "Let us eat and drink ... " but it adds the words "for tomorrow we die."

In private musings directed to "my soul," the rich man thinks only of himself and his

ON REFLECTION

Nowhere is true detachment better described in the New Testament than when the Apostle Paul wrote to the church at Philippi:

"For I have learned to be content with whatever I have. I know what it is to have little, and I know what it is to have plenty. In any and all circumstances I have learned the secret of being well-fed and of going hungry, of having plenty and of being in need. I can do all things through [Christ] who strengthens me" (Phil. 4:11-13).

How can we pull ourselves free of the great American acquisition game? Why is it so hard to find the balance that Jesus teaches and that Paul embodied?

Soren Kierkegaard wrote: "Can there be something in life that has power over us which little by little causes us to forget all that is good? And can this ever happen to anyone who has heard the call of eternity quite clearly and strongly? If this can ever be, then one must look for a cure against it.

"Praise be to God that such a cure exists—to quietly make a decision. A decision joins us to the eternal. It brings what is eternal into time. A decision raises us with a shock from the slumber of monotony. A decision breaks the magic spell of custom. A decision breaks the long row of weary thoughts. A decision pronounces its blessing upon even the weakest beginning, as long as it is a real beginning. Decision is the awakening to the eternal."

And so the choice, the decision, comes back to our awareness. Will we continue to build more barns, or will we pause and put on an apron?

"The will of God," writes Robert Farrar Capon, "is not a list of stops to make to pick up mouthwash, razor blades, and a pound of chopped chuck on the way home. It is God's longing that we will take the risk of being nothing but ourselves, desperately in love."

Will we hear God's call to us and turn our lives around?

—H. King Oehmig

wealth. There is no consideration of others or recognition that the land itself is a gift from God (cf Deut. 8:11-20). He feels confident that he is secure and in control because of his many possessions.

But then God speaks, calling him "You fool!" and warning him that this very night he will die. Now who will possess all that he has stored up? There is nothing wrong with careful planning and management of one's resources, but possessions have no survival value for eternity.

Jesus ends the parable by saying, "So it is with those who store up treasures for themselves but are not rich toward God" (v. 21). When life is considered only in terms of material possessions, we live in fear and cut ourselves off from a richer relationship with God.

Jesus expands on this theme in verses 22-31 when he says, "Do not worry about your life" (v. 22). Instead, we are to strive for God's Kingdom.

The foolishness of the rich man illustrates that there is no connection between eternal life and an abundance of material possessions. In the end, we all die, whether we are rich or poor.

However, in Colossians 3, Paul proclaims that death is not the final answer, for we "have been raised with Christ" (v. 1). Therefore, we are to set our minds on "things that are above, not on things that are on earth" (v. 2).

Because of this new life in Christ, Paul urges the community to "put to death" certain vices that may be found among them. They are to rid themselves of anger, wrath, malice, slander, and abusive language. They are now clothed with a "new self," and in this new life "Christ is all and in all!" (v. 11), thus eradicating all former divisions.

Through Christ death no longer has dominion. The folly of living in bondage to material possessions is to be transformed into a new life of glory forevermore.

POINTS TO PONDER

1. Why do you think the man in the crowd asked Jesus to settle a dispute with his brother? How would you explain the response Jesus gives him in Luke 12:14?

2. In verse 15, Jesus warns against an "abundance of possessions." How do possessions influence our lives? How might your life be changed if you had less "stuff"? What do you have that would be the most difficult to give up, and why?

3. As you read the parable beginning in verse 16, describe the actions of the rich man. How would you characterize him? Why do you think God calls him a fool?

4. What does it mean to be "rich toward God" (v. 21)? How does one attain this "wealth"? What do you count as riches in your own life? How do the values found in this passage compare with those held by our contemporary culture?

5. How is the Gospel reading further illuminated by the other Lessons appointed for today?

TRANSFIGURED

Exodus 34:29-35; Psalm 99; 2 Peter 1:13-21; Luke 9:28-36

O
n the Feast of Jesus' Transfiguration, August 6, our readings focus on the *revelation of the glory of God,* beginning with the experience of Moses on Mt. Sinai.

When Moses came down from the mountain after receiving the law from God, the people were afraid to come near him, as "the skin of his face was shining" (Ex. 34:30).

Moses' experience of a direct encounter with God changed him so profoundly that it was *visible.* When Moses spoke with the Lord, the reflection of God's glory remained on his face.

The people became afraid to approach Moses, since to encounter the Divine face to face meant death. What mortal could possibly sustain the awesome majesty and holiness of the Divine presence?

Once Moses realized the source of their fear, he covered his face with a veil. He removed it when he spoke with God and communicated the Word of God to the people.

The words of the Psalmist reflect the awesome holiness and majesty of the Lord that Moses and the Israelites experienced. Thus, in response, the people are to praise and worship the Lord: "Extol the Lord our God, and worship at his holy mountain; for the Lord our God is holy" (99:9).

The Gospel passage begins with a reference to "sayings" that had occurred eight days earlier: Peter's confession of Jesus as "the Messiah of God" (9:20); Jesus' first prediction of his Passion (9:21-22); and then his teachings on the true cost of discipleship (9:23-27). This is a turning point in the ministry of Jesus as he begins the journey to Jerusalem.

While Jesus is praying, "the appearance of his face changed, and his clothes became dazzling white" (v. 29). Like Moses' shining face (Ex. 34:29), the change in Jesus' appearance is an indication of holy transcendence.

Then Moses and Elijah appear and talk with Jesus about his departure—literally his "exodus" or coming death in Jerusalem. Only Luke includes this information about the content of their conversation; and it is only in Luke that Moses and Elijah appear "in glory" (v. 31). However, the glory of the two prophets is an indication of their risen and heavenly life; whereas the glory of Jesus is a manifestation of his Messiahship.

Moses and Elijah have had their own mountain experiences of the Divine, and tradition said that the reappearance of these two prophets would be a sign of the coming of the Messianic age. They link Jesus with Israel's past and show that Jesus was in accord with the law and the prophets. Jesus will also face rejection, as did Moses and Elijah.

In another detail particular to Luke, we read that Peter and the other two Apostles were "weighed down with sleep" (v. 32a). Similarly, the three men will fall asleep while Jesus prays on the Mount of Olives the night before his crucifixion (22:45-46).

PRAYER FOR THE DAY

Lord Jesus, the Light of the World, who revealed your glistening radiance to chosen witnesses on the holy mountain, so anoint us in the grace of your Holy Spirit, that we may know your eternal majesty as the Beloved One, who has come from the Father to transfigure all things in Divine love. *Amen.*

Suddenly Peter, "not knowing what he said" (v. 33b), proposes that they erect dwellings or booths on the site in commemoration of the three figures. Although Peter had previously confessed Jesus as the Messiah, he still did not comprehend that Jesus was far superior to Moses and Elijah, or that this experience could not possibly be contained or preserved.

At this point, the Apostles are terrified as they are overshadowed by a cloud (cf Ex. 13:21; 24:15-18). The cloud is a manifestation of the presence of God. A cloud led the Israelites in the journey through the wilderness (Ex. 13:21-22; 24:15-16), and would appear again at the Ascension of Jesus (Acts 1:9).

Then a voice came from the cloud saying, "This is my Son, my Chosen; listen to him!" (v. 35). These words echo those spoken to Jesus at his Baptism (Lk. 3:22); however, this time they are also heard by Peter, James, and John. Jesus is not only the *beloved* of God, but the *chosen* of God. And they are to *listen to him!*

Jesus is not just another prophet—he is the Son of God. He has revealed to them that the Messiah will be killed and then raised on the third day. To be a disciple is to take up the cross and follow him (Lk. 9:21-25).

After the voice has spoken, Jesus is alone, and the men with him are silent. What could possibly be said after such an experience with

ON REFLECTION

With Peter's confession at Caesarea Philippi and the subsequent confession of Jesus that the Son of Man must suffer and be rejected by the establishment, killed and raised again on the third day, the disciples could easily have looked upon their own future as little more than a relentless, joyless grind. What did they have to look forward to besides a discipleship that constituted a double-decker sandwich of heartache and gloom—another day, another bite.

But into this bleak picture—through prayer, Luke emphasizes—comes the spine-tingling, unforeseen extravagance of the Holy transfiguring the Chosen Son and transfixing his closest friends.

As always, after any encounter of this kind, the disciples are forever changed. How could anybody, waking from a nap to behold Moses and Elijah conversing with a Jesus transfigured in light—even given all inherent human tendencies to deny or minimize—walk down the mountain unchanged, business as usual?

They could no longer resort to convenient unconsciousness in matters where Jesus, as Lord, was authoritative. Luke records that Peter, James, and John "kept silent and in those days told no one any of the things they had seen" (9:36).

Deepak Chopra wrote in How to Know God (Running Press, 2001) of the first American to be canonized as a saint, Frances Cabrini. "When she was still an impoverished nun in Italy, Mother Cabrini was praying when another sister broke into her room without knocking. To her astonishment, the room was filled with a soft radiance.

"The sister was speechless, but Mother Cabrini remarked offhandedly, 'This isn't anything. Just ignore it and go on with what you were doing.' From that day on the saint made sure that her privacy was securely kept, and the only clue for outsiders was a faint light that occasionally crept out underneath her door. It is a mark of the true miracle worker to be comfortable with God's power."

—H. King Oehmig

such unimaginable implications? So it says that the Apostles "kept silent and in those days told no one any of the things they had seen" (v. 36).

It was not until the events surrounding the Resurrection unfolded that they could begin to understand what they had witnessed. Thus the Transfiguration stands as both an affirmation of Jesus' Messiahship and a foreshadowing of what was to come.

The experience of the Transfiguration of Jesus is recalled in the second letter attributed to Peter. What the disciples saw is the guarantee of the validity of the Apostolic teaching they had been given. *They truly were with him* on the mountain and were witnesses of his revealed majesty (1:16). They heard the Divine voice. Indeed, the words were addressed directly to them in order that they might know and obey.

The writer of the letter also carefully points out that these words, like the prophecies revealed in Scripture, are directly inspired by God's Holy Spirit. None of this is meant to be merely a matter of human interpretation or hearsay, but comes as a result of holy people responding to the guidance of the Holy Spirit for the benefit of the entire Church.

POINTS TO PONDER

1. We read in Exodus that the Israelites were afraid of Moses when he came down from the mountain because his face shone. Why do you think this frightened them? In addition to fear, what other responses does contact with the Divine elicit from us, and why?

2. What is the picture of God that emerges from Psalm 99? How do the images here compare with your own experience of God?

3. What do we learn about the nature of Divine revelation from the Epistle reading?

4. As you read the Gospel passage, pay particular attention to the actions of the Apostles who were with Jesus. How would you explain their reactions as the events unfolded? What importance do the words of God in Luke 9:35 have for us today?

5. In these passages we read how Moses and Jesus were physically changed by their direct encounters with God. How have you personally been transformed by the presence of God in your life?

_____

_____

_____

_____

_____

KEEP WATCH

Isaiah 1:1, 10-20; Psalm 50:1-8, 23-24; Hebrews 11:1-3, 8-16; Luke 12:32-40

The opening verse of the first Isaiah scroll identifies the prophet as a son of Amoz, who delivered his oracles during the reign of four particular Judean kings. The last of these kings was Hezekiah, one of the few who did what was right in the sight of the Lord.

Through much of the first Isaiah's life, the Word of the Lord that came to him was a threat of judgment. Thus 1:10 calls Judah's leaders "rulers of Sodom" and its inhabitants "people of Gomorrah."

Isaiah's words of judgment reject the sacrifices by which the Judeans had sought to buy God's favor: "I have had enough of burnt offerings of rams and the fat of fed beasts" (v. 11). All the usual trappings of worship have become offensive to the Lord, including the festivals and assemblies (vv. 12-14). No longer will the Lord listen to the prayers of those whose hands are stained with blood (v. 15).

However, the prophet does hold out a prospect of escape from God's condemnation if the people will "cease to do evil" (v. 16) and seek justice by aiding the oppressed and helpless. If they change their ways, their sins, which are like scarlet or crimson, shall be washed clean like snow or wool (v. 18). Their obedience will bring back God's favor, and they will be able to "eat the good of the land" (v. 19). However, if they "refuse and rebel" (v. 20), the consequence will be certain doom. Thus the Lord has spoken.

The Lord, "the mighty one," also speaks and does not keep silent in Psalm 50. God calls together those loyal followers who have bound themselves to the Lord with a covenant sealed by sacrifice. God does not accuse worshipers because of their sacrifices, or because of the lack of them—but the Lord does recognize those who offer the sacrifice of *thanksgiving.* They are the ones who truly honor God and will obtain salvation.

The anonymous author of the letter to the Hebrews defines faith as "the assurance of things hoped for, the conviction of things not seen" (11:1). Faith is commitment to a reality we cannot prove, but that we know by experience.

By faith we come to know that the universe was created as the expression or Word of God's purpose. The passage goes on to give several examples of persons of faith from the Hebrew Scriptures.

Verse 4 speaks of Abel, who trusted in God's guidance to offer a proper sacrifice. Therefore, he was acknowledged by God as righteous, even beyond the limit of his life on earth. Enoch's trusting faith in God raised him from earthly life to eternity in God's presence, with no need to undergo physical death.

Verse 6 affirms that true faith is trust not only that *God exists,* but that *the Lord rewards sincere seekers.* Then follows the illustration of how faith moved Noah to obey a Divine

PRAYER FOR THE DAY

Gracious God, Source of all life, Author of all that is true and good: give us the wind of your Holy Spirit that we may venture beyond the safe confines of an easy faith, and step out bravely from false security to carry the Gospel of Jesus Christ to a perishing world. All this we ask in the unity of the Godhead and in the power of your Holy Name. *Amen.*

warning. When informed by God about events as yet unseen, he respected the vision and constructed an ark to save his household.

Verses 8-12 recount how trust in God's guidance enabled Abraham to leave all that he knew, and, with his aged wife Sarah, believe he would have his own heir—and descendants as the stars in the heavens (Gen. 22:17).

By faith, all of these persons received their respective blessings; but to the ultimate blessing they could only look from afar (v. 13). They acknowledged that they were aliens in this world, seeking a better country prepared by God, "a heavenly one" (v. 16a). Such a faith was to be counted as righteousness.

The Gospel of Luke gives us another way

ON REFLECTION

Anthony de Mello, S. J., tells this story:

To a fearful religious visitor, the Master said, "Why are you so anxious?"
"Lest I fail to attain salvation."
"And what is salvation?"
"Moksha. Freedom. Liberation."
The Master roared with laughter and said, "So you are forced to be free? You are bound to be liberated?"
At that moment the visitor relaxed and lost his fear forever.

Today's Gospel continues to teach the importance of giving up for the Kingdom: "Sell your possessions, and give alms ... " Yet it is not so much a matter of giving up as of refocusing, of "making purses" that will not wear out, that count for eternity, that have value in God's ongoing reality of Kingdom life that begins here and now.

This admonition goes against the grain, not only of our culture's "gospel"—but of our own instinctive drive for self-protection, for personal "salvation," for survival in tough times.

We have learned along with the disciples that building bigger barns is not the answer. No matter how much our self-worth seems directly connected to our net worth—there is something offering greater reward than money in the bank, societal approval, and long-term earthly security.

Krister Stendahl has written: "Our age and that age of the first century have more in common than we think. ... Both times can be characterized as cosmically scared, frightened ages, caught under principalities and powers where tiny little human beings just know that they cannot do much, that they are not in control, that they are just caught."

No wonder we desperately grasp for money and the power it represents. Embedded in a world in which we feel limited and weak, we are ever looking for an external source of peace and certainty.

Luke was writing at a time when the once fervent expectation of Jesus' return was waning, "heresy" and systematic persecution were on the horizon, and some Christians were trying to combat this growing anxiety by wresting control of their lives.

But "fear not, little flock," Jesus assures them. Look instead for security in the Spirit, for "wallets" that are thief-proof, moth-proof, and death-proof.

—H. King Oehmig

to understand faith. Jesus has told the parable of the rich fool (Lk. 12:16-21), which warned against the false security of material possessions. Now he gives teachings to illustrate that *living a life of faith frees us from the fears and anxieties of daily life* (12:22-31).

The passage for today opens with words of assurance from Jesus: "Do not be afraid, little flock, for it is your Father's good pleasure to give you the kingdom" (v. 32). Because of the promise that they will be the recipients of God's Kingdom, Jesus counsels his followers to dispose of possessions through almsgiving. By doing so they will acquire treasure in heaven that will never be lost through theft or damage. Moreover, such actions draw the heart of the person to the realm of God, where it is secure.

Verses 35-40 consist of a warning to be watchful. The disciples must live in readiness for the coming of the Son of Man, who will bring reward to loyal servants. This portion of Luke suggests that Jesus expected an early end to human history in which the Son of Man would come to judge the world.

Facing such a prospect of final judgment, the true follower was to practice vigilance. As told in the parable in verses 35-39, the disciples were to be prepared and to live each day as though it were their last.

Thus they were to be "dressed for action" (v. 35), which is a reminder of the hasty flight from Egypt (Ex. 12:11). They were also to have prepared their lamps against the approach of darkness.

They were to be like servants who keep alert for the return of their master who has gone to a celebration. Here Luke uses the familiar biblical theme of a wedding banquet (Mt. 22:1-14; Mk. 2:19; Lk. 5:34-35). Although the hour of the master's return is not known, he must not be kept waiting at the door.

There is good fortune for those who have kept the proper watch and can open to the master at once. Their reward goes beyond what the servants expect, for the positions of the master and servant are reversed: *the master will come and serve them* (v. 37).

The servants are to keep watch especially when it seems darkest—in the middle of the night or just before dawn—as he gives no more notice than would a thief (vv. 38-39).

Jesus will return as the glorified Son of Man to be among his beloved at an unexpected hour (v. 40). This is the message of faithful promise underlying the warnings of the passage. We are called to live securely in God's love, alert and ready to receive the fullness of grace.

POINTS TO PONDER

1. Why do you think Jesus addresses his followers in Luke 12:32 as "little flock"? What does this phrase suggest to you about the relationship between Jesus and his disciples?

2. Jesus also says, "Do not be afraid." What is the connection between fear and faith? How can our fears affect our ability to receive the Kingdom into our lives? What is the treasure of which Jesus speaks in verse 34?

3. Describe the responsibilities of the servants who await their master's return in verses 35-38. What will be their reward for their vigilance? What must we do today to prepare for our master's return?

4. In verses 39-40, Jesus talks of a householder and a thief. What is the main point of this story in relation to the previous story about waiting servants?

5. The Epistle reading from Hebrews defines faith and gives several examples of those whose lives exemplify faithful living. How would you define faith? Can you name people who have served as models of faith for you?

FIRE ON THE EARTH

Isaiah 5:1-7; Psalm 80:1-2, 8-18; Hebrews 11:29—12:2; Luke 12:49-56

I saiah's Song of the Vineyard begins as a poem and ends as a judgment against God's people. The vineyard that the Lord planted represents the house of Israel, and its seedlings are the people of Judah. Nothing has been spared in the preparation and planting of the vineyard. A tower enabled the vintner to overlook the safety of the vineyard, and a winepress was fashioned to process the grapes.

But despite the loving care put into the vineyard, it yielded wild grapes. What more could the Lord have done? And what should God do now? The vineyard did not deserve its protective hedge or wall. *Therefore, let it be ravaged, trampled, and made a desolation.* From Israel and Judah the Lord had expected justice and righteousness, but instead God's people brought forth bloodshed and the cry of the oppressed.

Psalm 80 continues the allegory of the vineyard, with God's people described as the vine that the Lord brought out of Egypt and planted in the promised land. The Lord prepared the ground, and the vine flourished and "filled the land" (v. 9). But now the walls are broken down so that passersby eat the fruit. The vines have been ravaged by wild animals, burned, and cut down.

The Psalmist appeals to the Lord to "look down from heaven, and see; have regard for this vine" (v. 14). The present disasters are the result of the nation's turning away from God's purposes. But the people vow never to turn away again if they can be returned to the Lord's favor: "Restore us, O Lord God of hosts … that we may be saved" (v. 19).

The Gospel also speaks of God's judgment. In last week's Gospel reading, Jesus told his followers to *be ready,* as they do not know when

God's Kingdom will become reality. Now Jesus warns that the coming of God's new world will bring division and conflict.

The passage for today can be divided into two parts. Verses 49-53 of Luke 12 are addressed to the disciples as Jesus describes his mission. Then Jesus turns his attention to the crowd in verses 54-56, as he rebukes them for not being able to interpret the signs of the times.

Jesus begins by proclaiming that he comes "to bring fire to the earth" (v. 49). In biblical usage fire represents the Divine action in the world, often in terms of purifying judgment. (God is described as a "devouring fire" in Deut. 4:24 and a "consuming fire" in Heb. 12:29.) In these instances, fire symbolizes destruction because of its power to consume and extinguish evil.

The words of Jesus here recall the actions of the Prophet Elijah, who called fire upon the prophets of Baal (1 Ki. 18:36-40). Earlier in Luke's Gospel, Jesus rebuked his disciples for wanting to command fire from heaven to consume the Samaritans (9:54).

Yet later, Jesus proclaims that the coming of the Son of Man will be accompanied by "fire

PRAYER FOR THE DAY

Eternal and immortal God, dwelling in light inaccessible, from before time and forever: place in our hearts the desire to know and serve Jesus Christ, that we may experience the peace that supersedes all understanding, and then share that peace with all whom the Holy Spirit brings to us. This we ask in the power of your blessed Name. *Amen.*

and sulfur from heaven" like the destruction of Sodom (Lk. 17:29). Here Jesus speaks of the trial and destruction of the earth as he calls for the reordering of priorities.

In verse 50, Jesus predicts his own trials in what can be taken as a foretelling of his Passion. In the Gospel of Mark, when Jesus asks James and John if they are able to share his trials, he uses the figures of cup and baptism to represent the sufferings he is to endure (10:38). Here he expresses impatience for the fire and baptism—his suffering and death—to be completed.

Jesus goes on to declare that he has come to bring division and not peace (vv. 51-53). His words here are harsh and uncompromising and are in opposition to the image of Jesus as the Prince of Peace.

"From now on"—in the age to come—the followers of Jesus will have to decide whether they will stand with him or against him. These divisions are not just abstractions, but will be seen in every household (v. 52). Even sacred family relationships (Ex. 20:12; Dt. 5:16) will be jeopardized, as parents and children turn

ON REFLECTION

Francis MacNutt in his work Healing *(Ave Maria Press, 1999) explains an important distinction between two kinds of suffering. He points out that Jesus carried the cross of persecution, the kind of suffering that comes from outside of a person, because of the wickedness of others. Jerusalem hardened its heart toward him; scribes and Pharisees accused him of demonic activity; his family thought him crazy.*

He was scourged, mocked, and spit upon. This caused Jesus internal suffering. But its source was outside of himself. It was suffering, in other words, for the sake of the Kingdom. The division within families that today's Gospel reading speaks of is also part of this suffering.

But the suffering that Jesus sought at every turn to alleviate was that which tore people apart from within—*whether it was physical, emotional, or spiritual.*

Can you imagine Jesus telling the leper that he wasn't going to heal him of his ghastly disease because it would make him more saintly if he itched and burned and stayed ostracized from the community? Of course not.

Healthy suffering is redemptive; sick suffering destroys. When he spoke of the destructive fall of the tower of Siloam and Pilate's slaughter of Galilean worshipers (Lk. 13:1, 4), he made it clear that these people did not suffer because they were terrible (worse-than-us) sinners—though there was warning in cataclysm for everyone to repent.

So—what is this fire of which Jesus speaks? Is it a kind of torch that we ourselves carry forward?

Macrina Wiederkehr has written in The Song of the Seed *(HarperSanFrancisco, 1997): "Jesus prays that we will be consecrated in the truth, that we will all be one, and that each of us will be open to receiving God's glory into our lives. What is this glory? It is the brightness of God living on in each of us. It is the Divine Presence as revealed in our lives. ...*

"Throughout this day I attended those four beautiful words, live on in me. *These words also put me in communion with my parents and all the beloved ones in my life who have died. I called out to them, 'Live on in me.' I remembered those who died heroic deaths in their stand for justice. To them I cried out, 'Live on in me.' I believe that the glory of their lives, even now, can energize and heal me in my efforts to live as Christ in the world today."*

—H. King Oehmig

against one another. The peace that Jesus brings comes with a cost.

In verse 54, Jesus turns his attention to the crowds and questions their ability to read the signs of the time. They are able to predict the weather from the signs of nature—clouds in the west indicate rain, and a south wind foretells "scorching heat" (v. 55). In fact, their very survival depends upon their ability to accurately read these signs if they are to plant, grow, and harvest crops.

It is no less important for them to be able to "interpret the present time" (v. 56). The signs of God's Kingdom are all around, despite the fact that the disciples and the multitudes refuse to heed them. However, there is no doubt that God's Kingdom is coming, and these words of Jesus serve as a warning to the world to be ready.

The portion of the letter to the Hebrews for today provides encouragement for those who strive to be faithful disciples. Earlier in chapter 11, faith was defined (v. 1), and then followed by stories of earlier saints who serve as inspiration to the present generation. The letter continues with further accounts of heroes from the Old Covenant, beginning with the Red Sea crossing (11:29), and those who witnessed the fall of Jericho—mentioning also Rahab, Gideon, Barak, Samson, and Jephthah. Then Samuel, David, and the prophets who performed mighty deeds through faith are listed. Verse 35 mentions women who "received their dead by resurrection."

Thus "surrounded by so great a cloud of witnesses," the current generation can persevere in the race that is set before them (12:1). Those who have already gained sanctity are helping us now to lay aside burdens and sins.

But even more important than the example of the ancestors is that of Jesus himself. He endured the shame and persecution of the Cross for the ultimate joy of taking his place at the "right hand of the throne of God" (12:2b). And so we today also look to Jesus as the author, the pioneer and perfecter, of our faith.

POINTS TO PONDER

1. As you read the Gospel passage in Luke 12, what do you think might have been the reaction of Jesus' listeners to these words? What is your initial response to what Jesus says here?

2. In verse 49, what is the fire that Jesus brings? What will be the results of its burning? What is the nature of the baptism that Jesus proclaims in verse 50? How is our own baptism similar and yet different from the baptism that Jesus describes here?

3. Jesus says that he comes to bring division and not peace (v. 51). What are the divisions that result from Christ's ministry? How do these separations manifest themselves today? How are we personally called to mend these divisions?

4. How does Jesus' warning in verses 54-56 continue to be true for us today? Why do you think he refers to those in the crowd as hypocrites?

5. What do we discover here about the mission of Jesus? What do we learn about what it means to be a follower of Jesus?

"YOU ARE SET FREE"

Jeremiah 1:4-10; Psalm 71:1-6; Hebrews 12:18-29; Luke 13:10-17

The Prophet Jeremiah lived during one of the most turbulent periods in Jewish history. As a witness to the events leading to the destruction of Solomon's temple and the beginning of the Babylonian exile, Jeremiah chronicled the last days of the southern kingdom of Judah.

As we learn in the opening verses of the first chapter (vv. 1-3), Jeremiah served as the Lord's prophet from the thirteenth year of the reign of King Josiah (627 B. C.) to the captivity of Jerusalem in 587 B. C. He was from the tribe of Benjamin and of the priestly lineage of Eli (1 Sam. 1-4).

In Rabbinic tradition, Jeremiah is often likened to Moses. He served the Lord for forty years; but whereas Moses led Israel out of bondage, Jeremiah saw his people exiled from the promised land. Jeremiah himself ended his days as an exile in Egypt.

In the passage for today, Jeremiah gives his own account of his call and commission, which begins with the prophetic formula: "Now the word of the Lord came to me ... " (v. 4). Although Jeremiah has a clear sense that his call is predestined (v. 5), he is reluctant to accept it because of his youth. And, like Moses (Ex. 4:10), he protests that he is not able to speak eloquently for God (v. 6).

The Lord immediately counters his objections with the assurance that he need not be afraid; God will be with him and tell him what to say (vv. 7-8). God then touches Jeremiah's mouth, symbolizing the prophet's commission to speak for God. Jeremiah is given some hard words. As a prophet to the nations (v. 5b), and not just to Israel, his mission included messages of destruction: "to pluck up and to pull down, to destroy and to overthrow ... " (v.

10). But there is a note of redemption here as well, a promise of building and planting.

Psalm 71 is a prayer for help in a time of distress, a cry that shows trust in God's strength and presence. The Lord is like a "rock of refuge" and a "strong fortress" (v. 3). The Psalmist looks to the Lord for rescue from the injustice and cruelty of the wicked, and has relied upon the Lord from birth. Thus the writer can say that "my praise is continually of you" (v. 6).

As Jesus continues his ministry in the Gospel, he encounters increased antagonism from the Pharisees, who disagree with his attitudes toward the Sabbath. Today's passage is unique to Luke, and is the third of four controversies over acceptable Sabbath practices.

In the first of these conflicts, Jesus was criticized for allowing his disciples to pluck and eat grain as they walked through the fields on the Sabbath (6:1-5). On another occasion, Jesus healed a man with a withered hand while teaching in a synagogue on the Sabbath (6:6-11). The final controversy took place when Jesus healed a man with dropsy while dining with a group of Pharisees on the Sabbath (14:1-6). In

PRAYER FOR THE DAY

Grant us, gracious God, the gift of recognition, that we may come to see your hand at work in the world about us: may we, through the indwelling of the Holy Spirit, come to exalt Jesus as Lord and serve the Gospel of your love with imagination, boldness, and gladness of heart, to your glory. *Amen.*

all of these situations, Jesus makes the point that the welfare of individuals is more important than religious observance.

In 13:10f, Jesus was teaching in a synagogue on the Sabbath when a woman appeared "with a spirit that had crippled her for eighteen years." As a result, she was bent over and unable to stand up straight. Although she does not approach Jesus or make a plea to him for relief from her infirmity, Jesus calls her over and says, "Woman, you are set free from your ailment" (v. 12).

He then lays his hands on her, and she is able to walk standing up straight once again. The woman's response to this miraculous healing is to praise God. To this point, the incident is an example of a healing that becomes an occasion to glorify God.

But the episode takes on wider significance when the leader of the synagogue immediately takes exception to the actions of Jesus. After all, there are six days in the week for work, or in this case, healing—but it is not to be performed on the Sabbath.

Jesus answers by calling the leader and his colleagues "you hypocrites!" (v. 15). If they are permitted to untie—unbind—their domestic

ON REFLECTION

John Sanford in his classic study The Kingdom Within, *states in regard to entering the Kingdom:* "It is those who have recognized that they have been injured or hurt in some way in life who are most able to come into the kingdom. There is no virtue in our weakness or injury as such … but unless a person has recognized his own need, even his own despair, he is not ready for the kingdom, as those who feel they are self-sufficient, whom life has upheld in their one-sided orientation, remain caught in their egocentricity" *(p. 69).*

In today's Gospel Jesus has been teaching in a synagogue when a crippled woman who has been bent over for eighteen years appears before him. He calls her over, lays his hands on her, heals her, and sets her free from the confining ailment.

But it is the Sabbath—and Jesus has pushed the limits of his authority by this act of compassion extended in a moment of need.

"You hypocrites!" he addresses the dissenting leaders. "Does not each of you on the sabbath untie his ox or his donkey from the manger, and lead it away to give it water?" Should not this long-bound woman be liberated and receive kindness at least *as would a brute beast?*

As Gregory of Nazianzus put it: "A soul in trouble is near unto God." Need itself can be a door, an entrance, a path to the only security and hope available: surrendering to the power and mercy of God.

The suffering that Jesus sought at every turn to alleviate was the division within—that which was destroying people's lives physically, emotionally, or spiritually. This was suffering caused by evil in the world that always threatens to corrupt and devastate our lives.

Can you imagine Jesus looking down at the woman and saying, "Sorry"—he wasn't going to heal her because of the circumstances, the day, the hour, the witnesses? It might get him in trouble …

It is impossible to imagine, because, as someone has said, the door to the Kingdom is just narrow enough and high enough for one person on her knees to enter. And she did.

—H. King Oehmig

livestock from the manger to take them to water on the Sabbath, ought not it also be permissible for this woman to be released or unbound from her affliction on the Sabbath as well? In fact, as one who has been in bondage to infirmity for many years, it is *fitting* that she should be set free on the Sabbath day.

Here Jesus states that she has been bound by Satan, which gives rise to the concept of being enslaved by evil. But now God's activity will counteract the evil present in the world. The Jewish tradition of Sabbath applies not only to a time of rest, but also to the notion of release from bondage or slavery to affliction.

These words of Jesus put his opponents to shame, and the crowd rejoices at all the wonderful things he is doing.

Just as Jesus called for new understandings about the observance of religious practices, the letter to the Hebrews addresses the differences between the promises of the Old and New Covenants. Christ's death has inaugurated a whole new world of reconciliation and forgiveness, as opposed to the former world of fear and vengeance.

But despite its post-Resurrection confidence in God's loving care, the letter contains a note of warning. However awesome were the experiences of Israel in the Exodus—the flaming mountain, the blaring voice from which the hearers begged to be spared—Christians have come into a presence far more awesome.

The true Mount Zion to which they were called, the city of the Living God, was not designed to seem fearsome. Yet to be there was to face an innumerable company of angels, as well as the Lord Almighty exercising judgment. Also present would be the spirits of those already made perfect—along with Jesus, who is the mediator of their New Covenant.

Their Messiah's shed blood would appeal for pardon, as contrasted with the plea of Abel's blood of vengeance (12:24). God's voice at Sinai shook the earth, and at the final judgment the heavens shall also be shaken. There will be great turbulence and fear among the people. But what will be preserved for the people of God is a heritage that cannot be moved.

Therefore, we are to give thanks and offer to God our utmost worship in true reverence. God is indeed a consuming fire; but the purifying flames that envelop us are those of unquenchable love (v. 29).

POINTS TO PONDER

1. How do Jesus' words and actions put his opponents to shame in today's Gospel passage? What do we learn from his example about pleasing God rather than other human beings?

2. What new understandings about observing religious practices do you find in this text? How will they affect your own observance of worship and practice as a Christian?

3. How is Jesus an awesome presence to us today?

4. As you read the other Lessons appointed for today, what are the warnings and promises that you find?

5. What do we learn about freedom in Christ from these words of Jesus? What are we called to do in response?

_____

_____

_____

_____

HUMBLE YOURSELF

Jeremiah 2:4-13; Psalm 81:1, 10-16; Hebrews 13:1-8, 15-16; Luke 14:1, 7-14

hapters 2 through 6 of the Book of Jeremiah are a call to repentance directed at Jerusalem and Judah.

In verses 5-7 of the reading for today, God asks why Israel has abandoned the Lord, who brought them out of bondage in Egypt and led them safely through the dangers of the wilderness to a land of plenty.

Now they have "defiled my land, and made my heritage an abomination" (2:7b). Not only the people, but also the leaders have deserted the Lord—the priests, the scribes, the rulers, and the prophets who now follow the false god Baal. In pursuing worthless things, the people have themselves become worthless.

Thus the Lord accuses them and their future generations. Not even in foreign lands has such a thing happened that the people have deserted the God who has cared for them. They have forsaken the glory of the Lord "for something that does not profit" (v. 11).

God's people have committed two evils: They have turned from God, who is like a "fountain of living water," and have chosen instead "cracked cisterns that can hold no water" (v. 13). Thus they have abandoned the life-giving presence of the Lord for the stagnant waters of false gods.

The Psalmist in Psalm 81 also calls Israel to remember the Lord who brought them out of Egypt. God's people have forsaken the ways of the Lord to follow their own stubborn counsel. If Israel will return to the Lord, God will defeat their enemies, and they will partake of prosperity. The Lord will feed them with "the finest of the wheat, and with honey from the rock" (v. 16).

In the Gospel reading for today, Jesus dines with a group of Pharisees on the Sabbath.

There is a growing antagonism among the Pharisees toward Jesus, particularly regarding ritual observance. Luke tells us that they were watching Jesus closely to find some way to discredit him (11:53-54).

In the verses omitted from today's reading (14:2-6), when a man with dropsy appears, Jesus asks the Pharisees and lawyers whether it is lawful to do a healing work on the Sabbath. When Jesus' query is answered with silence, Jesus heals the man and sends him on his way. Jesus then goes on to justify his action with words based on Deuteronomy 22:4, and asks who among them would not rescue livestock from a ditch, even on the Sabbath. Again the words of Jesus are met with silence.

In today's verses, Jesus is dining with a group of Pharisees. His hosts were accustomed to receiving respect, which they considered their due. Luke already mentioned that the Pharisees "love to have the seat of honor in the synagogues" (11:43), and they expected this privileged status on social occasions as well. Thus Jesus uses this opportunity to teach by telling a parable about the seating at a wedding banquet.

PRAYER FOR THE DAY

Gracious Lord of all, in whose will there is contentment even in suffering: empower us, through the might of your Holy Spirit, to be the living expression of Jesus Christ and to carry our own crosses wherever you lead, and always to your glory and the well-being of all people. *Amen.*

If someone selects the seat of honor at the banquet, that person may suffer the disgrace of later being asked to move to a lower place. Therefore, it is better to sit at a less prestigious place at the table, with the possibility of being invited to move up.

By choosing the lowest place, the worst that can happen is that you will be left in the same position. Or you *might* be asked to move up to a place that befits true importance. There is greater approval for people who demand less than what is due them, than toward those who expect more.

These words of Jesus reflect the wisdom tradition of Israel as expressed in Proverbs 25:6-7: "Do not put yourself forward in the king's presence or stand in the place of the great; for it is better to be told, 'Come up here,' than to be put lower in the presence of a noble."

But to this wisdom, Jesus adds a phrase repeated elsewhere in the Gospels: "For all who exalt themselves will be humbled, and those who humble themselves will be exalted" (v. 11). These words are especially powerful, because they describe the ministry of Jesus himself (Phil. 2:5-11), as the one who humbled himself through

ON REFLECTION

When we live life on the surface, for how we look in a gorgeous building, or at the speaker's table, or in a sleek vehicle surrounded by other stunning people—we are living our lives according to the perceptions of others. We are outer-driven.

Our positive feelings about ourselves derive from how others perceive us. We look for more—for benefits and approval from people who are also looking for the same. And those people's neediness butts head with our neediness—and the result is that nobody comes away with anything of substance.

The people in the parable vying for the most prominent seats at the table are engaging in an endless game of musical chairs. There isn't enough prominence, enough approval, enough perks, enough winning that will ever compensate for their insecurity. And there is always the lurking possibility that someone more prominent or "in" will come along and painfully knock them down a notch.

The inevitable result of living life on the surface of "me and my needs/desires/demands" to win status and approval is a tragic one. These things distract from our uniqueness as children of God. The true needs of the soul can easily be overshadowed by the gotta have it *spirit.*

Only when we begin to live out of our deep, creative self will we be undeterred by and immune to the outer, surface signs of success. When we learn to live attentively out of this inner self—which has been unshackled through the love of Christ Jesus—we are free to be who we are and to allow others to discover who they are. We will have come to know ourselves—and others—primarily as children of the Most High.

This is our common identity. We have been embraced through Baptism by the Unconditional; therefore, we are able to see others not as competitors to be outdone (worshiping, dining, dwelling in better places than they do), but as sisters and brothers in whose elevation we will rejoice—no less than we would exult if the host at a banquet told US to "Move up higher."

By grace, we will no longer live to win, but to serve.

—H. King Oehmig

death on the cross and was then exalted.

In the final three verses, Jesus goes on to advise his hosts about who should be invited to dinner. When one sets out a banquet, it should not be for social equals or rich neighbors who will invite you in return. Instead, invite the poor, the maimed, and the blind who cannot repay you. In this way you will be blessed, and "you will be repaid at the resurrection of the righteous" (v. 14).

Once again Luke reverses the expectations of social convention. True hospitality consists of taking care of those in need for the sake of the Kingdom and expecting nothing in return.

The first five verses of today's passage from Hebrews give concrete examples of how we are to love and care for others, reflecting the ethical concerns of the biblical tradition. We are to "show hospitality to strangers" (13:2), who may in fact be embodiments of God's presence (Gen. 18:1-15).

Thus we are to offer what we have to others, never knowing the ultimate effect. Such love is also a manifestation of humility, considering the needs of others as no less important than our own.

Hospitality to the stranger is only one aspect of radical, unfailing love for others. We are also challenged to live out our empathy and kindness to those who are in prison or are being tortured (v. 3). Furthermore, we are to have respect for the marriage relationships of others.

The life of believers is to be marked by contentment with one's lot in life rather than a desire for wealth, since God promises: "I will never leave you or forsake you" (v. 5b). Thus we can live without fear and in confidence. With the Lord present, *what can anyone else do to us?* (v. 6b).

We are also admonished to remember our leaders and to imitate their example. The passage ends with words of eternal promise that empower us to live in faith and love toward one another, for: "Jesus Christ is the same yesterday and today and forever" (v. 8).

POINTS TO PONDER

1. As you read the parable in verses 7-11 of the Gospel passage in Luke 14, what do you understand to be the main point Jesus is making?

2. In verses 12-14, Jesus gives advice to those who would be hosts. Who should be invited to dinner and why?

3. According to this passage, what are we to expect when we help those less fortunate than ourselves? What is the blessing Jesus promises in verse 14?

4. Jesus speaks of the differences between humility and self-exaltation in this passage. How would you define humility? Identify some individuals who exemplify true humility for you. What are the challenges we face in our contemporary world in order to live in such a manner?

5. In both the Gospel and Epistle readings, life in the community of faith is contrasted with life in the world. What changes are we called to make in our lives if we are to reflect God's Kingdom?

_____

_____

_____

_____

THE CROSS AND DISCIPLESHIP

Jeremiah 18:1-11; Psalm 139:1-5, 13-17; Philemon 1-21; Luke 14:25-33

The image of God as the Creator who directly forms the material creation is found throughout Scripture (cf Gen. 2:7; Is. 43:1, 21; 44:21; Ps. 95:5; 104:26; Rom. 9:20-24). Today Jeremiah highlights this role of God as he pronounces judgment against Judah and Jerusalem.

God sends Jeremiah to the potter's house, where he observes the craftsman reworking a ruined vessel. Using the analogy of *God as the potter* and *the clay as God's people,* the Lord declares that nations can be plucked up and destroyed if they do not heed the word of the Lord. However, God can reverse that decision if the nation "turns from its evil" (18:8).

Conversely, if a righteous nation turns to evil, "then I [the Lord] will change my mind about the good that I had intended to do to it" (v. 10). Like the potter, God can form a new vessel from the old, depending upon the choice the people make for good or for evil. The passage ends with a warning to the inhabitants of Jerusalem to repent and avoid destruction. Here we see God as a powerful presence who actively shapes people and nations.

The verses of Psalm 139 appointed for today also speak of God's awesome presence in every aspect of an individual's life. The Lord knows our innermost being, since, like the potter, "it was you who formed my inward parts; you knit me together in my mother's womb" (v. 13).

Thus the Psalmist gives God praise for the mystery and miracle of his very existence (v. 14-15). According to a Rabbinic tradition, there is a book that contains the names of all people, and the Psalmist marvels that his life was included there even before he was born. Although God's thoughts are far beyond the understanding of the Psalmist (cf Is. 55:8-9), he declares his undying faith in the mystery: "I come to the end—I am still with you" (v. 18).

The Apostle Paul, in his letter to Philemon, presents another choice. The letter was written to make arrangements for the return of the runaway slave Onesimus to his master Philemon. This exchange reveals Paul's pastoral response to a particular situation, and illustrates how the life of the community is defined by mutual love in Christ Jesus.

After Paul's greeting from prison (vv. 1-3), the letter itself (vv. 8-20) is an eloquent and carefully crafted request to Philemon, urging him to take Onesimus back into his household without any repercussions. Although Paul is "bold enough in Christ" (v. 8) to command Philemon to do the right thing, he prefers to appeal to Philemon's love and sense of compassion instead. As one who can claim authority as an Apostle and who endures imprisonment for his faith in Christ, Paul nonetheless addresses Philemon as a colleague: "our dear friend and co-worker" (v. 1).

PRAYER FOR THE DAY

Grant us the grace, Holy Lord, to see one another—from every race, nation, and condition—as your children and worthy of our unconditional love. Set us free in the unity of the Holy Spirit to show forth your sacrificial love for the world, made manifest in the priceless gift of Jesus Christ, the Savior and Lord of all. *Amen.*

During their time together, Onesimus has become a Christian, and he and Paul have forged a strong friendship. Paul refers to him as "my child, Onesimus, whose father I have become during my imprisonment" (v. 10). Paul would like to keep Onesimus with him (v. 13); but he appeals to Philemon to welcome Onesimus back as a slave no longer, but a beloved brother in Christ (v. 16). Paul is willing to assume any debt that may be due Philemon in behalf of Onesimus. After all, Paul will not press the fact that Philemon owes his very life to Paul (v. 19).

Although Paul does not address the issue of slavery itself here, he encourages Philemon to lay aside legal considerations of treating slaves as property, and receive Onesimus as a fellow Christian, just as Philemon would receive Paul himself (v. 17). The letter concludes with Paul expressing his confidence that Philemon "will do even more than I say" (v. 21).

In the Gospel reading, Jesus presents the choices necessary if one is to become his disciple. As he continues on his way to Jerusalem, Jesus challenges the large crowd that is traveling with him by offering three teachings on the cost of discipleship (Lk. 14:26, 27, 33) and two parables on making decisions (vv. 28-32). Becoming a follower of

ON REFLECTION

Giving up our security for the sake of the Kingdom is the necessary cost of following Jesus. The reality of the spiritual surrender that Jesus called for in response to the Gospel served to confront his hearers with a choice. *This choice was between old attachments and the new life, and it was a difficult one for many.*

For instance, the only time in the Synoptic Gospels where Jesus is said to have loved *anyone is when he looked at the rich man before telling him that he needed to get rid of all his "baggage" before he could follow Jesus on the way (Mk. 10:21).*

Jesus was genuinely sympathetic to the wealthy man's struggle to decide between attachment and longing. Yet Jesus was unwavering. The man had to go one way or the other.

The same teaching, with a different twist, is presented in the Gospel reading for today about "hating" one's family in order truly to align oneself with the Gospel. Here too, the would-be disciple must decide.

Why is this so? Why does Jesus pose the apparent choice of "all or nothing"? Because it is only when we have deeply committed our lives to Christ that we experience the profundity of the Kingdom of God—its wonder and joy and its new way of seeing.

Grasped by this new reality of grace, we realize that the old attachments are not of ultimate value, but nevertheless they continue to lay claim to our allegiance.

Jesus declares that this "defining decision" of spiritual surrender is not to be entered into unadvisedly or lightly—just as no smart contractor would build a tower without first doing a cost analysis, or a general would send his troops into battle without sufficient ammunition.

Why? Because "the way" of Jesus is as arduous as it is fulfilling. As the words of Martin Luther King, Jr., remind us, "Jesus gave us a new norm of greatness. If you want to be important, wonderful. If you want to be recognized, wonderful. If you want to be great, wonderful. But recognize that he who is greatest among you shall be your servant. That's your new definition of greatness."

—H. King Oehmig

Jesus means to live a life of self-denial, and one must weigh the costs carefully before making a commitment.

The conditions that Jesus sets forth here for true discipleship are radical, uncompromising, and even harsh. First, he calls for the denial of close family ties and even life itself (v. 26). Our most cherished relationships must be renounced if they stand in the way of faithful discipleship. Eventually, even giving up one's life may be required.

The second requirement is cast in the metaphor of bearing the cross (v. 27), which calls forth the necessity of entering into suffering and death. But this relinquishment ultimately leads to an entirely new way of life.

Finally, disciples must be willing to give up their material possessions (v. 33). More than in the other Gospels, the relationship between discipleship and possessions is a frequent theme in Luke. As with family relationships, one must be willing to renounce anything that stands in the way of a commitment to full discipleship.

Becoming a follower of Jesus also requires careful discernment; thus, Jesus offers two parables on decision-making. Each is presented in the form of a question. First, if one does not plan the building of a tower carefully, there will not be enough materials to finish what was started, and such a builder will be ridiculed (vv. 28-30).

Second, a king must know what his military strength is in relation to his enemy (vv. 31-32). If he is greatly outnumbered, he can arrange a peace treaty instead; otherwise, he could face complete annihilation.

In each situation, one must sit down and consider all options wisely before taking action. Likewise, those who would choose to become Jesus' disciples must seriously weigh the costs and consequences of such a decision. The demands of discipleship are great and call for radical changes in our lives. But the promises are likewise great and the blessings eternal.

POINTS TO PONDER

1. What are the specific conditions for discipleship that Jesus lays out in the Gospel passage? What is your initial reaction to these requirements?

2. Why do you think Jesus made these particular demands of those who would follow him? As you read these words of Jesus, how are the priorities of your own life challenged?

3. How are we to understand and obey these requirements in our lives today? Which of these demands would be the most difficult for you to follow and why?

4. What do the short parables in Luke 14:28-30 and 31-32 tell us about decision-making? Why do you think Jesus includes these illustrations here?

5. In verse 27, Jesus challenges his followers to "carry the cross." In your own experience, what are some of the challenges as well as the unique blessings of being a follower of Jesus in the world today?

THE LOST IS FOUND

Jeremiah 4:11-12, 22-28; Psalm 14; 1 Timothy 1:12-17; Luke 15:1-10

I n the Old Testament reading for today, Jeremiah continues to warn Judah and Jerusalem of the coming destruction. In his vision of judgment, Jeremiah compares the imminent invasion of Judah to a "hot wind" (4:11) that will sweep down upon the people from the desert. This is not a cleansing wind, but the dry and parching sirocco wind that brings unbearable, suffocating heat. Because God's people are ignorant and tend to do evil instead of good, all of creation suffers.

In a reversal of God's act of creation in Genesis 1:1—2:3, the earth is "waste and void" (v. 23), and darkness prevails in heaven. The mountains quake, and the birds are gone. The once fruitful land has become a desert, and the cities are in ruins. The earth itself mourns. Although the Lord will not turn back from what has been spoken, there is a note of hope in verse 27 that the destruction will not be total.

Psalm 14 also speaks of the foolish and corrupt ones who reject the Lord, saying, "There is no God" (v. 1). With a few variations, this Psalm is a duplicate of Psalm 53. The Lord looks down on the acts of human beings and finds that humanity is perverse, and "there is no one who does good, no, not one" (v. 3). Yet God is with the righteous and will be their refuge. And the Psalm that begins as a lament ends with a note of hope and joy that God's people will be delivered. *When the Lord restores the fortunes of the people, Jacob will rejoice and Israel will be glad (v. 7).*

Chapter 15 is often described as the very heart of Luke's Gospel, as it contains three parables about the joy of finding what has been lost, and is a beautiful expression of God's grace and mercy. Today's reading looks at the first two of these parables: the lost sheep and the lost coin, both of which follow the pattern of *losing, searching, finding, and celebrating.* The stories tell us that each person is precious to God and that the Kingdom will be incomplete until all the lost are found.

In the opening verses of the passage, the Pharisees and scribes are grumbling about Jesus because he "welcomes sinners" and eats with them. Sharing table fellowship was an indication of social acceptance, and how could God's people be expected to share meals with such unworthy people? In a reversal characteristic of Luke, it is these same outcast tax collectors and sinners who come to *listen* to Jesus—while the religious leaders murmur against him.

Thus Jesus tells them a story that begins with a question about shepherding. If you had one hundred sheep, would you not leave all of them to search for one that is lost? To leave an entire flock to fend for itself in order to search for just one would be economically irresponsible, and such a question would give further evidence to the Pharisees of Jesus' incompetence.

PRAYER FOR THE DAY

O God of unrestricted love and limitless grace, by the gift of your Holy Spirit may we daily be willing to set aside unforgiveness of any sort: may we aspire to that Kingdom love that empowered our Lord Jesus Christ to forgive his executioners even as he was perishing on the Cross, and this we ask in the power of your Name. *Amen.*

However, although what Jesus suggests may be bad economics, it is faithful shepherding. Ezekiel 34:1-24 provides the example for Luke's shepherd, as God promises to seek the lost and bring back the strayed. Jesus follows this model and challenges conventional thinking by putting the relationship of the shepherd to the sheep before practical considerations. When he finds the lost sheep, he carefully "lays it on his shoulders and rejoices" (v. 5)—thus providing an enduring image of Jesus himself as the good shepherd.

As the shepherd returns home, he calls his friends and neighbors together to share his joy. The recovery of this one lost sheep is cause for community celebration: "Rejoice with me, for I have found my sheep that was lost" (v. 6). The point of the shepherd's extravagance here is that Jesus came "to call not the righteous but sinners to repentance" (Lk. 5:32). Jesus ends the parable by declaring that the joy in heaven of one repentant sinner is more than that over ninety-nine righteous ones who do not need to repent.

ON REFLECTION

Being found by God changes everything. Being loved by God into repentance turns us around, reestablishes our position, rewrites our address.

When we find the courage to realize that WE stand with the sinners Jesus describes, then we can accept that the ultimate tale of redemption, with its tragedy AND triumph, is about us and our destiny. We acknowledge that Jesus, our Good Shepherd, has delivered us and will continue to go to any length to bring us back.

We too will learn compassion and a better way of life with him. And we will be enabled to recognize the lostness in our brothers and sisters that compels us to model Jesus' own redemptive work in our treatment of them. We will find that the paradox of the Gospel story can manifest its deepest truths through us—when we live by mercy and not by our feeble merit.

The surprises will be many. The lost become seekers themselves, the found, rejoicers. Dean Sluyter has written: "Jewish wisdom teaches, rather than expecting the gratitude of those you help, you should be grateful to them for giving you the opportunity to do a mitzvah, a kindness."

And, if none of this makes exact logical sense—reversal of roles and welcoming of the unworthy—Sluyter adds: "In the Talmudic tradition, some ethical problems, even after centuries of debate, are given a good Jewish shrug and tagged TEIKU, an acronym for 'It will be resolved when Elijah returns.'"

And so, what is the true meaning of the lost and the found in today's Gospel? Jesus calls sinners to repentance—something that sheep and coins can't experience. But C. S. Lewis in Mere Christianity *explains:*

"This repentance, this willing submission to humiliation and a kind of death, is not something God demands of you before He will take you back and which He could let you off if He chose: it is simply a description of what going back to Him is like. If you ask God to take you back without it, you are really asking Him to let you go back without going back. It cannot happen."

And so the Gospel message is one of total love, of relentless pursuit, and of reunion that leads to joy eternal. In God's story of redemption, the lost are not only found—they are brought Home.

—H. King Oehmig

While the parable of the lost sheep has a parallel in Matthew 18:12-14, the parable of the lost coin is unique to Luke. As is often the case with Luke, this is an example of a pairing of similar stories, one with a female main character and one with a male. As in the previous parable, one item—here a coin—out of ten is lost, and the woman searches diligently until she finds it. And again, when the coin is finally found, she calls her friends and neighbors to celebrate with her. As in the previous parable, Jesus concludes with a statement of the joy in heaven "over one sinner who repents" (v. 10).

As was true with the shepherd, the woman's behavior in searching for her lost possession is extravagant and illustrates the overwhelming abundance of God's love and forgiveness in seeking the lost and welcoming them back. This is the answer to the Pharisees as to why Jesus eats with the tax collectors and the sinners, and the joy of God here stands in direct contrast to the grumbling Pharisees.

Chapter 15 concludes with the parable of the son who was lost, which gives an even more complex picture of repentance and forgiveness (vv. 11-32).

Today's Epistle also states this mission: "Christ Jesus came into the world to save sinners" (1 Tim. 1:15). Paul speaks out of his own experience, as he offers thanks for the mercy and grace of Christ who has appointed him to his service—despite the fact that he has been a "blasphemer, a persecutor, and a man of violence" (v. 13). He had no valid claim on God's forgiveness because he was the worst of sinners, thus confirming that anyone could come to Christ through repentance.

In the life of Paul, Jesus had manifested the "utmost patience" (v. 16); and so Paul persevered in his task. Rejoicing in the reality of his salvation, he never ceased to ascribe honor and glory to the one immortal and invisible God.

The mission of Jesus remains: to love sinners into repentance—to relentlessly seek us out and never give up until the lost is found. This is the God who never rests until all are brought home again. And when any who have been lost are found, there is joy in heaven, the exuberant celebration of saints and angels.

POINTS TO PONDER

1. As you read the two Gospel parables, consider the main character in each one. How do you think each one felt upon realizing the respective losses? What do you think motivated their relentless searches? How are these two individuals models for us today?

2. In the parable of the lost sheep, imagine what it might have been like to be the sheep that was lost and then found. When have you been lost, and what was it like to be found?

3. Both the shepherd and the woman call together their friends and neighbors to celebrate the return of the sheep and the coin. What do their actions tell us about the importance of community celebrations, and how is this relevant to our Christian tradition? What is there for us to celebrate today in these parables?

4. What does the sequence of loss, search, and joy in these parables tell us about life in the Kingdom? What do these stories reveal to us about the mission of Jesus, and by extension, the task of the Church today?

5. Also read the experience of Paul in the Epistle for today in 1 Timothy 1:12-17. When have you felt God's grace and forgiveness in your own life?

GOD OR WEALTH

Jeremiah 8:18—9:1; Psalm 79:1-9; 1 Timothy 2:1-7; Luke 16:1-13

The Old Testament reading is a poignant lament by the Prophet Jeremiah, as he expresses his personal grief over the plight of his people. The specific disaster that has befallen Judah is not named, but it is enough for Jeremiah to say that his joy is gone and his heart is sick.

The people cry throughout the land because the Lord is no longer with them. Jeremiah 8:19b is probably a later insertion, and would imply that God is angry because of the people's sin of idolatry. The nation faces famine, for the time of the harvest and ingathering of the summer fruits has passed.

Thus the prophet identifies with "the hurt of my poor people" (v. 20) and mourns with them. The plea, "Is there no balm in Gilead?" (v. 22) symbolizes the prophet's sense of futility and despair. (Gilead was the area east of the Jordan River, known for a healing resin that was extracted from local plants and exported.)

The lament concludes with Jeremiah's expression of anguish that he "might weep day and night for the slain of my poor people" (9:1). Although it has been the mission of Jeremiah to prophesy judgment and destruction against the people, here he expresses his heartfelt love and despair on their behalf as well.

Psalm 79 is a cry for deliverance, which was probably composed after the Babylonian invasion and destruction of Jerusalem. Verses 1-3 describe the devastation of the city and the death of its inhabitants. As a result, Judah is now mocked by the other nations. The people ask that the Lord's anger be poured out "on the nations that do not know you" (v. 6), and they appeal to God for compassion and forgiveness. "Help us, O God of our salvation, for the glory of your name" (v. 9).

In the Epistle, Paul offers Timothy instructions on the prayer life of the community. They should all lift up "supplications, prayers, intercessions, and thanksgivings" (1 Tim. 2:1) offered for everyone. Then, as now, the Church prays that those in authority may govern with wisdom and justice. In particular, Paul urges prayers for kings and those in positions of power, who are to bring peace, dignity, and godliness to those under their rule. The Lord desires that all be brought into fullness of life with God and "knowledge of the truth" (v. 4).

Verses 5-6 form a statement of belief, beginning with the affirmation that "there is one God" (v. 5a). From there the statement moves to describe Jesus as the "one mediator between God and humankind, Christ Jesus, himself human" (v. 5b). This same Jesus died as a "ransom for all" (v. 6).

The passage concludes with the author's declaration of his own vocation as herald, Apostle, and "teacher of the Gentiles in faith and truth" (v. 7). He received his commission from the Lord to proclaim the truth that *all people are included in the promise of salvation*

PRAYER FOR THE DAY

O God, whose property is always to have mercy and to give regardless of merit, may we forever realize that we are saved by grace through faith in our Lord Jesus Christ; therefore, by the overflowing power of the Holy Spirit, may we go forth to serve our neighbors and the world with joy and singleness of heart. *Amen.*

through Jesus. Thus the community enters into a life of prayer together, and thereby lives out a new vision of salvation.

After the comforting parables of the joy of *finding the lost* in chapter 15, Luke's Gospel continues with the enigmatic parable of the dishonest manager, which reflects Luke's ongoing concern with the proper use of wealth and possessions.

After addressing the crowds following him, Jesus now turns his attention to his disciples and tells them this parable, unique to Luke. The story involves two main characters, a rich man and his manager. The rich man was probably an absentee landowner who had entrusted the day-to-day oversight of his property to the manager, as his agent for business transactions.

The rich man learns that his manager has been "squandering his property" (16:1). The exact charges against the manager are not specified, but the word *squander* was also used in the preceding parable of the prodigal son to indicate waste and carelessness (15:13).

When the rich man confronts the manager and asks for an "accounting of your management, because you cannot be my manager any longer" (v. 2b), the manager does not dispute the charges against him. It is

ON REFLECTION

Greg Rickel retells this story about a man who collects pearls.

One day, while walking through the downtown, he sees in a store window the most beautiful, the largest, most magnificent pearl he has ever seen. Instantly he knows he must have it. So he enters the store and an old guy enters from the door to the rear of the showroom.

The man addresses the storekeeper, "I want that pearl. How much is it?"

The storekeeper says, "How much you got?"

"Well, I have $300 in my pocket."

"Good, I'll take that. What else you got?"

"Well, I have a Chevy Suburban outside, low mileage, about two years old, paid off."

"Good, I'll take that too. What else you got?"

"Well, I have two CDs worth about $18,000."

"Good," says the storekeeper, "I'll take those too. What else you got?"

This goes on and on. The man gives away his house, his property, even his family. Until finally the storekeeper says, "OK, here. The pearl is yours."

The man turns to leave the store. But as he is walking out the storekeeper stops him and says, "Hey, you know what? That family of yours? I don't need a family. So I'm going to give them back to you. But remember, they are mine now, not yours. You must take good care of them. And that house in Connecticut, well, I don't need a house so you can have that back too. Although it does belong to me, I just want you to care for it. And as for the CDs and the stocks and the Suburban and even this $300, you can have it all back too. But remember, it is all mine. Take it. Use it wisely. Care for it for me."

So the man left with everything he had when he walked into the store—plus the great pearl.

But there was a big difference. He walked into the store owning everything he had. He walked out owning nothing. Instead, everything he had before was now a gift. That is Christian stewardship.

—H. King Oehmig

important to note here that the central issue in the manager's dismissal is his failure to carry out his duties as a competent manager.

In verses 3-4, the manager assesses what he will do now that he is unemployed. He acknowledges that he is not physically suited for manual labor, and he does not want to face the social stigma of becoming a beggar. He decides to take action so that he will not lose his social and economic status, and so that "people may welcome me into their homes" (v. 4).

In verses 5-7, he quickly puts his plan into action by contacting his master's debtors and reducing the amount they owe. A man who owes one hundred jugs of olive oil pays only fifty, and another who owes a hundred containers of wheat is charged only eighty. It was accepted practice for a manager to collect a commission on goods taken in loan repayment to his master, so it could be that the manager relinquished his own commission.

In an unexpected twist at the end of the story, the master commends the dishonest manager for acting shrewdly—not for his original dishonesty, but *for taking prudent action in a crisis situation to insure the future.*

The shrewdness of the manager actually is held up as a model for the disciples—"the children of light"—because he is adept at assessing a dire situation and acting accordingly (v. 8). The followers of Jesus cannot hold themselves apart from the world, and, in fact, can learn from the prudence of the "children of this age."

Verse 9 could be interpreted as having end-time implications, as the disciples are encouraged to make good use of their material possessions in the present—as by almsgiving—so that they will be welcomed "into the eternal homes."

Verses 10-12 contrast faithful/unfaithful conduct with possessions. Good stewardship is equated with faithfulness, and vice versa. If one cannot be trusted with "dishonest wealth" or worldly possessions (v. 11), how can one be trusted with the true riches of eternal life?

The final verse is a general warning against putting too much reliance on possessions: "You cannot serve God and wealth" (v. 13). Faithful stewardship is an act of service to God, and God alone must be served.

POINTS TO PONDER

1. Read the parable in Luke 16:1-8a, and focus your attention on the two main characters. What do you think the two men were like, and how would you describe their relationship? What was the dilemma faced by the manager, and how did he resolve it? What do you think you might have done if you were in his situation?

2. Why was the dishonest manager praised by his master? How is this manager paradoxically a model for us?

3. What is unexpected about this parable? What further issues or questions does the story raise for you? What does the parable say about the differences between the way "people of the world" and devout believers manage their affairs?

4. According to this story, what is the relationship between the wise use of worldly resources and seeking the Kingdom of God?

5. Read the final verses of the Gospel reading (vv. 9-13) in which Jesus expands on the theme of the parable. Reflect on the meaning of this parable for you personally, as well as its implications for the mission of the Church.

THE RICH MAN AND LAZARUS

Jeremiah 32:1-3a, 6-15; Psalm 91:1-6, 14-16; 1 Timothy 6:6-19; Luke 16:19-31

After many dire predictions concerning the coming destruction of Judah, the Prophet Jeremiah now brings a message of hope for the future by purchasing a plot of land. At the time (588 B. C.), Jerusalem was under siege by the armies of Babylon, and Jeremiah himself was imprisoned by King Zedekiah for proclaiming that God would deliver Jerusalem to the Babylonian King Nebuchadnezzar.

The Lord came to Jeremiah and told him to purchase a field in Anathoth from his uncle Shallum upon the request of his cousin Hanamel. According to the right of redemption (Lev. 25:25-28), a relative had the first right to buy a piece of property in order to keep it in the family. Thus Jeremiah made the necessary arrangements to purchase the land.

The significance of the purchase is revealed in Jeremiah 32:15: the redemption of the field at Anathoth, which was already in enemy hands, was evidence of *faith for the future of God's people.* Despite the present destruction, the Lord would redeem Israel, and there would be a time of prosperous houses and fields and vineyards.

The beautiful poetic imagery of Psalm 91 expresses trust in the Lord's protection. God is our refuge, who provides deliverance from pestilence. God's faithfulness is "a shield and buckler" (v. 4). Thus we need not fear the darkness or hostile arrows. In verses 14-15, God declares deliverance and protection to those who call upon the name of the Lord. We can be assured that God will answer our call in times of trouble and bring us long life and salvation.

Jesus' parable of the rich man and Lazarus focuses on the ongoing concern for the right use of wealth and power, an issue that is emphasized throughout the Gospel of Luke.

Following the parable of the dishonest manager (16:1-13), Jesus continued with a series of teachings that included the warning that "what is prized by human beings is an abomination in the sight of God" (16:15b). But the Pharisees, lovers of money (v. 14), ridiculed Jesus for his teachings about riches. To their way of thinking, wealth was an indication of God's blessing.

Whereas the rich man in this story dressed in fine clothes and "feasted sumptuously every day" (v. 19), Lazarus was a poor man who longed to eat even the scraps from the rich man's table. The fact that the rich man wore expensive purple is an indication of his elevated wealth and status.

Lazarus lay outside the gate of the rich man's home, and was covered with sores instead of fine purple linen. The wretchedness and outcast status of Lazarus as compared to the extravagant lifestyle of the rich man is dramatically illustrated by the fact that dogs came to lick his sores.

When both men die, the contrasts continue: whereas the poor man "was carried away by the

PRAYER FOR THE DAY

Lord Jesus, who taught with freedom and authority, and called us to follow you in the way that leads to abundant life: give us the grace of your Holy Spirit, that we may with sure confidence and a steadfast faith express your will to draw all people to know the Holy God in the intimate way you have shown. *Amen.*

angels to be with Abraham" (v. 22a), the rich man found himself tormented in Hades. In a reversal of the previous situation, Lazarus is now exalted and resides in comfort, while the rich man is cast out and endures in agony.

Like Lazarus, who formerly lay far away at the gate longing for scraps of food, the rich man now looks across the chasm from Hades and begs for mercy. Hades is the Hebrew realm of the dead or *Sheol*, but here it is seen as a place of punishment.

As the rich man begs for relief from his torment, he tells "Father Abraham" to "send Lazarus to dip the tip of his finger in water and cool my tongue" (v. 24). The rich man has not yet grasped the significance of what has occurred, and acts as though his former status remains. He asks Lazarus to do what he himself never did for Lazarus.

In life, the rich man had "received your good things" and Lazarus "evil things" (v. 25); but now the reverse is true. Lazarus will be

ON REFLECTION

"There was once a rich man ... " begins this familiar story of the Rich Man and Lazarus. How could such a man, master of all he surveyed, imagine that he need even listen to the plight of a poor beggar grubbing outside his gates?

But such self-assurance—being convinced of one's God-given right to "lord" it over the misfortunates who "could have worked harder"—is a far more dangerous course than it seems. Anthony de Mello reminds us in The Heart of Enlightenment: *"To know exactly where you're headed may be the best way to go astray. Not all those who loiter are lost."*

And Grant Gallup observes that it IS possible to take notice and take action: "When Albert Schweitzer heard the story of the Rich Man and Lazarus, he was converted. He saw at once that Europe was the Rich Man, and that Beggar Africa starved at his doorstep. He heard Moses and the Prophets clearly, and went off to a hospital in Lambarene, to tend the running sores of poverty and oppression and to serve the Risen One. Most of the privileged of the world, individuals or nations, have not followed Jesus or Albert into that service."

The litany of excuses that the Rich Man (commonly called "Dives") probably ran through in his time must have been as predictable as they were lame as they were self-righteous (though we have no record of any of this):

Lazarus is a bum and doesn't deserve assistance.

To help him when he begs for food outside the compound not only means Lazarus would continue to show up regularly and disturb the family—but the guests at my swim party would have to look at him!

Any assistance I'd give would just turn out to be counter-productive, furthering his "beggar's syndrome" of shiftlessness and dependency.

So ... don't even set out the table scraps ... then maybe he'll get the message, turn his life around, and become a hard-working, God-fearing, deserving person (like me). Until then, let the bleeding hearts down at the soup kitchen or the welfare agency take care of him.

But God's ways are not our ways. If the Gospel has one message for us, exemplified in Jesus' being companioned by sinners and "outcasts"—it is that thinking yourself righteous is worse than loitering.

—H. King Oehmig

comforted and the rich man will experience anguish.

Furthermore, the chasm that now exists between the two men is so wide that it cannot be crossed. In death, the rich man is now as powerless as the poor man had been in life. The rich man finds himself in this situation because he misused his wealth and position; he could have helped Lazarus, but he did not.

The rich man seems to realize that there is nothing more he can do to alter his own immediate situation, so he turns his attention to his family. He tells Abraham to send Lazarus to warn his five brothers "so that they will not also come into this place of torment" (v. 28). He still sees Lazarus as an inferior who is available to do his bidding, but his concerns are limited to his immediate family and not to the wider world.

But Abraham will have none of this. He replies that the brothers do not need a visit from Lazarus; they already have the words of Moses and the prophets (v. 29) to tell them how they should conduct their lives, particularly in regard to the poor.

The rich man continues to insist that they will repent only if "someone goes to them from the dead" (v. 30). But if his brothers have ignored the words of Moses and the prophets, not even the witness of someone from the dead will make a difference (v. 31).

The rich man finds himself in torment because he did not heed the words of Scripture; he abused the wealth and power that had been given to him by disregarding his obligation to the poor and oppressed. He did not grasp that his lack of compassion toward Lazarus was against the will of God.

The Epistle offers similar advice to Timothy by warning against the temptations of material possessions: "For the love of money is a root of all kinds of evil" (1 Tim. 6:10). Timothy himself is to live a virtuous life and to "fight the good fight of the faith" (v. 12) which leads to eternal life. He is to keep the commandment until the coming of Christ Jesus, who is the "blessed and only Sovereign, the King of kings and Lord of lords" (v. 15).

But in this present age, those who are rich are not to be haughty, but are to set their hopes on God (v. 17b). Rather than seeking transitory wealth, they are to be generous and "rich in good works" (v. 18) so that they may inherit eternal life—"the life that really is life" (v. 19).

POINTS TO PONDER

1. Compare the life and character of the two men in the parable, both before and after their deaths. How did each man handle his respective situation in both this life and the afterlife?

2. How did the rich man's outlook change after his death and why? According to this parable, what are the responsibilities associated with wealth and privilege?

3. Who are the Lazaruses of our world today? What is our responsibility toward such people?

4. How do you think this parable might be understood by a person living in poverty or any other condition of oppression today? How does this story speak to you personally?

5. Also read the Old Testament Lesson and the Epistle text for today. How do these readings relate to the Gospel passage? What are the challenges presented? What are we as the Church, as well as each of us as individuals, called to do?

MUSTARD SEED FAITH

Lamentations 1:1-6; Psalm 137; 2 Timothy 1:1-14; Luke 17:5-10

Although the Book of Lamentations specifically recounts the destruction of Jerusalem and the exile of the people in 586 B. C., it has come to represent the grief and sadness of all the disasters that have befallen the Jewish people.

The five chapters of the book contain evocative poetic language that relates the consequences of God's punishment for Israel's sins. In the passage for today, Jerusalem is compared to a widow who mourns and "weeps bitterly in the night" (1:2). She has been abandoned by her friends, who have now become her enemies. The image of a widow speaks of loneliness and despair, as well as a sense of vulnerability.

The "suffering and hard servitude" (v. 3) that Judah endures is reminiscent of Israel's slavery in Egypt. The once vibrant city of Jerusalem is now deserted, since the temple has been destroyed, and no one comes for the religious festivals.

Israel's enemies prosper and have become masters over Israel. But the text explains how God's people have brought this punishment down upon themselves because of their sins (v. 5). The majesty of the city is no more, and her leaders have "fled without strength before the pursuer" (v. 6).

Psalm 137 is also a lament over the destruction of Jerusalem, as the people weep when they remember Zion. Their captors torment them by asking them to "Sing us one of the songs of Zion!" (v. 3). But how are they to sing their songs in a foreign land?

Thus the Psalmist vows never to forget Jerusalem: "If I forget you, O Jerusalem, let my right hand wither!" (v. 5). The Psalm concludes with a plea to God to avenge those who destroyed Jerusalem and sent her people into exile.

The tone of the Epistle and Gospel today are in marked contrast to the first two Lessons, as they speak of faith and what it means to put full trust in God.

Although the Book of 2 Timothy is usually attributed to Paul, it was most likely written by one of Paul's followers. However, these opening verses of 2 Timothy chapter 1 do emphasize the need to suffer for the love of God, as an imprisoned author gives thanks for the faith of his colleague Timothy.

The author is reminded of the faith that was instilled in Timothy through his grandmother Lois and mother Eunice (1:5). Through these faithful witnesses, Timothy became a believer. He is now encouraged to renew the Spirit that has been bestowed upon him, to proclaim the Gospel without embarrassment, and bravely to accept suffering (vv. 6-8).

The strength to carry out this calling comes from God, who calls us according to the Divine purpose and grace (v. 9a), which has

PRAYER FOR THE DAY

Gracious and ever-faithful God, friend of sinners and sanctifier of the faithful: suffuse us in the wonder and power of the Holy Spirit, that we may know the Gospel of Jesus Christ as a banquet of liberation, a celebration of the magnificence of your love. And may we witness, in word and deed, to this eternal truth unto the ends of the earth. *Amen.*

been revealed through the appearance of "our Savior Christ Jesus, who abolished death and brought life and immortality to light through the gospel" (v. 10).

The author was called to be a herald, Apostle, and teacher of this very Gospel, and for this he is willing to suffer and hold fast because of his trust in God's purposes.

Jesus also offers encouragement to those who aspire to a life of faith. In the verses that precede the Gospel reading for today (17:1-4), Jesus teaches his disciples concerning life in the community of faith. They are to take care not to lead others astray inadvertently (vv. 1-2); and when one person wrongs another, repentance and unlimited forgiveness are required (vv. 3-4).

Upon hearing these words, the Apostles turn to Jesus and exclaim, "Increase our faith!" (v. 5). Jesus answers that if they have faith the size of a mustard seed, they can command a mulberry tree to be uprooted and planted in the sea (v. 6). The point is that it is not the quantity but the *genuineness* of faith that matters.

ON REFLECTION

Frederick Buechner, in his book Whistling in the Dark *(HarperSanFrancisco, 1993), reminds us of the seeking ones, the hoping-for-faith souls Jesus chose (and chooses) to go out and plant his mustard-seed Kingdom-in-the-making:*

"Not the spiritual giants but 'the poor in spirit' ... Not the champions of the faith who can rejoice even in the midst of suffering but the ones who mourn over their own suffering because they know for the most part they've brought it down on themselves. ...

"Not the strong ones but the meek ones in the sense of the gentle ones, i. e., the ones not like Caspar Milquetoast but like Charlie Chaplin, the little tramp who lets the world walk over him and yet, dapper and undaunted to the end, somehow makes the world more human in the process. ... Not the ones who are righteous but the ones who hope they will be someday. ...

"Not the winners of great victories over Evil in the world, but the ones who, seeing it also in themselves every time they comb their hair in front of the bathroom mirror, are merciful. ... Not the totally pure but the 'pure in heart,' to use Jesus' phrase, the ones who may be as shop-worn and clay-footed as the next one but have somehow kept some inner freshness and innocence intact" (pp. 19-20).

In other words, they are such as we would-be followers of Jesus today often find ourselves.

A lifelong venture of faith sounds like such a high-minded aim: a trusting-God-in-all-circumstances state of being. Who could measure or calibrate something of such value? Is faith a commodity one can build, or that can be passed on, hand to hand?

Jesus does begin this teaching with a comparison. "If you had faith the size of a mustard seed, you could say to this mulberry tree, 'Be uprooted and planted in the sea,' and it would obey you."

The mustard seed, a grain so tiny that it proverbially indicated whatever was very small, nevertheless had mass and some dimension. And mulberry tree or mountain (cf Mt. 17:20)—this was a promise of real moving capability.

Yet—there was also a new dimension at work here, one previously unaccounted for. It was Jesus' own power in performing the will of the Father, all the way to the Cross.

—H. King Oehmig

Even the smallest, most infinitesimal grain of faith will bring God's power to bear upon the needs of the world. Nothing would be impossible to the disciples if they were open to and reliant upon the power of God to work through them.

The fig-mulberry type of tree is relatively large with an extensive root system, which would make it extremely difficult to uproot and throw into the sea. In a parallel saying in Matthew 17:20, faith as a mustard seed can move a mountain. That the mustard seed is "the smallest of all the seeds" is also noted in Matthew 13:31-32 and Mark 4:31.

The point Jesus makes here with such an exaggerated and unlikely promise is an explanation of *the power of the gift of faith, which we cannot create or earn.* This faith is absolute reliance on God, in which there is no dependence on one's own intelligence or talents or influence.

Thus the image of the mustard seed conveys the point that even the minutest amount of trust in the power of God can bring about inconceivable results—such as moving a mulberry tree or a mountain—or practicing unlimited forgiveness.

Nor can we ever in any way put God under obligation to ourselves, as Jesus shows in the parable in verses 7-10. The parable begins by describing any situation in which a worker, here a slave who plows the field or tends the sheep, serves at the pleasure of the master.

Although the slave may have completed a day of hard work, the master expects to be served before the slaves have their meal. Their eventual right to eat and drink is not to be seen as a reward for any special services. Rather, they simply receive what is their due at the proper time.

In the final verse, Jesus tells his Apostles that when *they* have performed every appointed duty, they are to acknowledge that they have done no more than what they were obliged to do: "We have done only what we ought to have done!" (v. 10b). They are not to expect special gratitude for simply doing what they are commanded or expected to do.

Thus the disciples can make no special claim on God. The duties of a servant of Christ are to be performed with humility, and without expectation of commendation.

Furthermore, the power to accomplish these tasks always comes from God; and living faithfully day to day is possible only through the *love of Christ* and the *power of the Holy Spirit.*

POINTS TO PONDER

1. In Luke 17:6, Jesus responds to his disciples' plea for increased faith. What point does Jesus make by using the image of the mustard seed in connection with faith? What other metaphors can you think of that convey your own understanding of faith?

2. Recall times in your own life when your personal faith has been increased. What were the particular circumstances in which your faith was empowered? What role does your faith community play in the growth of your faith?

3. What gets in the way of nurturing your faith? How are you able to overcome these obstacles? What does the parable in Luke 17:7-10 tell us about our relationship to God?

4. What do we learn from today's Lessons about the cost and the reward of faithful discipleship?

5. In the Epistle for today, we learn that Timothy's faith came through his grandmother Lois and his mother Eunice. Who are the people who have increased your own faith?

HEALING FAITH

Jeremiah 29:1, 4-7; Psalm 66:1-12; 2 Timothy 2:8-15; Luke 17:11-19

It is the year 597 B. C., and Jerusalem has been overcome by the Babylonians and its inhabitants sent into captivity by King Nebuchadnezzar.

Chapter 29 of the Book of Jeremiah consists of a letter from the God of Israel to the priests, prophets, elders, and all those carried off into exile. Jeremiah begins by telling them to build houses, eat the produce from their gardens, and marry and raise families. They are not to give up their identity. Instead, they are to "multiply there, and do not decrease" (v. 6).

Moreover, they are to seek the welfare of the city of Babylon by praying on its behalf to the Lord, since the well-being of God's people is ultimately dependent upon the continuance of Babylon itself. Thus, the Israelites are to accept their stay in Babylon and to build lives for themselves and their families for at least two generations.

The letter continues with warnings against those who would offer false hopes of rescue before the seventy years of captivity are over. At that time, and not before, the Lord's promise of a return to their homeland will be fulfilled.

Thus the Israelites are to trust in the promises of the Lord and wait until the appointed time for a return to their homeland. They are admonished that, even in exile, they will search for and find the Lord.

Psalm 66 offers confirmation of the hope of Israel for deliverance in a hymn of praise and thanksgiving for the awesome deeds and power of the Lord: "All the earth worships you; they sing praises to you" (v. 4).

Through the power of the Lord, Israel passed through the Red Sea and crossed the Jordan River into the promised land of Canaan (v. 6). The Lord keeps watch over the nations and has kept Israel safe. Though God's people have been tested, they have been strengthened by these experiences, and have been brought to a place of safety and prosperity: "a spacious place" (v. 12).

The unknown author of the second letter to Timothy encourages the disciple to be faithful just as God remains faithful, despite the risks to be faced and the suffering to be endured. As an example, Paul himself is willing to be imprisoned—"chained like a criminal" (2:9)—for the sake of the Gospel.

There can be no divided loyalty in which one would hesitate to follow the Messiah as our example. Blessed by birth that made him an heir of David, Jesus offered himself up for others and was vindicated by being raised from the dead.

Verses 11-13 comprise an early hymn promising that *with Christ we have died to the world*, and *with him we shall receive the crown of victory*. But if we fail to persevere and so deny Christ by our lives, we will likewise be denied.

PRAYER FOR THE DAY

Holy God, author and giver of peace, source of all well-being: instill in our hearts through the working of your Holy Spirit a true sense of gratitude, that we may show forth the boundless riches of knowing Jesus Christ as Lord, living in the power of your creative abundance, and this we pray in your holy Name. *Amen.*

However, Christ will be faithful whether we are steadfast or not, as faithfulness defines Christ's nature.

This is our witness as the people of God that we are to manifest in our lives: "Do your best to present yourself to God" as an approved worker (v. 15).

In the Gospel Lesson, God's power to offer healing and wholeness is demonstrated through the actions of another outsider. The story of the ten lepers is unique to Luke, but has similarities to the healing of Naaman in 2 Kings 5:1-14 and the healing of a leper earlier in Luke's Gospel (5:12-14).

The passage begins with a reminder that Jesus is on his way to Jerusalem, where the Cross looms before him. We are told that he was traveling in the area between Samaria and Galilee when ten lepers approached him as he entered a village (Lk. 17:11-12).

ON REFLECTION

This was not an easy case. The ancient Torah, revered by both Jews and Samaritans, viewed all skin eruptions—from elephantiasis, psoriasis, and vitiligo, to any other cases of lesions—as "leprosy." Such conditions were considered contagious and the cause of ceremonial impurity. And so those classified as "lepers" could not freely associate with other people nor enter into their faith's religious rites.

One of the lepers in today's story had another condition. He was a Samaritan, an alien. How ironic that it is his story that embodies the classic characteristics of healing on another level—beyond physical restoration from the skin-disease problem.

Here was a man who offered thanks, who returned joyously to Jesus to express his heartfelt gratitude. This man's life was not merely rescued from alienation, it was saved. This healing was not only skin-deep but clearly also heart-deep.

Your faith has made you well …

Here was an example of true life-healing in one who, as a foreigner, had less of a reason than the other nine to return to Jesus and express his thankfulness to God.

His example comes down to us today as emblematic of one who did the extraordinary, who took the time to turn back, to complete his own healing process with evidence of true salvation.

Author Marcus Borg has said in an interview:

"In the Bible, salvation is mostly concerned with something that happens in this life. Even in the New Testament, the primary meaning of the word 'salvation' is transformation in this life. One can see this in the roots of the English word salvation, which comes from 'salve,' which is a healing ointment. Salvation is about healing. We all grow up wounded, and salvation is about the healing of the roots of existence. …

"Faith is not primarily about believing a set of claims to be true—that's what goes with the earlier vision of Christianity. The understanding of faith that goes with the emerging vision is about a relationship of trust in God and faithfulness to God. The ancient meaning of the word 'believe' is 'to commit oneself, to be loyal to.' The Middle English word is 'beleve,' and that means to love or be loved. So faith is about loving God and loving that which God loves—which is the whole of creation."

—H. King Oehmig

In Scripture, leprosy is more often a general term for a variety of skin diseases than what we refer to today as Hansen's Disease. Those afflicted were subject to a number of social taboos and religious purification requirements (Lev. 13—14). The law stipulated that they remain isolated from the community (Num. 5:1-4); and they were to warn others not to come close (Lev. 13:45-46).

Thus the lepers called to Jesus from afar: "Jesus, Master, have mercy on us!" (v. 13). That the lepers address Jesus as "master"—i. e., as a person in authority—is unusual. This is the only time Jesus is addressed this way by someone other than a disciple. The plea for mercy could have been a request for alms or for healing.

The next sentence begins with: "When he *saw* them" (v. 14). Because their condition was considered God's judgment against them, lepers were shunned as invisible people in society. The fact that *Jesus saw them* is an indication of his compassion for those who suffer and are marginalized.

In accordance with the requirements of the Law, Jesus tells them to go and show themselves to the priests, who alone had the authority to determine whether they could be accepted back into the community. As the lepers went on their way, "they were made clean" (v. 14).

But then one of the lepers realizes that he has been healed. He immediately offers loud praise to God as he returns to Jesus, prostrates himself at his feet, and offers thanks. The spontaneous response of this man shows that faith is grounded in obedience and thanksgiving. "And he was a Samaritan" (v. 16b).

As a leper and a Samaritan, this man was doubly cursed as an outsider. But like the Samaritan of the parable in Luke 10:25-37, he is an example of faithful living.

In Luke 4:27, Jesus refers to the healing of another foreigner, the Syrian Naaman, as an example of a non-Israelite who received Divine healing when the lepers of Israel rejected God's saving help. This is further emphasized when Jesus asks about the other nine lepers who were cured. "Was none of them found to return and give praise to God except this foreigner?" (v. 18).

Turning again to the Samaritan, Jesus tells him to go on his way, as "your faith has made you well" (v. 19)—which could also be translated as "your faith has saved you."

POINTS TO PONDER

1. Try to imagine the scene described in the Gospel passage. What do you think life might have been like for a leper in first-century Palestine? How do you think these lepers might have felt when they realized that they were no longer infected with leprosy?

2. Why do you think the nine lepers continued on their way without coming back to Jesus? How would you describe Jesus' attitude toward the nine?

3. Look carefully at the specific actions of the grateful leper in Luke 17:15-16. What do we learn here about a grateful response to God?

4. In verse 19, Jesus tells the tenth leper that his faith has made him well. Within the context of this story, how would you define faith?

5. Now that they were no longer afflicted with leprosy, these ten individuals could once again be a part of society. Who are the "lepers" of our contemporary culture—the invisible people that we ignore? What are we called to do as the Church and as individuals to reach out to such people and welcome them into our faith communities?

PERSISTENCE IN PRAYER

Jeremiah 31:27-34; Psalm 119:97-104; 2 Timothy 3:14—4:5; Luke 18:1-8

The Prophet Jeremiah warned Judah of the coming destruction of Jerusalem and exile in Babylon; but at the same time, he also held out the promise of redemption for God's people and the restoration of the nation.

Today's reading is a part of a vision of future salvation that came to Jeremiah in a dream. "I awoke and looked, and my sleep was pleasant to me" (31:26).

The days are coming when God's people will return to their land to rebuild and repopulate. The same words that were used in the call of Jeremiah (1:10) appear again—to *pluck up, break down, overthrow, destroy, build, plant* (v. 28) as an indication of the punishment as well as the restoration of the people under the watchful eye of God.

Quoting from Ezekiel 18:2-4, Jeremiah makes the point that in the future people will be punished only for their own sins (vv. 29-31). Most importantly, there will be a new and fuller understanding of the covenant that was made with Moses after the exodus from Egypt. Now the law will be written on the hearts of the people.

"I will put my law within them, and I will write it on their hearts" (v. 33). The further words that "I will be their God, and they shall be my people" signify the covenant between God and Israel (Lev. 26:12; Jer. 7:23; 24:7).

But now there will be a new spirit in the nation such that it will not be necessary to teach the people about the Lord, "for they shall all know me" (v. 34).

Finally, the sins of the people will be forgiven and forgotten with this new and deeper covenant relationship with God. Thus the message brought by the Prophet Jeremiah was not only about judgment against Israel, but also about hope for the future and renewed relationship with God.

The implications of this new covenant written in the hearts of the people as proclaimed by Jeremiah is reflected in the words of the Psalmist in Psalm 119, who declares, "Oh, how I love your law!" (v. 97). The Psalm is a celebration of the law that verges on the mystical as it extols the Torah as the source of wisdom, understanding, and inspiration.

Devotion to the law and keeping its precepts protects the author from evil and false ways. "How sweet are your words to my taste, sweeter than honey to my mouth!" (v. 103).

The Epistle also encourages devotion to God's Word through persistence in witness: "Proclaim the message; be persistent whether the time is favorable or unfavorable" (2 Tim. 4:2).

Timothy had been taught the truth of "salvation through faith in Christ Jesus" (3:15) from childhood. This truth came through the Scriptures, which are inspired by God to be used for teaching, verification, correction, and

PRAYER FOR THE DAY

Almighty and merciful God, you alone can order our wills and affections: through the wisdom of your Word, Jesus Christ, assist us in distinguishing what is holy and lasting in life from what is transient and not worthy of our allegiance, so that, through the working of the Holy Spirit within and among us, we may know where true joys are to be found. *Amen.*

right training, so that "everyone who belongs to God may be proficient, equipped for every good work" (v. 17).

This message is urgent and must be presented *persistently* and *patiently* so that people hear the truth and not what they want to hear. Thus Timothy is reminded to *be steadfast and ready to endure trials and suffering* as he continues to carry out his ministry as an evangelist until Christ comes again.

Luke alone of the Gospel writers tells the parable of the unjust judge and the persistent widow. This story appears near the end of Luke's travel narrative (9:51—19:27), and immediately follows the discourse in 17:22-37 in which Jesus predicts his Passion and warns of the coming judgment.

The story of the widow and the judge has elements of humor that break the tension of the preceding passage and give a sense of hope. It is found in Luke 18:2-5, and is framed by interpretation in verses 1 and 6-7. Verse 8 provides a link with the theme of the coming of the Son of Man at the end of chapter 17.

ON REFLECTION

Perhaps the widow didn't laugh all the way to justice … but she certainly must have smiled. And one can imagine her heart's affirmation: There IS a God!

And with this God, asking *is the sacrament of desire. It is also the heart of prayer. To explain the parable, Jesus teaches the disciples at the end of it (Lk. 18:6-8) that GOD IS, and that GOD HEARS US.*

God is not an unjust, self-centered tyrant. SO: How much more will God hear and answer us—if even a measly human authority such as this local judge finally gets it right?

The purpose of prayer is not to put a headlock on the Almighty God, forcing God to cry "Uncle!" and give us what we want. Prayer is not a wrestling match, Jacob's experience notwithstanding.

Yet neither is it High Tea. It is a dance between importunity and surrender, a sure shot between missing the mark and hitting it, a combination of concern for the self and self-sacrifice—that is the mix of human prayer.

But Jesus seems to be teaching here that the only way to err in our praying life is not to do it. I cannot recall an instance in which a disciple is rebuked by Jesus for asking wrongly in prayer.

James and John, the sons of Zebedee, once came forward to ask Jesus, "Teacher, we want you to do for us whatever we ask of you" (Mk. 10:35). Did Jesus quail at their brashness, or leave in a huff because of their self-centeredness in pushing their own agenda?

When they asked Jesus to let them sit on his right and left hands in glory, Jesus did correct them for their obtuseness and told them he could not grant their request; but he did not lambast them for their importunity.

Had they not asked him, they never would have learned about true service and its cost— and they would have remained in their ignorance of what true discipleship is.

The good news is that, no matter what we ask, God will work with us to bring about good, and a continuing relationship that demands more—but yields greater blessing, too.

—H. King Oehmig

As an appointed official, the judge held a position of authority in the local community; we read that he had no particular concern for what others thought of him.

In contrast, the widow was among the most vulnerable members of society. The law made provisions for widows (Dt. 24:19-21; 26:12-13; 27:19); but without a husband or other family members to care for her, a woman's very survival was in jeopardy.

Every day when the judge emerged from the courthouse he was confronted by the widow, who demanded justice. Finally the judge relented because he became tired of the widow's constant harassment. "I will grant her justice, so that she may not wear me out" (v. 5). Although the judge had no regard for other people, he did not want his authority as a magistrate to be brought into question.

Thus, though Jesus explained that the story was told to emphasize the "need to pray always and not to lose heart," the parable also provides encouragement to those who seek justice over oppression. The dogged determination of the widow is a model for us, and an important example of the efficacy of prayer.

However, as we move to verses 7-8, further issues are raised. Jesus makes the point that if this unjust judge will finally grant justice, we can be assured that our merciful God will do even more for God's imploring people. Although it may seem to take a long time, God's justice will prevail.

Nonetheless, the purpose and result of constant prayer is not to change God's mind, but instead, persistent prayer allows the ongoing presence of God to have power over our lives and brings us into fuller relationship with God.

Another question is raised in verse 8b: Even if we *are* persistent in prayer—when the Son of Man comes, will there be any faithful ones like the widow to receive him? The point of the parable has been turned back on us. We are to pray always, but we must pray *with faith*.

POINTS TO PONDER

1. How would you describe the two main characters in the Gospel parable? Why do you think the judge finally changed his mind?

2. What do we learn from the actions of the widow? What is the example she sets for us here?

3. Jesus tells us that we are to "pray always and not to lose heart" (Lk. 18:1). How has your own life been changed by prayer?

4. As you read verses 6-8, what else can be learned from the actions of the widow and the judge? What other truths do you discover from this story?

5. In today's Epistle (2 Tim. 3:14—4:5), Timothy is encouraged to "carry out your ministry fully" (4:5). What tools for ministry are mentioned in the passage, and how can we use these resources in our lives today to fulfill our call to God's service?

ACCEPTED BY GOD

Joel 2:23-32; Psalm 65; 2 Timothy 4:6-8, 16-18; Luke 18:9-14

Unlike the other prophetic writings, the Book of Joel does not take place in a specified time, but the events portrayed in it present a theological summary of the history of Israel.

The first two chapters tell of the devastating effects of a plague of locusts, and call the people to repentance. Beginning in 2:28, and continuing through the end of the book, Joel proclaims a vision of future judgment and God's blessings.

The verses assigned for today begin by calling upon God's people to "be glad and rejoice in the Lord your God" (2:23), for their fortunes have been reversed after the widespread destruction of the locusts. The rains have returned, the harvests will be plentiful, and the people shall once again have enough to eat. They are to *praise the Lord their God who dwells among them* and are assured that such misfortune will not happen again. For God's people "shall never again be put to shame" (vv. 26b, 27b).

Joel now proclaims a glorious future in which God's Spirit will be poured out upon all people, no matter what their age, gender, or social status. God will be revealed through prophecy, dreams, and visions.

The apocalyptic imagery of vv. 30-31 of "blood and fire and columns of smoke" (v. 30), when the sun is turned to darkness and the moon to blood, are images of war and natural phenomena that describe the coming judgment: "the great and terrible day of the Lord."

In those days, the ones who call upon the name of the Lord will be saved. On the day of Pentecost, Peter quotes these words of Joel (Acts 2:17-21) in his call to faith and salvation at the coming of the Holy Spirit.

The words of the Psalmist in Psalm 65 reflect the joy the people of Israel might have felt as their land was renewed after the plague of locusts, as described by the Prophet Joel.

In this exuberant and beautiful hymn, the people praise God for answering their prayers and forgiving their sins. They give further thanks to God as the creator and sustainer of the earth's bounty.

The final words of the second letter to Timothy were composed by Paul's admirers as a tribute to the Apostle a generation or more after his martyrdom.

As Paul's days draw to an end, he can confidently claim that he has "fought the good fight" and "kept the faith" (4:7). He pictures receiving the "crown of righteousness" (v. 8) from the Lord much as an athlete receives the crown of victory. But this recognition is not just for Paul himself; it is for all who have served faithfully and longed for Jesus' return.

He laments that he has been deserted by some of his former companions who did not come to his defense when he was imprisoned.

PRAYER FOR THE DAY

Eternal God, in you we find genuine peace and the strength to love: draw us ever closer to you through the mediation of the Holy Spirit, that you may love others through us. May we live no longer for ourselves alone, but for the Gospel of Jesus Christ in the supreme virtues of faith, hope, and love. *Amen.*

But he does not hold this against them, since he was strengthened by the presence of the Lord and used his situation to proclaim the Gospel to the Gentiles.

Using the metaphor of being saved from the lion's mouth (cf Dan. 6:19-22), Paul expresses his confidence that the Lord will rescue him from attack and give him deliverance (v. 18). Paul knows that the Lord will save all believers and bring them safely into the glory of God's heavenly Kingdom. "To him be the glory forever and ever. Amen" (v. 18b).

The parable of the Pharisee and the tax collector is unique to Luke, and provides further teachings on prayer and patterns of reversal. The story is addressed to "some who trusted in themselves that they were righteous and regarded others with contempt" (18:9). Previous descriptions would suggest that Jesus is specifically referring to the Pharisees and lawyers (16:14-15); but his words have wider application as well, and set up a comparison between the spiritual pride of the Pharisee and the humility of the tax collector.

ON REFLECTION

Robert Farrar Capon in his book Parables of the Kingdom *refers to the nature of parables as "roundabout, analogical devices." When Jesus was asked why he used parables in his teaching, he said he taught that way so that "they may indeed look, but not perceive, and may indeed listen, but not understand" (Mk. 4:12a).*

Although Jesus would teach more straightforwardly when alone with his disciples, such directness was no guarantee they would grasp the mystery any more accurately.

On three separate occasions, Jesus pronounced quite clearly to his followers predictions of his dying and rising in Jerusalem. But when those mighty acts did come into being, it was as though they had never heard of such a thing.

Still, it is little wonder why Jesus used parables to instruct, even though they were hardly ever comprehended. In the manner of a chemistry professor attempting to explain to students the mysterious particles inside an atom, the instructor might use the comparison of electrons circling the nucleus in the way that planets whirl around the sun. Comparisons can lock analogies into place.

But, as Capon points out, Jesus differed from the chemistry professor in that his "explanations" were not used to clarify points for the listeners' satisfaction, but to call attention to the unsatisfactoriness of all their previous explanations and understandings.

Had he been the chemistry professor, Jesus would have pushed the comparison to its ultimate, mind-boggling conclusion: "The solar system is mostly great tracts of empty space, so too is matter, and that which we had previously thought of as solid stuff consists almost entirely of holes."

Jesus' underlying truths were just this mind-boggling. When we apply this principle of pushing on to the ultimate logical conclusion to today's parable of the Pharisee and the Publican, our old beliefs are instantly shattered as to who is acceptable to God.

In the words of Blaise Pascal: "Experience makes us see an enormous difference between piety and goodness." That is the difference between the Pharisee and the repentant Publican for us today.

—H. King Oehmig

The two characters in the story provide a stark contrast. The Pharisee was a person of elite status, education, and respectability who knew and meticulously followed Mosaic Law. He would have been held up as a model citizen of the community.

At the opposite end of the social spectrum was the tax collector. In first-century Palestine the responsibility of collecting Roman taxes was usually contracted out to Gentile and Jewish agents who could charge any tax rate they wished, as long as the government received its due. By keeping the difference, the tax collectors could, and did, become quite wealthy.

Since many devout Jews regarded the paying of any tax to a foreign power as treason against God, any Jew participating in and profiteering by such treachery was considered a collaborator of the worst sort. For this reason, a tax collector was counted among the worst of sinners and banned from Jewish religious and social life. Though tax collectors could repent, the chances of their doing so were slim, because of the sizable repayments they would have to make to those they had cheated.

Jesus tells us that both men went to the temple to pray. The Pharisee gives thanks that "I am not like other people ... or even like this tax collector" (v. 11). He does not violate the commandments against robbery or fraud or adultery. In addition, he fasts twice a week and tithes his income. Surely he is different from sinners such as the tax collector.

In contrast, the tax collector prays for mercy. "God, be merciful to me, a sinner!" (v. 13). His actions themselves demonstrate a sense of humility before God. He stands far off, keeps his face lowered, beats his breast, and begs for mercy. Thus, the tax collector goes down to his home "justified rather than the other" (v. 14).

The tax collector is "justified," or made right with God, because he recognizes that he is a sinner in need of God's grace and forgiveness (Rom. 3:21-26). Tax collectors and sinners are portrayed throughout Luke's Gospel as being receptive to the message of Jesus, while the religious establishment rejects him (3:12; 5:27-32; 7:29-30, 34; 15:1-2).

Jesus, echoing his words in 14:11, again declares that "all who exalt themselves will be humbled, but all who humble themselves will be exalted" (v. 14). Jesus himself is the prime example of this, as the one who humbled himself for the redemption of the world (Phil. 2:6-11).

POINTS TO PONDER

1. Describe the two main characters in the Gospel parable. Why do you think Jesus singled out a Pharisee and a tax collector for this story? Who are some contemporary representatives of these two people?

2. According to the opening verse, to whom did Jesus direct this story, and why? How do you think those who heard this parable might have reacted?

3. Compare the prayers of these two men, as well as their physical actions while praying. What do you think each of these men might have been thinking as he prayed?

4. In Luke 18:14, Jesus says that the tax collector was justified. What do you think it means in this context to be "justified"?

5. What does this story suggest about our relationship with God? About confession, grace, and mercy? What conventional assumptions about piety are called into question in this parable? What are the inherent warnings here for us today as we strive for deeper spiritual awareness?

FOR ALL THE SAINTS

Daniel 7:1-3, 15-18; Psalm 149; Ephesians 1:11-23; Luke 6:20-31

In today's Gospel passage Jesus defines the way of life exemplified for us by the saints.

Luke's "Sermon on the Plain" (6:17-49) contains material that is similar to Matthew's "Sermon on the Mount" (Mt. 5-7), and both include what we have come to call the "Beatitudes." However, Matthew's body of teaching is much longer and it covers nine Beatitudes (5:1-11) instead of Luke's four, and without Luke's corresponding woes.

Luke here focuses on social concerns, and so: "Blessed are you who are poor" (6:20). Matthew's Beatitudes are more spiritualized: "Blessed are the poor in spirit" (Mt. 5:3). Luke's four blessings are paired with contrasting woes: poor/rich; hungry/full; weeping/laughter; and rejection/acceptance. The word *blessing* is used here in the sense of inner happiness.

In the verses immediately preceding today's reading (6:12-16), Jesus had spent the night on the mountain praying to discern which of his disciples would be chosen as his inner circle. The next day he named the Twelve, and came down with them to a "level place" before a large crowd (v. 17). The crowd sought healing from disease and release from unclean spirits, as they attempted to touch Jesus and benefit from his power (v. 19).

Jesus begins by blessing the poor, those who suffer from economic deprivation (v. 20). They have no illusions about their own self-sufficiency, and are thus more likely to turn to God—in contrast to the rich, who put their trust in wealth. Thus Jesus proclaims: "But woe to you who are rich" (v. 24). The consolation of the poor is the Kingdom of God, which is everlasting; the consolation of the rich is their temporal wealth and power.

"Blessed are you who are hungry now, for you will be filled" (v. 21a). Like the poor, the hungry have the promise of future abundance; but those who are full now will be hungry later (v. 25a).

"Blessed are you who weep now, for you will laugh" (6:21b). This is the only place in the New Testament where the word *laugh* appears. For those who trust in themselves, their "laughing" or present success will ultimately turn to failure, resulting in mourning and weeping (v. 25b).

"Blessed are you when people hate you" (v. 22a). Those who are hated, excluded, reviled, and defamed for their allegiance to Jesus should have joy, since they will be rewarded in heaven. Just as the former prophets were persecuted, so Jesus and his followers could expect to suffer. But Jesus warns of woe to those who revel now in the world's acclaim; they are false prophets who tell people what they want to hear instead of the truth (v. 26).

Here Jesus, by contrasting the way of the righteous with the way of the wicked, points to a final judgment and reversal of fortunes, in which the hardships of this present life will disappear in God's Kingdom.

PRAYER FOR THE DAY

Gracious Lord, who sent your Son Jesus Christ to deliver us from the power of evil and make us your children by adoption and grace: may your anointing with the Holy Spirit guide us into becoming "little Christs" to all whom you give us, that we may be transparent to your unfailing Presence in the world as your saints. *Amen.*

The visions of Daniel also bear out the promise of the inheritance of God's Kingdom to the faithful. Although composed in the second century B. C. to provide consolation to those facing persecution under Antiochus Epiphanes, the dream in today's passage is set in an earlier time, at the beginning of the reign of King Belshazzar of Babylon (553 B. C.) to give the sense of an ancient oracle.

In this first of four visions recorded in chapters 7-12, Daniel saw "four great beasts" stirred up by the "four winds of heaven" (7:3) emerging from the great sea. In ancient Near East mythology, images of the sea and sea monsters are associated with the destructive powers of chaos controlled by God at creation (cf Job 26:12-13; Ps. 33:6-7; Is. 27:1).

The four winds represent the four kingdoms of the Babylonians, the Medes, the Persians, and the Greeks. In a judgment scene in verses 9-14 the fourth beast (the Greeks) is killed, and the power of the remaining three taken away and given to "one like a human being coming with the clouds of heaven" (v. 13).

ON REFLECTION

The Apostle Paul makes it abundantly clear in the Book of Romans that claiming to be a Christian is equivalent to being a saint (1:7). The baptized in Christ are already counted among their number.

Perhaps we miss this point about the imperfection and everydayness of sainthood because we have forgotten the attraction of the holy and have been repulsed by the holier-than-thou.

We have forgotten being prayerful and put in its place being pious. We have seen "holiness" as best applied to those who get a kick out of being "better" or more "world-denying" than others—thus vindicating Ambrose Bierce's acidic definition of a saint: "a dead sinner revised and edited."

But "saints" are as apt to admit being as flawed and flaky, as faint-hearted and fat-headed as any backslider around. Not to mention just as sinful. The difference is: "saints" claim that God uses them anyway. Despite their own corruption and personal demons, they stand before God willing to be used, ready to be God's troubadours. And the world is enriched by their song.

So if saints aren't always the best examples, look pretty much like the rest of us, and don't live perfect lives—how do they live?

Joan Chittister, a Benedictine sister, best-selling author, and popular lecturer writes in her book Called to Question *(Sheed & Ward, 2004) about going beyond the "comfortable answers." "It was years," she admits, "before I figured out how change and failure were among the best friends of the soul."*

And no matter how much we seek to be obedient, faithful saints, regular in attendance at church, reading Scripture, doing good deeds—saintliness is really more about being than doing. More about listening than talking. More about readiness to fit into God's plan than following a course of spiritual improvement aimed at sainthood.

Nevertheless, it helps to keep on keeping on. Chittister reveals: "I am never closer to God than in the moments when I am busiest. It is in those times that I throw myself on the mind of God and listen to know if the direction is right, if the words are right, if the ideas are right. Then God becomes the radar by which I steer."

—H. King Oehmig

Daniel is troubled and frightened by this vision and asks for help in interpreting what he has seen. He is thus told that the four beasts are the kings of the four kingdoms, but that it is the "holy ones of the Most High" who shall possess the kingdom "forever and ever" (v. 18). These "holy ones" are the angelic host, or perhaps those who have survived tribulations. In the context of All Saints' Day, we are reminded of the promises of God's Kingdom to those who are faithful.

The writer of the letter to the Ephesians also speaks of the promises of the Kingdom manifested in *the salvation that comes through Christ.* Believers are marked with the "seal of the promised Holy Spirit" (1:13).

The genuine faith of this community at Ephesus is acknowledged with an assurance of continuing prayer for their further spiritual enlightenment. This will provide understanding of the hope to which God calls them, as well as appreciation of the glorious inheritance God provides. They must understand the boundless scope of God's power on behalf of believers, as demonstrated in the rising of Christ from the dead.

They are to acknowledge Jesus' establishment in heaven above all powers, temporal and eternal—whether of the present or the coming age. This exalted Christ has been made head over all existence for the sake of the Church his Body. Through his presence all things are brought to completion. God the Father raised Christ from the dead and seated him at God's "right hand" in the heavenly places (v. 20).

Therefore, Christ has dominion over all in this age and in the age to come (vv. 21-22). He is the head of the Church, his Body, the fullness of "him who fills all in all" (v. 23).

Thus on this day of celebration we are called to follow the example of the Psalmist as we praise God with dancing and music. The Lord "adorns the humble with victory" (Ps. 149:4) and brings glory for all faithful ones. *Praise the Lord!*

POINTS TO PONDER

1. Read both versions of the Beatitudes, in Matthew 5:1-12 and Luke 6:20-26, and reflect on the following questions: What are the similarities and differences in the two passages? How would you define "blessed" as it is used here? When have you felt blessed in your own life?

2. What is the relationship between God and those who are blessed?

3. How does the vision of *blessedness* described in these passages compare with blessedness as it is commonly defined in our contemporary culture?

4. The Beatitudes describe a way of life that Jesus expects of his followers. How are we called to live here? What are the challenges that are presented to us by this vision?

5. What does it mean to be a "saint"? Who are some individuals in your own life who exemplify the qualities of a saint, and in what ways?

_____

_____

_____

_____

_____

_____

_____

ZACCHAEUS' NEW LIFE

Habakkuk 1:1-4; 2:1-4; Psalm 119:137-144; 2 Thessalonians 1:1-4, 11-12; Luke 19:1-10

The Prophet Habakkuk wrote in the turbulent times of the late 7th and early 6th centuries B. C., when the Chaldeans posed a threat to Judah. The first two chapters consist of a dialogue between God and the prophet, with a concluding prayer in the final chapter.

Habakkuk begins by questioning why God allows violence and injustice to prevail. "O Lord, how long shall I cry for help, and you will not listen?" (1:1). The law is disregarded, the righteous are surrounded by the wicked, and judgment is perverted.

However, despite the corruption around him, Habakkuk continues to have ultimate faith that God is the eternal Holy One, the Rock whose eyes are too pure to look at evil. Thus, in trust, the prophet will await God's reply to his complaints: "I will stand at my watchpost ... to see what [God] will say to me" (2:1).

The Lord speaks in 2:2 by commanding the prophet to "Write the vision." God's time is not our time (v. 3), and we must trust that the Lord will act when the time is right. For our part, we are to wait and watch in faith, for "the righteous live by their faith" (v. 4b).

Habakkuk's faith in God's justice is reflected in Psalm 119, a lengthy and formal meditation on God's Torah or Instruction. The verses for today declare that "You are righteous, O Lord, and your judgments are right" (v. 137).

The Psalmist expresses indignation that his enemies forget God's word. Although he is of little account himself: "I am small and despised" (v. 141), he recognizes God's everlasting justice. Amid the trials in his life, he takes delight in the commandments that give him *understanding* by which he can maintain his life.

Although 2 Thessalonians seems similar to other letters of Paul, scholars debate whether or not Paul was actually the author.

The opening of the letter includes a prayer for God's grace and peace toward the church at Thessalonica (1:1-2), followed by praise to the people for their growing faith and increasing love for one another, as well as their steadfastness in enduring persecution (vv. 3-4). Their sufferings glorify God and make them worthy of their calling as God's people.

The verses that are left out (5-10) speak of punishments intended to be inflicted upon the persecutors and oppressors. The fate of the believers is contrasted to that of those who "do not know God" and "do not obey the gospel of our Lord Jesus" (v. 8). While the end of those who deny the Lord will be to suffer eternal separation from God's presence, those who are faithful will be instruments of further glory in and through Christ.

It is by God's power that these things will be accomplished; yet the writer admonishes the people to continue to grow in worthiness and fulfillment of their own calling as witnesses, to the end that *they themselves may be more like*

PRAYER FOR THE DAY

Grant us, gracious Lord God, the blessing of humility through the gift of your Holy Spirit: anoint us that we may understand ourselves as sons and daughters of the Most High. Let us forever seek to express the holy will of Jesus Christ, who humbled himself and died on the Cross, liberating the world from the power of sin and death. *Amen.*

Christ. This is the true grace and peace prayed for at the beginning of the letter.

The protagonist in today's Gospel story is Zacchaeus, the chief tax collector in Jericho, and thus a very wealthy man. In first-century Palestine, private individuals contracted with the Roman government to collect taxes. As long as the government received its due, the tax collectors could charge whatever they liked and pocket the difference.

Thus they were in a position to make unregulated profits and were much despised. Jews considered such collaboration with a foreign occupying power an act of treason since it perpetuated the defiling of their land by Gentile oppressors. Their treachery and

ON REFLECTION

It's been years since Zacchaeus has shimmied up a tree, but he spots a lonesome sycamore that's just right.

Luke says that Jesus spied the little IRS agent perched in the tree, which must have made quite a spectacle: bulging veins, heaving chest, and the Debeer's 8-carat ring twinkling on the finger of the little guy. No wonder Jesus spotted him. Not many in the crowds have ever climbed out on a limb just to glimpse him.

After all the preachers Zacchaeus has heard on TV, and what he dimly recalls from the yeshiva—and knowing full well his way of life has been financed by living anything but kosher—Zacchaeus expects from the lips of Jesus that which he knows he deserves. "You greedy, treacherous little wretch! You are a worm and no man! There's a place in hell for you that could melt the Arctic Circle. Get outta my sight."

But what actually happens is the magic of story—the unimaginable. Instead of lambasting Zacchaeus into the darkest recesses of Sheol, Jesus tells him that he's going to room at his mansion.

The little shyster can't believe his ears. He nearly falls out of the tree in an effort to consummate the deal. All the way to the ground, he wonders to himself, "Where's the catch?"

Fighting back his doubts, Zacchaeus calls off his goons and personally opens the door to the limo for a smiling Jesus—who steps inside to the sound of boos and hisses from the crowd. Zacchaeus wastes no time getting on his cell phone to his wife to tell her to be ready. The private plane will pick her up within the hour. He calls ahead to the chef and tells him it will be Chateaubriand with the '76 Beaujolais. Spare nothing.

Later in the evening, over Courvoisier, Jesus unveils the miracle of Gospel love. God is not an angry father with a belt in his hand, but the shepherd who leaves the ninety-nine to seek out the wayward lamb—to retrieve even the shamelessly rich. Underhanded tax collectors whose righteousness could possibly fill only the first line item on a 1040 form.

The story line continues to amaze. God desires fellowship with Zacchaeus, regardless of his past—even if he is a public and moral disaster. God wants him happy, joyous, and free—not locked up like a littleneck clam. Zacchaeus hears, accepts, rejoices—blessed be he.

We could call it The Gospel in Sycamore. Seamy human nature is confronted by the unflagging Divine affection for sinners. The outcome is a turn-around that only God could bring about. It is Amazing Grace in all its splendor, a gem of a story, indeed.

—H. King Oehmig

greed ranked tax collectors among the dregs of society, those who were regarded by the rabbis as thieves. Tax collectors could not hold communal office or give testimony in the Jewish courts, nor were they welcomed into the synagogue. Devout Jews avoided contact with these agents of Rome as much as possible.

As a chief tax collector, Zacchaeus would have been considered a sinner of the worst sort; therefore, it is ironic that his name means "pure" or "innocent."

As Jesus entered the city of Jericho, Zacchaeus wanted to see him; but because he was short in stature (19:3), Zacchaeus could not see through the crowds of people. Thus he ran ahead and climbed a sycamore tree along the route where Jesus would pass.

When Jesus noticed Zacchaeus in the tree, he called to him. There is a sense of urgency here; Zacchaeus was to *hurry* since Jesus *must* go to the home of Zacchaeus *today*—emphasizing that this visit was necessary for the saving purposes of God.

Zacchaeus joyfully welcomed Jesus into his home. Zacchaeus, as a tax collector, probably would have had few social invitations. The fact that Jesus accepted people for who they were, even if he did not condone their activities, raised objections from more conventional folk.

Thus the crowd began to grumble when they saw Jesus go "to be the guest of one who is a sinner" (v. 7). This was not the first time that such objections to Jesus' chosen company was raised (Lk. 5:30; 7:34, 39; 15:2).

But Zacchaeus' next words indicate that he is not an unrepentant sinner, as he pledges to give half of his possessions to the poor as well as repay fourfold anyone he has defrauded (v. 8). He thus meets and even exceeds the demands of the law, which required the original sum plus one fifth in repayment for anything stolen (Lev. 6:5; Num. 5:7).

Zacchaeus' admission of wrongdoing and his intention to amend his life prompt Jesus to say that "Today salvation has come to this house ... " (v. 9)—as Zacchaeus receives Jesus and voluntarily gives of his wealth to the poor.

Furthermore, Jesus bestows upon him the title of "son of Abraham" (v. 9) as an indication that he has been restored to the community and is entitled to inherited blessings. The actions of Zacchaeus indicate that he is open to receive the Kingdom of God, and that repentance has led to transformation. "For the Son of Man came to seek out and to save the lost" (v. 10).

POINTS TO PONDER

1. As you read the Gospel passage, put yourself in Zacchaeus' place. How do you think he might have felt as the events unfolded? Why do you think he was so eager to see Jesus in the first place?

2. How do you think Zacchaeus' life was changed by his encounter with Jesus?

3. In what ways do you identify with Zacchaeus? How is he an example for us today?

4. Why do you think Jesus invited himself to the house of Zacchaeus? We read that Zacchaeus was happy to welcome Jesus into his home (Lk. 19:6). How have you welcomed the presence of Jesus into your own heart?

5. Refer to the other readings for today and discuss what these passages, as well as the Gospel, suggest to us about sin, repentance, and forgiveness. In the final verse (v. 10) of the Gospel passage, Jesus proclaims that he "came to seek out and to save the lost." Who are the lost in our world today? How are we as individuals and as the Church called to take part in this ministry?

RESURRECTION LIFE

Haggai 1:15b—2:9; Psalm 145:1-5, 18-21 or 98; 2 Thessalonians 2:1-5, 13-17; Luke 20:27-38

Although the Book of Haggai gives no indication as to the identity of its author, the writer is very specific about chronological details. The four oracles that comprise the book take place between August and December of the year 520 B. C., during the reign of Darius the Great, who ruled over the Persian Empire between 522 and 486 B. C.

The exiles had returned to Israel from captivity in Babylon and had started to rebuild their lives. But in the first oracle of Haggai, addressed to Zerubbabel, the governor of Judah, and to Joshua the high priest (1:1-11), the people are rebuked for building houses instead of rebuilding the ruined temple. As a consequence, the land itself suffers under a severe drought. The people, energized by these words of the prophet, "came and worked on the house of the Lord of hosts, their God" (1:14).

In the second oracle in the verses for today, the Lord asks if anyone remembers what the temple looked like before it was destroyed. The prophet then goes on to assure the people of God's presence and promises when they were led out of captivity in Egypt. "My spirit abides among you; do not fear" (2:5b).

In the days to come, the Lord will act so that the abundance of gold and silver in tribute from other nations will make the splendor of the new temple even greater than that of the first, "and in this place I will give prosperity, says the Lord of hosts" (2:9).

Haggai probably did not see the completion of the temple (circa 516 B. C.), but his visions reminded the people of Israel of the unfailing presence and abundant promises of God.

The second letter to the Thessalonians also reminds the community that God's promises can be trusted. There were those whose faith had been shaken because of being told that "the day of the Lord is already here" (2:2). However, Paul reminded them that a time of rebellion and opposition to Christ could be expected before his coming again (cf Mt. 24:11-14, 23-24).

The portion of the letter for today goes on to assure the Thessalonians of God's continuing presence in their lives, both now and for eternity. They have been chosen by God "as the first fruits for salvation through sanctification by the Spirit and through belief in the truth" (2:13b). Thus the action of the Holy Spirit within them makes them holy and implants in them a saving faith.

They were called for a distinct purpose through Paul's proclamation of the good news so that they might obtain the glory of Christ. Thus they have the responsibility to hold fast to the traditions that they have received and to live their lives accordingly.

Paul goes on to pray that the converts may be strengthened in their life in Christ in the knowledge that, through Christ and God the Father, they have received "eternal comfort and good hope" (2:16). All this is so that they might be strengthened in "every good work and word" (v. 17).

PRAYER FOR THE DAY

O God of grace and glory, in whose service we find perfect freedom and true purpose, by the invisible working of your Holy Spirit, keep us forever awake to the needs of the world and alert to respond in the Name of Jesus Christ our Lord, until the end of the age. *Amen.*

A Psalm of praise expresses Paul's own confidence: "I will extol you, my God and King, and bless your name forever and ever. ... Great is the Lord, and greatly to be praised; his greatness is unsearchable" (Ps. 145:1, 3).

In the Gospel passage, Jesus holds out the promise of eternal life. During Jesus' ministry there was a widespread belief and hope of resurrection that was shared by Jesus and his disciples. It had become a common belief that the righteous dead would be raised to share in the eternal glories of God's ultimate victory.

Eternal life was not understood, however, as the immortality of a disembodied soul—an idea that arose among the Greeks. Rather, God was to create a new heaven and a new earth in

ON REFLECTION

The Sadducees have come to represent religionists of all times and faiths who insist on majoring in the minors. They remind me of the crotchety old lady who once cornered her priest after church and exclaimed at him: "If our Lord Jesus could hear this newfangled liturgy, he would roll over in his grave!"

Rather than asking Jesus a profound question about the nature of the Kingdom, or when God might restore Israel to Davidic preeminence, the Sadducees ask Jesus a question that is a cross between how many angels can fit on the head of a pin and how many Episcopalians it takes to change a light bulb.

Medievalists debated the first perplexity for years. The answer to the second is easy: It takes two. One to make the martinis and the other to call the electrician.

But these Sadducees, having a rather low view of the afterlife (really, none at all) pose the one-bride-for-seven-brothers mind-teaser for Jesus. With the gallows looming before him, it is surprising that Jesus gives them any answer at all. But answer them he does—and this is the only answer he gives in the first three Gospels on the subject of resurrection (cf Mk. 12:18-27).

First, Jesus tells them that those who enter into the "resurrection of the dead" don't have to worry about marital contracts. Resurrection is a wholly new, unparalleled state of being—not a continuation of earthly existence with its institutions of binding agreements.

Resurrection is beyond all of those terms, making it inconceivable in human language. Despite the hype of "life-after-death" bestsellers, what happens to us after death is ultimately a mystery, an incomprehensible, all-embracing reality grounded in God's love and faithfulness.

So the brothers—and the poor woman to whom all of them would have been married— don't have to fret about who belongs to whom. After they become like "angels" and "children of God" in the resurrection, blood tests and marriage licenses will be totally obsolete. They will be as useless in heaven as the ark was to Noah after he reached Mt. Ararat.

Jesus also sets the Sadducees straight on another count. Citing the encounter between Moses and God at the burning bush, where Moses speaks of the Holy One as "the God of Abraham, the God of Isaac, the God of Jacob"—even though these patriarchs were long gone from the face of the earth—Jesus instructs the Sadducees that God lives even if we die. And that we go on living in God, who is the only indestructible and imperishable reality.

Luke ends the scene on an upbeat note. Some of the testy, nitpicking Sadducees seem to turn out to be teachable after all. They commend Jesus for his wisdom (v. 39). The rest just keep quiet.

—H. King Oehmig

which people would have a physical body. This understanding was supported by the Pharisees and was affirmed by Jesus as well.

However, one party among the Jews, the conservative and aristocratic Sadducees, strongly denied this view that the dead could be raised. It was not only incomprehensible, but even repellent to them. The Sadducees appear in today's Gospel reading for the first and only time in Luke, as they pose a convoluted and hypothetical problem to Jesus concerning the resurrection of the dead (cf Mt. 22:23-33; Mk. 12:18-27).

They present Jesus with the unlikely case of a woman who marries seven times according to the terms of an ancient custom. Deuteronomy 25:5-6 asserts that a man whose brother has died without siring children must marry the deceased brother's wife and have children for him. Thus no man's family would die out, as the first son born of the new union would inherit the deceased husband's name and lands.

Polygamy was allowed; however, by the time of Jesus, observance of the custom had become rare, though not unknown. The question posed to Jesus was: in the supposed resurrection, whose wife would she be, since she had been married to all seven brothers?

It was typical for rabbis to pose such riddles to one another—to test, amaze, and baffle their audiences and students, as well as to ridicule their rivals. But here Jesus simply points out that resurrection life *is not meant* to be a mere continuation of earthly existence. Rather, it is a transformation into a completely different, unimagined state of being. In this eternal life, God's reign would be fully established.

Although marriage is necessary in this life, it is unnecessary in future life. And while, in this new existence, our personal identity will survive, it will be as a transfigured personality comparable to that of the angels. "Indeed they cannot die anymore, because they are like angels and are children of God, being children of the resurrection" (Lk. 20:36).

Not only did the Sadducees not believe in resurrection, they also denied the existence of angels. Thus the Sadducees are among those "who belong to this age" (v. 34), and are so preoccupied with temporal matters that they cannot envision something as miraculous as resurrection. The Sadducees' question is simply irrelevant to the quality of resurrection life.

Jesus goes on to present further proof of his claim for resurrection by referring to the words of Moses at the burning bush, when the Lord is identified as the God of the Hebrew patriarchs. The statement in the present tense, "I am the God of Abraham, Isaac, and Jacob," is an assertion that the patriarchs still live. Thus the Lord is "God not of the dead, but of the living; for to him all of them are alive" (v. 38).

Children of the resurrection are God's own children who share in God's eternal life. In response, one of the scribes afterward declared, "Teacher, you have spoken well" (20:39), and they dared question him no more.

POINTS TO PONDER

1. As you read the Gospel Lesson, what do we discover here about Jesus himself and his ministry? In particular, what do we learn about dealing with situations of conflict?

2. What is the understanding of resurrection that Jesus articulates?

3. How are we "children of the resurrection" (20:36)?

4. What does it mean that God is God of the living? How does Jesus illustrate this point?

5. What is the difference between the soul's immortality and the resurrection of the body? How would you express your own understanding of life after death?

THE DAY OF THE LORD

Isaiah 65:17-25; Canticle 9 (Isaiah 12:2-6); 2 Thessalonians 3:6-13; Luke 21:5-19

Jesus delivers a discourse on the end times in his final days in Jerusalem before the Passion. This climax of Jesus' public teaching in Luke 21 reflects similar material in Mark 13 and Matthew 24. However, whereas Matthew and Mark speak of the end of the world, here Jesus refers specifically to the destruction of Jerusalem and the temple. The passage for today can be divided into three parts: a prediction of the destruction of the temple (21:5-7); signs that the time is near (vv. 8-11); and the coming persecutions (vv. 12-19).

As the reading begins, someone in the crowd remarks upon the beauty of the temple. After the return from exile in Babylon, the second temple was completed around 515 B.C., replacing Solomon's temple, which had been destroyed in 586 B.C. In the time of Jesus, Herod the Great was enlarging and refurbishing this same temple.

Jesus responds by saying that in the days to come the temple would be destroyed: "Not one stone will be left" on another (v. 6). The temple was at the heart of Jewish religious and national identity. As Jesus foretells the destruction of the temple, he is also proclaiming that the religious institutions of Israel have lost their life-giving properties, as he points to a new kind of temple in the Kingdom of God.

When the people ask when this will occur and what will be the signs, Jesus replies by offering a series of images. First, he warns them against false prophets who will attempt to lead them astray with misleading predictions of the end times.

Jesus tells his followers not to be afraid when they hear of "wars and insurrections," for although these things must take place, "the end will not follow immediately" (v. 9). There will be political upheavals as nations go to war against each other (v. 10), as well as cosmic disturbances, famine, plague, and "great signs from heaven" (v. 11).

But even before these signs of the end, his followers will be persecuted and arrested. They will face the hostility of the synagogue, imprisonment, and even death at the hands of governors and kings. They will be betrayed by family and friends and "hated by all because of my name" (v. 17).

Yet all of this they can face without fear, as this persecution will provide opportunities for them to testify. They do not need to prepare a defense in advance, for when the time comes, Jesus will give them words and "a wisdom" that none of their opponents will be able to withstand or contradict (v. 15).

Moreover, "not a hair of your head will perish" (v. 18). By their endurance and faithful persistence they will gain life (v. 19). Thus they must not become discouraged or distressed, but take courage in light of God's final victory.

Much of what Jesus spoke of here would take place within the lifetimes of those who heard him speak. The temple was destroyed in

PRAYER FOR THE DAY

Almighty God, we ask for the coming of your Kingdom and glory in all its fullness; and, we pray, anoint us with the Holy Spirit that we may live out the giftedness with which we have been blessed: that Jesus Christ may be proclaimed in thought, word, and deed until his coming again in glory. *Amen.*

the rebellion of A. D. 70, and the persecution of Jesus' followers would be recorded in the Book of Acts (4:1-22; 5:17-41; 22—26).

The faith community at Thessalonica was also concerned with the coming day of the Lord, but so stressed the idea that *the Second Coming was near* that some were ready to forsake work and wait for the new life. Thus the writer of the Epistle warns against joining those who engage in such idle or disorderly conduct. They are to follow the example of those such as Paul, who could have properly claimed support from others, but instead earned his keep by practicing his own trade.

ON REFLECTION

Imagine how the Jews of Jesus' day felt, being told that the temple was at risk. It stood at the heart of all Jerusalem—the most sacred, prominent structure in the Holy City. The temple occupied the center of Hebrew culture. The nation's identity, its whole reason for being, was derived from this seat and symbol of God's dwelling place among the Covenant people.

Hardly anyone living in Jerusalem did not have some kind of connection with the temple from a commercial standpoint. Craftspeople were needed to provide ritual objects and to keep them repaired. The site also brought traders who dealt in sacrificial animals.

A priestly hierarchy that consisted of High Priest, priests, and Levites lived and moved and labored throughout the temple—overseeing all ritual and cultic observances.

Hordes of pilgrims arriving at the temple created a vast "tourist" industry that offered lodging and food service to visitors. Currency changers, or temple bankers, made their living around the temple, as almost all the people of Jerusalem, rich or poor, deposited their money there.

Herod the Great, rebuilding this third and most sublime version of Solomon's original temple, had 10,000 unskilled laborers put to work on the project, along with 1,000 priest-masons who worked on the most sacred parts of the structure.

Herod had started the stupendous project in 20 B. C., and most of the construction had been finished within ten years. But the arduous "trim work" had continued for years on end, leading some Pharisees to observe that "this temple has been under construction for forty-six years" (Jn. 2:20).

And the finished product? The historian Josephus, unmatched chronicler of the ancient world, wrote in his work The Jewish War: *"The exterior of the building wanted nothing that could astound either mind or eye. For, being covered on all sides with massive plates of gold, the sun was no sooner up than it radiated so fiery a flash that persons straining to look at it were compelled to avert their eyes, as from the solar rays."*

How could such an edifice be subject to destruction and tragedy?

Within a week of making this prophecy, Jesus would be dead. In his death, his words about the destruction of the temple would be regarded as less dangerous than mere delusion. He had been destroyed, not Herod's grand edifice.

Yet, within a few short years, the temple would come crumbling down at the hands of the Romans—and Jesus' prophecy would hold true.

—H. King Oehmig

The end indeed is promised by God; but no one can predict when it will be. Therefore, all Christians are called to quietly carry out the responsibilities given to them in this world as preparation for God's new order.

While Luke and 2 Thessalonians do both hold out the promise of the coming reign of God, the eloquent words of the Prophet Isaiah describe what this transformed world will be like. Indeed, God is "about to create new heavens and a new earth" (65:17) unlike anything that has ever been. Throughout the Old Testament, evidence of the work of the Lord can be seen in nature; thus this new age will be such that *former things will be forgotten.* The prophet is not saying here that the world will be destroyed but that it will be transformed.

God will "create Jerusalem as a joy, and its people as a delight" (v. 18). In contrast to the sorrow of the past, no longer will the sounds of weeping and distress be heard. Long life was seen as a blessing of the Lord, and in this new creation, people could expect to live beyond a hundred years.

They shall live in the houses they build and enjoy the fruits of their vineyards; no longer will others have the advantage of their labors. God's chosen and their descendants shall enjoy the work of their hands.

During the former times of despair, God was silent. Now no prayer would be in vain: the Lord will answer before the suppliant has completed the request.

God's reign will be a time of peace that is once again manifested in nature: "the wolf and the lamb shall feed together, the lion shall eat straw like the ox" (v. 25), and none shall fear danger from the venomous serpent. In God's holy mountain, hurt and destruction will be unknown. Such a vision of joy, peace, and blessing goes beyond our imagination.

In the earlier writings, the Prophet Isaiah composed a song of thanksgiving that also described the ideal age. The verses of Canticle 9 follow an oracle in chapter 12 that describes

the restoration of Israel under the leadership of a Davidic king. The passage begins with a thanksgiving for God's salvation. There is no need to be afraid, for the Lord God is our strength and our might.

Life-giving water is a sign of God's salvation; therefore, "with joy you will draw water from the wells of salvation" (v. 3) and proclaim the Lord's mighty deeds throughout the earth. Thus Israel can shout with joy, "for great in your midst is the Holy One ... " (v. 6).

POINTS TO PONDER

1. What are some of the signs that Jesus describes as indications that Jerusalem and the temple will be destroyed? How are his followers to respond to these crises?

2. In Luke 21:8, Jesus warns against impostors who come in his name. How can we identify and avoid such false prophets in our world today?

3. Jesus also warns his followers that they can expect persecution (v. 12). What adversities do we as Christians face today?

4. Persecution will provide Jesus' followers with "an opportunity to testify" (v. 13). How will they be guided when this happens? What are the opportunities that we have today to defend our faith?

5. What promises does Jesus make here to those who would follow him? How are we inheritors of these promises today as well?

_____

_____

_____

LORD OF LORDS

Jeremiah 23:1-6; Canticle 4 or 16 (Luke 1:68-79); Colossians 1:11-20; Luke 23:33-43

On this last Sunday of the Church Year, Christ the King Sunday, we proclaim that Jesus is "the King of kings and Lord of lords" (Prayer Book, p. 236). The Lectionary for today shows us what it means that *Jesus is King.*

The Prophet Jeremiah lived during one of the most turbulent periods in Jewish history. As a witness to the events leading to the destruction of Solomon's temple and the beginning of the exile in Babylon, Jeremiah chronicled the last days of the southern kingdom of Judah.

He served the Lord for forty years, saw his people exiled from the Promised Land, and ended his days as an exile in Egypt. In today's passage, Jeremiah denounces the leaders of Judah (23:1-4), but also looks to a future when Israel and Judah will return from exile and again be united under a Davidic king (vv. 5-6).

In the ancient Near East, and in the Old Testament itself, the image of a shepherd is often used in reference to kings and rulers. The shepherd's responsibility was to protect the sheep from danger, just as a king was to provide for the security of the nation.

Here Jeremiah pronounces God's judgment against the rulers of Judah whose faithlessness has resulted in defeat and exile: "It is you who have scattered my flock, and have driven them away … " (v. 2).

Thus the Lord will gather the remnant of the flock and bring them back to their fold. The Lord also promises to find faithful shepherds to guide and keep them. Once again they "shall be fruitful and multiply," in accordance with the Divine blessing at creation (Gen. 1:28).

In the days to come, the Lord will "raise up for David a righteous Branch" (v. 5)—a king of David's lineage who shall reign with wisdom, justice, and righteousness. Judah and Israel will be reunited and live in safety. The word "Branch" itself (Zech. 3:8; 6:12) has messianic connotations.

Jeremiah goes on to say that the name of this king will be "The Lord is our righteousness" (v. 6), or deliverance.

In place of the Psalm today we read Canticle 4 or 16—the Song of Zechariah or the *Benedictus.* Zechariah, a priest, was stricken mute when he did not believe the angel Gabriel's announcement to him that his wife Elizabeth would bear them a son in their old age. He did not regain his speech until it was time for the child to be circumcised. At that time, Zechariah delivered a prophecy in response to the question of "What then will this child become?" (Lk. 1:66a).

In this hymn of praise, Zechariah recalls the fulfillment of God's promises to Israel and declares that this child, named John, will be the one to prepare the way for the Lord, who will bring a message of forgiveness and salvation. The hymn ends with a beautiful expression of hope for a world in which there will be light and peace.

PRAYER FOR THE DAY

Almighty and ever merciful God, whose purpose is to bring to consummation all things in Jesus Christ our Lord: give to all peoples of the earth, in spite of ongoing rebellion and division, the grace to come together under the rule of the King of kings and Lord of lords, through the unity of the Holy Spirit, who lives and reigns with you, one God, forever and ever. *Amen.*

The letter to the Colossians is a response to a dispute within that community as to what was actually accomplished in Christ. The author of the letter argues quite clearly that Jesus Christ is God's only Son, through whom comes the salvation of the world.

The passage that we read today begins with thanksgiving to God, who has rescued us from darkness and "transferred us" into the Kingdom (1:13). Through the Son, the power of evil has been defeated, and we have received forgiveness of sins.

The Christ hymn of verses 15-20 eloquently proclaims that Jesus is "the image of the invisible God, the firstborn of all creation" (v. 15). "All things have been created through him and for him" (v. 16b). The image of Christ perfectly reveals the invisible God, and as the "firstborn"

ON REFLECTION

There are so many warring images attempting to convey the reality of Jesus, some more biblically accurate than others. Of them all, perhaps the most confusing is the theme of our Lectionary readings today, "Christ the King" Sunday.

The problem is simple: how do we associate Jesus—our Lord on a cross—with any sort of monarchialism? What serves to connect the Nazarene carpenter, or the Suffering Servant, with the King of the now-and-future Kingdom?

What does Jesus have to do with Caesar?

How could a figure as apolitical as Jesus, who died without a penny to his name, be a king—since he had no apparent nation to rule?

Furthermore, how do we connect Jesus with a title that is so undemocratic and un-American? So politically incorrect?

How can we identify this person comfortably with the title: "King of kings and Lord of lords"?

Despite the setting of the crucifixion, Luke in chapter 23 does not treat the picture of this dying king as a tragedy. Paradoxes abound, as in the figure of the Lord of heaven dying between two thieves. Even in his agony, Jesus can turn to the penitent robber on one side and assure him that they will be together in paradise.

No picture, no likeness, no commentary can explain any of these off-the-scale truths. We can only believe ... and worship ... and take heart.

Huston Smith in his wonderful book Forgotten Truth *(HarperSanFrancisco, 1976, p. 101) counterposes these two thoughts:*

Paul in Romans 8:18:

"I consider that the sufferings of this present time are not worth comparing with the glory that is to be revealed [in or to] us."
and Gregory of Nyssa:

"You are made in the likeness of that nature which surpasses all understanding. ... Nothing in all creation can equal your grandeur. ... If you realize this you will no longer marvel even at the heavens. ... For the heavens pass away, but you will abide for all eternity with him who is forever."

—H. King Oehmig

Jesus has priority over all of created existence.

Every created thing—even celestial orders and worldly powers—has its origin in him and exists for him and his glory. Not only is Christ supreme over all creation, he is also the head of the Church—its origin, its source of power, its purpose for existence.

Christ is the "firstborn from the dead" (v. 18), thus assuring resurrection for all. Through him God's work of reconciliation on earth and in heaven will be accomplished, as God has made peace for us all through the blood of Christ.

The Gospel also affirms the supremacy of Jesus as God's chosen, but in different terms. For ultimately, the kingship of Jesus is expressed most eloquently by the Cross and through his acts of forgiveness and compassion.

As Jesus is crucified, his first words from the cross in Luke's account are "Father, forgive them; for they do not know what they are doing" (23:34). Even in his suffering, Jesus asks that God grant forgiveness to his tormentors and those who reject him out of their own ignorance.

As a brutal means of execution for the worst of criminals, crucifixion was considered to be a deterrent to crime. Thus a sign would be posted describing the person's offense. The inscription over Jesus' cross read: "This is the King of the Jews" (Lk. 23:38). He had been accused of blasphemy and sedition against Rome, and the words were meant to be an insult.

In fact, as he hung on the cross, the crowd mocked him, saying that if he really were King of the Jews—the Messiah—he should come down from the cross and save himself.

We are told that two other criminals were crucified with Jesus—one on his right and one on his left. Luke alone of the Gospel writers records their conversation. The first man joins in mocking Jesus, saying, "Are you not the Messiah? Save yourself and us!" (v. 39). He was interested only in his own well-being and reflected the attitude of those who followed Jesus for what they hoped to gain.

The second man had a very different attitude, and his words to Jesus have been characterized as the "Gospel within the Gospel." He recognized his own sin and the innocence of Jesus. " ... we are getting what we deserve for our deeds, but this man has done nothing wrong" (v. 41). He then turned to Jesus with a profession of faith as he asked that Jesus remember him in his Kingdom.

Jesus answered with an assurance of forgiveness and eternal life. "Truly I tell you, today you will be with me in Paradise" (v. 43).

POINTS TO PONDER

1. On this Christ the King Sunday, the Gospel reading focuses on a portion of Luke's crucifixion narrative. Why do you think this is a fitting passage for this last Sunday of the Church Year?

2. Pay particular attention to the conversation Jesus has with the criminals who were crucified with him. How would you describe the different attitudes of these two men?

3. What promise does Jesus make to the second criminal in Luke 23:43 and why? How is this condemned man an example for us today?

4. Also read the other passages for today. What do we learn from Jeremiah about the ideal king? What does the letter to the Colossians reveal to us about Jesus?

5. What will the world be like under the reign of Jesus? What can we do in our own lives to make this vision a reality in the world today?

Breinigsville, PA USA
05 October 2009

225288BV00002B/5/P